I0814524

Hell on Color, Sweet on Song

HELL ON COLOR, SWEET ON SONG

Jacob Wrey Mould and the Artful Beauty of Central Park

Francis R. Kowsky
With Lucille Gordon

AN IMPRINT OF FORDHAM UNIVERSITY PRESS
NEW YORK 2023

Funding for this book was provided by **Furthermore: a program of the J. M. Kaplan Fund.**

Frontispiece: Jacob Wrey Mould (1825–1886)

Visit us online at www.fordhampress.com/empire-state-editions.

Library of Congress Cataloging-in-Publication Data available online at https://catalog.loc.gov.

Printed in the United States of America

25 24 23 5 4 3 2 1

First edition

à la mémoire d'Hélène Kowsky

CONTENTS

PREFACE

Discovering Jacob Wrey Mould

Jacob Wrey Mould's reputation as an inventive and flamboyant High Victorian architect rests on his revolutionary design of New York's All Souls Unitarian Church and as the third creator, with Calvert Vaux and Frederick Law Olmsted, of Central Park. All Souls—constructed between 1853 and 1855 for the congregation of Henry Whitney Bellows, a respected Unitarian minister—introduced fully formed, colorful High Victorian design to America. Mould's brilliant designs for carved reliefs featuring plants, birds, and rural scenes, together with the beautiful tilework that embellish Central Park's Bethesda Terrace, testify to his genius for creating ornamental designs of all sorts. Numerous buildings he planned, many of which have followed All Souls to demolition, were also important in their day.

For many years, I and other architectural historians have wished to know more about this talented architect, especially his family background and early life in London before he came to America in 1852. In the 1990s, Lucille Gordon, a dedicated volunteer docent at Central Park, contacted me about Mould, whose sculptural reliefs, tile work, and structures in the park fascinated her, as they have many others since their creation in the late nineteenth century. She realized that few people were aware of his authorship of these works and of the existence of buildings elsewhere he had designed. Nor was he mentioned in any of the art history courses that she had taken as her undergraduate major at Queens College. After careers in book publishing and marketing and blessed with a life-long interest in art, architecture, and archaeology, she had decided to devote her retirement years to tracking down Mould's elusive history. This would entail cataloguing all of his architectural and other design creations and understanding his role in New York's musical scene, which was significant, in preparation for a whole biography of the man. Her graduate degree in library science from Pratt Institute prepared her well for the complicated pursuit.

When Lucille undertook her project, she found that little had been published about Mould's life and artistry. For scholarly reference, she had only David Van Zanten's excellent 1969 article in the *Journal of the Society of Architectural Historians* to consult for an overview of Mould's career. Nor did any diaries or collections of Mould's papers or office records exist. Lucille began by asking, Who was he? Did the information about him reveal anything of the man, the influences that informed his work, or help us to understand his contributions to the architecture and the society of the Gilded Age? Did the "bohemian" lifestyle he was said to have lived hint at scandalous excesses? It seemed to her, a woman who had spent many years working in the publishing business, that his striking architecture, colorful ornamental designs, and venturesome unconventional life would make a compelling biography.

Lucille started what became a lengthy and rewarding journey to find the real Jacob Wrey Mould. I was happy to assist her in this quest and would send her information on Mould whenever I came across something of note. Over the years, we had many long conversations in which she eagerly talked about the progress of her work. I was also pleased to share with her items that an earlier close friend, Dennis Francis, had sent to me regarding Mould. He, too, had been fascinated by Mould's career and had made inroads into understanding his art before his premature death in 1980. (In 1982, Joy Kestenbaum readied his entry on Mould for the *McMillan Encyclopedia of Architects*.) Lucille spent many hours tracking down leads in public records, journals, and archives. She came to correspond with many people in America and abroad who offered long-lost information about some aspect of Mould's life and his achievements in architecture, design, and music. Lucille traveled to England where she visited the scenes of Mould's ancestry, earliest life, and education. She soon found that many of the "facts" that we knew about Mould's life turned out to be myths. Yet, Mould, who contemporaries generally referred to as Wrey Mould, did have secrets. (Neither Lucille nor I have been able to ascertain why he preferred to use his middle name or why his parents chose to bestow it on him.) As she came to see, the richness of his actual life makes a splendid story. Although she could not gather in all the particulars of Mould's personal history, Lucille brought us closer than anyone has to this brilliant artist.

Unfortunately, aging intervened to prevent Lucille Gordon from completing her work. In 2019, her daughter Jamie contacted me with the sad news that her mother was then in a nursing home, unable to pursue her long labor of love. She asked if I would like to have the many folders of notes that her mother had amassed over the years. Not wishing to see that treasure of information lost, I agreed to take it with the promise that one day I would either carry on where Lucille had left off or find someone else who would do so. When the COVID-19 virus struck, and I was virtually confined to our home in Buffalo, I decided that I would pick up my friend's work and write that book on Mould. This is not the book that she would have written, but it could not have been written without her. In places, I have relied on her phraseology. But as an architectural historian, I have focused on Mould's works and their place in the history of nineteenth-century American architecture and design rather than sought to construct a traditional biography. I also undertook further research in newspapers and other resources that had not been available to Lucille or she had yet to discover. The book that follows rests on the foundation of Lucille Gordon's heroic efforts to raise from obscurity one of the geniuses of American architecture and a significant contributor to the world of music in his time. Mould's contributions to Central Park—the works that inspired Lucille Gordon to pursue his history—have been conserved by the Central Park Conservancy and continue to delight the eyes of thousands of visitors. One of those was Lucille Gordon, who died of COVID-19 in November 2021. She had begun her search for Jacob Wrey Mould at the Bethesda Terrace.

Francis Kowsky
Buffalo, NY

Hell on Color, Sweet on Song

INTRODUCTION

JACOB WREY MOULD OCCUPIED a significant place in American architecture in the last half of the nineteenth century. He was a pupil and friend of the esteemed British architect and designer Owen Jones (1809–1874), a fact that Mould publicized. Jones was England's greatest proponent of color in architecture. He had laid on the vivid hues that brought to life Joseph Paxton's enormous prefabricated metal and glass Crystal Palace, the venue for London's Great Exhibition of 1851 that attracted millions of visitors from around the world. Jones's remarkably comprehensive book, *Grammar of Ornament* (1856), became the bible of an age that cherished opulent decoration as much as it admired structural innovation in architecture. Jones also devoted his energies to the decorative arts, designing books, tiles, fabrics, monograms, and many other esthetically pleasing items. Well placed among his influential contemporaries—Augustus Welby Northmore Pugin, John Ruskin, William Morris, Christopher Dresser, and Eugene-Emmanuel Viollet-le-Duc—Owen Jones was a foremost representative of the design arts in the Romantic age. "It is impossible to exaggerate the authority and stature of Owen Jones during the middle of the nineteenth century," states architectural historian Carol Flores in her definitive monograph on Jones, "or to overestimate the influence of his theory and designs on his contemporaries and on subsequent generations."[1] As historian Mark Crinson points out, Jones, unlike Pugin and others, did not aim to produce a religious revival aided by medieval architecture and crafts;

instead, for him, "the secularism of the new age had to be accepted, new works derived from a new trinity—Science, Commerce, and Industry."[2]

Jones taught Mould to explore wider boundaries of the past for inspiration in his art, to look to Italy, Spain, and the Middle East—wherever there was a rich ornamental tradition to be mined. He also imparted his theories of color and design to his prize pupil and trusted assistant. Notable among them was that, in architecture, "construction should be decorated; decoration should never be constructed." For as much as he cherished ornament and history, Jones maintained that decoration should remain subservient to a building's general form and function and that architects should use the past as a font of ideas for new work, not as a source of wholehearted imitation. Moreover, as Flores states, Jones believed in the "emotional power of architecture and the analogous relationship between architecture and music."[3] Owen Jones had called for a glorious new architectural statement, a statement that would renew English architecture and connect it with modern times. With passion and artistry, his trans-Atlantic protégé would aspire to Jones's motto: *pulchritudo vincit omnia*—beauty conquers all.

The varied activities in Owen Jones's studio served to lay the foundation for Jacob Wrey Mould's future career. He absorbed lessons that Jones would codify in the *Grammar of Ornament* as a series of principles explaining how to go about enhancing structures with colorful patterns of polychromatic tiles and other durable materials. In America, Wrey Mould—he preferred to go by his middle name—would also replicate Jones's pursuit of art and beauty beyond the borders of architecture. On an 1869 handbill advertising his New York practice, Mould proudly proclaimed himself "pupil of Owen Jones, Esq., of London"—who by then the world knew as one of the giants of Victorian art. Mimicking Jones, Mould laid forth a cornucopia of talents, balancing architecture and "Art Design." Together with his capabilities for the design and superintendence of buildings, Mould catalogued the "several subsidiary arts" he had learned to love and master in Jones's busy Argyll Place atelier. These comprised the "decoration in color for the interior of churches, public buildings, or dwellings"; stained glass; and book design—including title pages, vignettes, ornamental borders and covers for "all forms of illustrated and illuminated works, designed and drawn, either on wood block or in lithography." It also registered bank note design; book binding; designs for pottery and porcelain; designs for "bronze, silver and ornamental glassware; organ cases; textile fabrics; wall hangings"; and "all other Designs . . . for subjects in any way co-relative with Ornamental Art." Upon Jones's recommendation, Mould went to work in the office of Jones's former master, the London architect Lewis Vulliamy. At the time, Vulliamy, who enjoyed a large and lucrative practice, was constructing and furnishing Dorchester House, the palatial London residence of England's richest man. After serving as Vulliamy's trusted assistant, Mould, at age twenty-six, determined, against the advice of Jones, to leave England for America.

Arriving in New York from London in 1852, Mould augmented the number of British architects—including Gervase Wheeler, Richard Upjohn, Calvert Vaux, and Frederick Clarke Withers—who had immigrated to the United States and obtained successful practices here. Within a year, Mould had the good fortune to secure the commission to design All Souls Unitarian Church. The red-and-white-banded marble "church of the Holy Zebra" became the talk of New York. Its success launched Mould on his transatlantic career. A representative of advanced High Victorian principles of design and expression, Mould, with his plans for All Souls, introduced the full-blown use of color—polychromy—to his American colleagues. His assertion, "I'm Hell on color," was a statement many of his contemporaries cheerfully remembered.[4] "Bold as a lion in the selection of his colors," declared the art magazine the *Crayon* of his interior design scheme for the home of an early client, "and grave as a judge in their combination, he dazzles with brightness, without offending the most fastidious taste; and as to design, we must pronounce it exquisite."[5]

Along with his mastery of color, Mould was the inventor of beautiful ornamental designs. These were his notable contributions to New York's Central Park, a project with which he became involved at its inception in 1858. Indeed, Central Park was where he lavished most of his life's labors. Today, it is the place where one can most fully appreciate Mould's talent for unprecedented work that is everlastingly enchanting. Together with Calvert Vaux and Frederick Law Olmsted, Mould pioneered the creation of that historic municipal park. His designs for carved ornament and tilework at the Bethesda Terrace are still among the chief delights that modern visitors enjoy there. Mould also added several structures to the park. The largest of these, the Sheepfold, came into being during the brief time when the populist Mayor William Magear Tweed named Mould, who was less committed than Vaux and Olmsted to the ideas embodied in the Greensward plan, the park's architect-in-chief.

During the 1860s, Mould advanced his career outside of Central Park with several important commissions. The West Presbyterian Church on Forty-Second Street in Manhattan was a highly original solution to the problem of fitting a large church into the tight confines of an urban streetscape. Malkasten, looking out over the Hudson at Tarrytown, New York, was the grandiose home and studio of the famous landscape painter Albert Bierstadt (1830–1902). Other prominent Gilded Age men of means who became his clients included John Davenport, a wealthy Upstate businessman and philanthropist; Thomas William Kennard (1825–1893), the brilliant railroad engineer and owner of the luxury steam yacht *Octavia*; and Edward C. Dubois, trans-Andean rail designer and agent for the Dreyfus bank in Lima, Peru. Yet a reputation for disregarding his client's budget hurt Mould's practice. "The truth is," wrote the art critic Clarence Cook who knew him well, "that people of only moderate wealth feared to put themselves in his hands, while ordinary folk dared not trust him at all." It was a pity, lamented Cook, that because of this, Mould was "so little employed."[6]

After two decades in New York, Mould, at age fifty, took the bold decision to abandon his adopted city and move to Lima, Peru. He did so at the invitation of Henry Meiggs (1811–1877), the flamboyant American entrepreneur who was financing the construction of the Trans-Andean Railroad and planning to transform Lima into a cosmopolitan metropolis. In March 1875, Mould and his wife left for Lima where he fully intended to become the major architect in South Pacific America. In this regard, as historian Jeffrey Cody notes, Mould "presaged the activities of many American construction-oriented professionals"—such as Walter Burley Griffin, Frank Lloyd Wright, and Louis Kahn—who, in the twentieth century, created significant work beyond America's borders.[7] Unfortunately, his generous patron became ill unexpectedly and died two years after Mould arrived. This and other events in Peru made it impossible for Mould to remain in Lima. In 1879, he was back in the States. By then, however, the architectural scene had changed, and he was unable to regain a strong foothold in the profession that followed the lead of Henry Hobson Richardson and his Richardsonian Romanesque style and the advocates of the international Neo-Classical tradition promoted by partisans of the École des Beaux-Arts in Paris. Mould resumed his association with the New York City Department of Public Parks where he worked on a variety of projects, notably the border walls of Morningside Park and the temporary tomb of President Ulysses S. Grant, Mould's last work.

Perhaps the best way to regard Mould's role in the profession of his day is as an architect's architect. He was not widely known to the public, but his reputation was high among his colleagues. His influence was by example, not directly through contact with other practitioners, as master of a large firm, or through theoretical writings—one doubts that he even had the patience to read his friend Leopold Eidlitz's 1881 hefty volume *The Nature and Function of Art, More Especially of Architecture*. The polychromatic palate that Mould employed at All Souls provoked other daring young men to articulate a new chapter in American architecture. During the last half of the nineteenth century, robust color would be an essential ingredient in the design of many buildings. When diarist George Templeton Strong reviewed long established Gothic Revivalist Richard Upjohn's proposal for new buildings for Columbia College, he saw the impact of Mould. "He's going to attempt Venetian pointed, to which he's an utter stranger," remarked Strong; "Ruskin has inspired him with the notion. Also he's going to use brick of divers colors for external work. Mr. J. Wrey Mould set him the example in the Unitarian meeting-house at the corner of Fourth Avenue and Twentieth Street. . . . I'm glad the precedent is to be followed."[8]

Many shared Upjohn's example. Calvert Vaux, who frequently collaborated with Mould, absorbed lessons of color from him. Vaux's handsome 1881 design for the façade of Samuel Tilden's house on Gramercy Park (the present National Arts Club) recalled, in the words of Montgomery Schuyler, that most perceptive and well-informed of our early architectural critics, "the best work of the most successful colorist in architecture whom we have had in New York—Mr. Wrey Mould."[9] Even so staunch a Gothic Revivalist as James Renwick Jr., architect of New York's Grace Episcopal Church and St. Patrick's Cathedral, warmed to Mould's Southern Gothic visions. For his now demolished Church of the Covenant of 1863, Renwick bowed to the rising tide of Mould's brand of modernism to create a colorful and picturesque building that abandoned British and French medieval precedent for the Italian middle ages. The same effect could be felt in Carl Pfeiffer's Church of the Messiah (1867; demolished), with its high-gabled rectory in the same style appended at the back. From the example of All Souls, Leopold Eidlitz, another leading light of the profession, boldly dared to create a vibrant polychromatic exterior for his Church of the Holy Trinity (1872; demolished). Eidlitz found his colorful building sharing with All Souls the reproach of wags who called it the "The Church of the Holy Oil Cloth." Eidlitz held Mould's work in high regard and maintained a fondness for him that endured Mould's personal-life transgressions. "Though antipodean in their respective attitudes towards life, and in everything else excepting their common love for Gothic architecture, [they] were sympathetic even when competitive," remembered Schuyler. He characterized them as "the respectable and responsible Bohemian" and "the Bohemian and irresponsible Anglican."[10]

Viewed in the broad perspective of American nineteenth-century architecture, Mould stands out as the earliest acolyte of British and Continental enchantment with Southern and Eastern European architecture. This strain of modern design developed in England and on the Continent through the endeavors of such architects as Owen Jones, Jules Goury, James Wild, Jacques Ignace Hittorf, Eugene Viollet-le-Duc, and Gottfried Semper. Fascination with the Islamic and Byzantine traditions of the East and their manifestations in medieval Spain and Italy, exemplified something different than purist Gothic Revival notions of Catholic Pugin and the Anglican ecclesiologists. They looked to native British architecture of the thirteenth and fourteenth centuries as the most suited of all styles to inspire Christian piety in modern worshippers. It would be John Ruskin, Mould's contemporary, who revised this thinking by praising the beauties of "oriental" Venetian Gothic, that admixture of Western and Eastern influences. Until Mould arrived in New York, this embrace of the architecture of Southern Europe and the Islamic world was largely unknown in America. "The only contemporary artist who endeavored to Italianize his Gothic in church architecture," observed Schuyler, "was that strange genius, Wrey Mould, and he did not get his commissions from the Episcopal Church." Yet, Mould's was a free-spirited use of Italian sources, and Schuyler praised him for his unconstrained originality. "Wrey Mould's churches were by no means 'examples' of Italian Gothic," he said, "nor, indeed, of any recognized style."[11]

Architectural historians regard the young Philadelphia architect Frank Furness (1839–1912) as the individual who most fully appreciated Mould's innovative designs. In the 1850s, Furness, the son of a Unitarian minister, studied architecture in New York with Richard Morris Hunt, an admirer of Mould's work. Like all followers of the local architectural scene, Furness surely took note of Mould's All Souls. Moreover, Henry Whitney Bellows, the minister at All Souls, was a friend of Furness's father and could have introduced the young student to his innovative church and its architect. The building Furness designed with George Hewett in 1871 for the Pennsylvania Academy of Fine Arts in Philadelphia, both outside and inside, seems pervaded by the influence of Mould's work. The façade displays eccentric proportions and patterned surfaces, and the interior glows with rich color and ornamental detailing, all features common to Mould's esthetic. "There is a curious analogy, without any specific resemblance, between his work in Philadelphia and that which Mr. Mould has done in New York," noted a contemporary observer of the Philadelphia architectural scene. The writer went on to assess the esthetic kinship between the two architects in the following terms: "Both are wonderful fertile and brilliant in invention, with a keen delight in color, which sometimes makes them forget that architecture is essentially an art of modelling with lights and shadows. The most brilliant performances of both are in picturesque rather than monumental designs; and of both it may be said, though of both with many qualifications, and with Mr. Furness with the more hesitation, that the decorator in them tends to overpower the architect."[12]

Other contemporaries of Mould audited his instruction. Both Russell Sturgis (1836–1909) and Peter Bonnett Wight (1838–1925) admitted to having been inspired to read John Ruskin and to wanting to become architects after seeing Mould's drawings for All Souls. "It was from seeing his exquisite working drawings, to which the builders gave me access, and the work as carried out after them, that I first realized what an architect was," stated Wight many years later.[13] Wight's National Academy of Design (1864), one of the lost masterpieces of High Victorian Gothic design (and which beat out Mould's own competition entry), can be easily paired with Mould's work. Until 1901, it stood only a few blocks north on Fourth Avenue from its progenitor. The young Henry Hobson Richardson, who started his architectural practice in New York in the mid-1860s, also learned from the example of All Souls.[14] Mould's design informed both the interior and exterior of Richardson's Brattle Square Church in Boston of 1869 and his unbuilt design of 1871 for Trinity Church in Buffalo. The admired architect Edward Tuckerman Potter (1831–1904), identified by Sarah Bradford Landau along with his younger half-brother William A. Potter (1842–1909) as "the two most important American practitioners of the High Victorian Gothic" period, also owed a debt of inspiration to the lessons of polychrome and festive expression that Mould's buildings taught. In his diary, E. T. Potter, who, like Mould, avowed a serious interest in music, confided his warm admiration for Mould's architecture.[15]

Temperamentally unsuited to manage others, Mould never had a large office like those of Richardson or Richard Morris Hunt that populated the next phase of the profession. Mould was often spoken of in the press as a talented genius but was looked upon as an outsider to his profession. He could be counted on to come up with an adept and original design for whatever commission he might receive, but he never enjoyed membership in the mainstream of the architectural profession of his time. One senses a certain bemused tone common to the remarks of numerous commentators that suggested they regarded him in the same endearing way that one might hold a child prodigy. But everyone admired his performance. Nor did Mould write much about his work or his theories of design. He had little inclination toward formulating grand architectural schemes like those of Calvert Vaux or conceiving original philosophical theories of architecture and society like his friend Leopold Eidlitz. Nowhere do we have evidence of his sharing his colleague Frederick Law Olmsted's brief for moral and social theories regarding modern domestic architecture or justifying the purpose of urban parks. Mould, like his mentor Owen Jones, sought single-mindedly to bring beauty into the world by means of sophisticated notions of color, pattern, ornament, and structure. His imagination, like the music he loved, was emotive. In his buildings, he delighted in picturesque massing, expressive contrasts of scale among design elements, interior spaces spanned by arching trusses, intriguing details, and color-loaded decorative schemes. The example of his work may have inspired many in various ways but failed to form a delineable movement or school of imitators. Nor did his mind incline toward grand projects. "It may be said in general," wrote Schuyler, "that his successes were in inverse proportion to the magnitude of which he undertook, and that while he was apt to fail in architecture properly monumental, he was uniformly and often brilliantly successful in architecture properly picturesque."[16]

In the century following Mould's death, the rise of Modernism consigned his contributions to the attic of architectural history. To International Style disciples of Mies Van Der Rohe's dictum "less is more," Mould's lush ornament, picturesque massing, and warm color schemes appeared relics of decadent Romanticism. At the time of the fire that destroyed All Souls, the authoritative architectural historian Henry-Russell Hitchcock was organizing the Museum of Modern Art's influential exhibition on the International Style. Monochromatic, rectilinear, unornamented, dispassionate, the International Style was all the things All Souls was not. Hitchcock left Mould out of his 1958 *Architecture, Nineteenth and Twentieth Centuries*, a lacuna he corrected in his 1968 essay "Ruskin and American Architecture, or Regeneration Long Delayed."[17] Postmodernism, the historic preservation movement, and generally a more sympathetic appraisal of the architecture and urbanism of the mid-nineteenth century have rehabilitated the reputation of Mould and his contemporaries.

While devoting most of his creative energies to his career in architecture and the design arts, Mould also acquired a reputation in musical circles in London and New York. In his childhood, his mother inspired a lifelong passion for music in her son. Like his mother, Mould became a skilled performer on the piano and organ. By late adolescence, he had united his love of music with his gift for languages to translate into English song lyrics and opera libretti from German, French, and Italian.

In New York, concert and operagoers were familiar with Jacob Wrey Mould as a regular at the city's fashionable musical venues. His presence at performances, score in hand, was a subject of remark by those who knew him. His knowledge of the music ran deep, as his essays about composers and past performances that accompanied his translations reveal. Indeed, Mould could be a severe critic of what he came to see and hear. When a performance of *Don Giovanni* displeased him because it departed from the composer's score, for example, he fumed: "Give us the Finale to the First Act as Mozart wrote it, and not a chorus, which he *never* wrote, consisting of the principal parts reduplicated! Give us a minuet properly danced, and not an exhibition of Monsieur this, and Mdlle that *en cavalier et en dame*. And, *more* than all, restore the last Finale; do not bring down the curtain (as at present) upon eighteen-penny-worth of red and blue fire, but give the true musical and dramatic finish to a mighty monument of human genius."[18] In addition to attending public performances, Mould invited talented young musicians to perform in his home where his soirees were of a high order. At times, Mould himself played the piano and organ at these gatherings.

For Mould, music, especially opera, was an enduring passion and source of income. He was closely associated with the English sheet music publishers Thomas Boosey and Antoine Jullien. He enjoyed a lifelong friendship with the music critic and historian William Rockstro and was compatriot to many of New York's leading musicians and operatic singers. Mould also promoted the cause of music among the public. He raised the money for the first free concerts in Central Park (most of which took place on a bandstand of his own design). He planned the programs and appeared at the concerts acting as a delighted host. In the 1870s, he supported the Church Music Association, an organization dedicated to performing lesser-known compositions of sacred music.[19]

Over the course of his venturesome existence, Mould had seamlessly stitched together the two fabrics of his creative life, architecture and music. He was rare among his professional colleagues for having music as such a strong and enduring avocation. Surely, the inherent emotionalism of his designs and the appeal to the senses in his decorative work represent crossover between the two spheres. Quoting Walter Pater—"All art constantly aspires toward the condition of music"—Charles Jencks explored the subliminal relationship between music and modern architecture.[20] Indeed, the closest counterpart to Mould in our time is David Liebeskind who is both an accomplished musician and an architect. He equates creating architecture with composing music and observes that just as composers of music put down their ideas on sheet music, architects initially envision their buildings with drawings and blueprints. Both he and Mould would certainly agree that the standard definition of music as the art of ordering tones or sounds in succession, in combination, and in temporal relationships to produce a composition having unity and continuity was analogous to their art of building.

Personally, Mould comes into view as a maverick who lived a life generally apart from his close professional associates. While Calvert Vaux was relaxing amidst the beautiful scenery of the Hudson River Highlands or going on sketching excursions in the Catskills, and Olmsted was enjoying the company of New York's cognoscenti at the Century or Union League Club, Mould (never a clubman) might have been cheering on a favorite diva at the opera or taking his pleasure on the water on board the *Octavia* with his extravagant friend Thomas Kennard. A generous host, Mould pursued a lavish lifestyle. Unfortunately, spendthrift ways and costly attachment to the finer things of life caused money to slip through his fingers. Public records show judgments against him by his tailor, grocer, and a furniture dealer. On one occasion, he was even jailed for what was referred to as "a money matter." He borrowed shamelessly from friends and acquaintances, rarely repaying.

Prone to be headstrong and egotistical, Jacob Wrey Mould led a restless, unresolved life. His need for recognition was rarely satisfied, and the wealth he imagined would be his always eluded him. Anxiety over money and resentment over lack of appreciation of his talents soured his spirit. Unsystematic, impractical, and immune from maturity, he displayed a singular indifference to the realities of architecture as a commercial enterprise. "In spite of an industry quite equal to his talent," observed Schuyler at the time of Mould's death, "he was so lacking in business qualities that he never took the place in his profession as a practitioner which belonged to him and was accorded to him as a designer. Indeed, his very best work was done when his own position was practically that of a draughtsman in another architect's office."[21] When he died, his wife had from him two hundred dollars and his house on East Twenty-Sixth Street in New York, which she sold several years later. He was interred in Brooklyn's Green-Wood Cemetery in the large plot owned by his mother's family, which had ever been kind to him. (The whereabouts of his spouse Mary Josephine's grave is unknown.) Mould's impulsive, romantic outlook dominated too frequently, and though he craved recognition, he was determined to follow his own vision and indifferent to how others viewed him.

His impulsive temperament and arrowy spirit unsuited him for ready acceptance by the wider world of his day. A slightly later age was more tolerant of aberrant social behavior of creative people. Arts and crafts pundit Elbert Hubbard and genius architect Frank Lloyd Wright, who violated marital norms in their time, were able to surmount social barriers. Mould's liaison with an unmarried woman, however, seems to have consigned him to the margins of polite society. "He was a man of talent and many genial traits, but was without moral sense," remarked his onetime friend, the artist Jervis McEntee. "But his behavior has been such that I could not recognize him and have had the pain of passing him in the street as a stranger." When news of Mould's death reached him, McEntee confided to his diary "he died almost friendless I learn, although the woman he called his wife stuck to him to the last."[22]

Time has not been kind to Mould's creations. His greatest achievement, All Souls Unitarian Church, burnt down in the 1930s. Albert Bierstadt's mansion, the West Presbyterian Church, Thomas Kennard's house, and Mould's fabulous band shell in Central Park have all disappeared. Sadly, images of these and other departed buildings survive only in black and white photographs or engravings. Fortunately, the large number of drawings he made for Central Park has survived and been conserved at New York's Municipal Archives. Otherwise, most of his architectural drawings, which were famous in their day for their beauty, are lost. To understand the master of color, the historian must rely all too often on the printed word or the eyewitness accounts of Mould's contemporaries. For this reason, readers of this book will be required to exercise their imagination, for written descriptions are sometimes the only record remaining of the original. And as for his contributions to the musical life of his times, the present age is nearly entirely unaware of them.

Few people commented on Mould's personal appearance other than George Templeton Strong who, while admiring him for his cleverness, regarded him as ugly. In fact, few images of Mould have survived. Most often reproduced is a group photograph with Mould and others taken in Central Park by the French American photographer Victor Prévost who chronicled the

Figure 1. Willowdale Arch in Central Park with early park creators (1862).

emerging park in September 1862. On September 23, he recorded the park's chief creators standing on Willowdale Arch. Mould is said to be the figure second from the right (fig. 1).

A few days before, Prévost took another photograph of Mould that shows him standing with studied nonchalance next to the easternmost pillar at the foot of the Bethesda Terrace. The freshly carved relief decoration emblematic of springtime is clearly discernable, but Mould's thirty-seven-year-old visage is not. The natty outfit of light-colored pants, slightly darker waistcoat and top hat with contrasting ribbon band, however, conforms to our understanding of his fondness for fashionable dress. His jaunty attitude holding a copy of *Le Messager Franco-Americain*—a French-language journal published in New York—suggests pride of authorship in the carved ornaments that grace the massive pier (fig. 2).[23] Prévost, who dedicated an album of thirty-five albumen prints of the nascent park to Andrew H. Green, the city comptroller who oversaw the park's construction, might well have captioned Mould's image with Clarence Cook's reflection: "He has such delight in his art."[24] It was Cook who published the most familiar image we have of Mould, a woodcut portrait in his 1869 book on Central Park. At that date, Mould would have been in his mid-forties. It must have

Figure 2. Mould standing next to the Spring pillar, Bethesda Terrace, Central Park.

derived from the same photograph tapped for the portrait published by *Harper's Weekly* at the time of Mould's death in 1886 (it appears as the frontispiece).

Almost as elusive as his physical appearance is the answer to the question, was Jacob Wrey Mould a Black architect? At the time of his death, his attending physician listed his "Color" as "white" on his death certificate. Nevertheless, thanks to Lucille Gordon's research, we know that his grandfather, Jacob Mould, went to the Gold Coast (modern Ghana) to work for the Company of Merchants Trading to Africa. He eventually became Governor Mould, the director of the Company's slave trade operations and lived in the infamous Cape Coast Castle. While in Africa, he appears to have married Sarah Miles (or she lived with him as his wife), the daughter of a Black African mother and white English father. In the terminology of the day, Sarah would have been a mulatto. If this story were true, and I believe it is, then the answer would be yes, the architect had Black ancestry. His father, also named Jacob Mould, the son of Sarah Miles and Governor Mould, spent most of his youth in England where he became an attorney. The actual term for Jacob Wrey Mould's racial status was "hexadecaroon," one-sixteenth part Black ancestry. In the arcane legal classification of races prevalent in the nineteenth century, many people held that one drop of Black blood made a person Black. In that case, Jacob Mould would probably have been considered a person of color. As far as we know, Jacob Wrey Mould never presented himself as having Black African ancestry or family association with the Gold Coast slave trade. Given the age and society in which he lived, this is understandable.

We can have confidence in the belief that Jacob Wrey Mould belonged to that small class of people known today as racially ambiguous. Legal scholar Daniel J. Sharfstein notes that since colonial times in America, people of color "have lived among white people, identified themselves as white, and been regarded by others—neighbors, strangers, government officials—as white."[25] Mould fits the description by Stanford University historian Allyson Hobbs that passing—the term used today to describe people of African American heritage who could pass for being white—"was possible in a society where whiteness was not based solely (or arguably, even primarily) on appearance, but also on dress, comportment, and social knowledge."[26] In New York, the presence of Mould's Caucasian mother, his British accent, and his impeccable English education and training—and, yes, even his liaison with an Irish-born woman—would have buttressed his credentials within the white community. We can assume that Mould knew he was living a life of passing, although no documentary evidence has surfaced to confirm the supposition. Whether or not his Oakley relatives were aware of his ancestry is likely but also uncertain. Did his mentor, Owen Jones, know? If so, might his stark warning to Mould on his departure for America have been motivated at least in part by this knowledge? In New York, Mould surely felt comfortable with his close professional associates, Calvert Vaux, another Englishman, and Frederick Law Olmsted, whose abolitionist credentials derived from his firsthand knowledge of the South. Within Olmsted's circle of friends was the explorer Clarence King who presented himself as African American and married a former slave. In the greater society in which Mould moved, however, including the world of music, to have been revealed as having African blood would probably have spelled serious trouble for him. In any event, surely he would have shared historian Robert Fikes's observation that whereas passing was a cause "for anxiety for white Americans fearing racial contamination and degradation," it made "laughable fools of those who countenanced notions of white racial purity and supremacy."[27]

1

Family Territory

England, Africa, Ireland, America

From the colonial era to the present, people of African ancestry have crossed the color line and faded into the world around them.

—Daniel J. Sharfstein, *The Invisible Line*

JACOB WREY MOULD DESCENDED from a middle-class British family whose members had careers in the church, commerce, and law. His great-great-grandfather, Jacob Mould, devoted his life to the Anglican Church in rural England. After working in Staffordshire as schoolmaster of the Wheaton Aston Free School and then curate of All Saints church in Lapley, he assumed the vicarship of the parish church in the small Worcestershire community of Pebworth. From 1759 until his death in 1805, the Reverend Mould served as vicar of St. Eadburgha's, a church dating to the Romanesque period, in the picturesque Cotswold village of Ebrington, Gloucestershire. He and his wife Sarah had several sons and daughters. Their oldest son, William (1763–1839), also became a clergyman, holding for over fifty years the post of rector in a parish in Devon. Another son, Jacob, was born in 1770. The family hoped that this younger scion would set himself up in a profession. They had in mind the law, which required, after schooling, a five-year apprenticeship as an articled clerk to a licensed attorney.

Young Jacob, however, lacked the necessary temperament for tedious legal work. His was a free spirit, an impulsive youth who hoped to advance himself without the grind of studies and apprenticeship. Eager for adventure, he sought to break free of bucolic Ebrington. When the opportunity offered itself to join the Company of Merchants Trading to Africa, Jacob was eager to enlist. Employment with the company offered the prospect of adventure in exotic Africa. While his brother William anticipated a comfortable sinecure in the church, Jacob set his sights on the Gold Coast from where he might return home a rich man. It was widely recognized that a young man hired as a writer—a junior officer charged with keeping company records—had the privilege of conducting his own trade as a private individual in such valuable commodities as gold dust, elephant's teeth, and Black slaves. This freelancing provision was meant both to expand trading with the native population and to foster initiative among the officers. Unfortunately, it also allowed the unscrupulous to enrich themselves at the expense of the company. Advancement promised to be relatively rapid because clerks rotated through different departments and, if one stayed, he might ascend to the governorship, which paid the handsome sum of two thousand pounds per year. Moreover, the claim on one's time was light; the work schedule required only three or four hours per day. Jacob Mould's father and two family friends, Richard and Stephen Taylor of Red Lion Street, London, stood young Jacob's bond. On July 28, 1786, he received an allowance of fifteen pounds to pay for his passage on the next supply ship bound for the Gold Coast, where he was admitted to the company with the position of writer.

The attraction of gold and slave labor for their West Indies plantations first brought the Dutch to the Gold Coast in the fifteenth century. Danes, Swedes, and other European merchants followed. English trade in West Africa started sometime later. After Queen Elizabeth I came to the throne in 1558 she chartered new trading companies and encouraged some already in existence. She even gave John Hawkins, the first Englishman to profit from the nefarious Triangle Trade, a ship from her fleet. In 1562, almost a century after the Portuguese, Hawkins made the voyage marking the beginning of the English slave trade. He left Plymouth bound for Africa with the express purpose of buying Black Africans along the Guinea Coast to sell as laborers on the plantations of the New World. A few years later, Hawkins's cousin Francis Drake joined in the lucrative commerce in "black gold."

For the next three centuries, Elizabeth's successors further developed the West African trade. In the seventeenth century, when Charles II authorized the Company of Royal Adventurers Trading into Africa, he added gold mining, ivory, palm oil, and other goods to the list of commodities. Traders bought Gold Coast ivory and palm oil, valuable cargoes to sell in

England, with ordinary British goods such as cloth, guns and ammunition, hardware, tobacco, cheap glassware, and alcoholic beverages.[1] Heading the list, however, was the lucrative trafficking in human beings for West Indies sugar plantations.

When the young Mould reached his post in Africa, he was plunged into the most difficult conditions. The heat was unparalleled in his experience. He was exposed to life-threatening diseases unknown in England, among them malaria and sleeping sickness. His colleagues died in horrifying numbers from these illnesses and from dysentery and various fevers. New employees sometimes perished aboard ship during the difficult journey. Others drowned within sight of the company's Cape Coast Castle headquarters when the canoe ferrying them from ship to shore overturned in heavy swells.

Every aspect of young Mould's new location must have seemed a radical change from Ebrington. The small coastal villages were crowded and dirty, and lacked even proper thoroughfares. Communication between towns was infrequent and difficult. Because of the coastal surf, transport by canoe was both uncomfortable and unsafe. The thick woolen clothing worn by the Europeans made death almost inevitable if the boat overturned. Traveling by land posed its own challenges. Most people journeyed on foot toting heavy rucksacks, for European pack animals were unreliable because they often succumbed to diseases carried by the omnipresent tsetse fly.[2]

Jacob Mould soon found himself living in a small community of Englishmen on the coast. Such places usually had fewer than forty officers of the company plus a contingent of soldiers. They were completely reliant on the local people for food, supplies, and services of every kind from the daily household chores of cooking, cleaning, and laundry to construction work, transportation, and communication with company employees at other locations. Far from the comforts of home, men like Jacob soon came to realize that survival and profit demanded they adapt to the indigenous cultures.

Successful trading could only come about with harmonious relations with the local people. The Fante ethnic group, England's primary trading partners, had an elaborate social system that was imperative for men like Mould to understand. Mould quickly mastered their language. He also absorbed the customs of the Asante and Dahomey, other trading partners each with a different social structure. Since few Englishmen ever went inland, trade was carried on through a network of African traders who brought slaves and products from the interior to the coast. The company conducted business in a string of trading posts scattered throughout the area of their charter. They ranged from small lodges staffed by a single trader and a soldier or two to larger trading posts called factories or forts. The forts had once been places for securely storing gold; they now became the dungeons where the company held captured people awaiting shipment as slaves by private merchants to the sugar plantations of the West Indies. The imposing Cape Coast Castle served as the administrative seat of the extensive enterprise. The large forbidding three-story white-washed building with a red tile roof was protected from enemies by heavy canons pointed at the only logical route of attack—the sea. Not far from the infamous "door of no return," the castle's chambers included comfortable "lounging rooms" for company officers.

Life in the castle was anything but comfortable and secure. The officers in charge struggled to maintain order among the English staff and to enforce the rules and regulations of the company. Many of the men suffered loneliness, boredom, and physical ailments. Malaria, yellow fever, smallpox, and Guinea worm often proved fatal. The oppressive climate fueled many angry outbursts, and ill feelings and quarrels were frequent and could be bitter. Not surprisingly, chronic drunkenness was a common problem. With dismissal recurring often and the mortality rate high, there were frequent openings in the company's hierarchy. Promotion was almost automatic. Young men like Mould could quickly move up into positions of authority.

Jacob's rise in the company structure is well documented by the London and Cape Coast meeting minutes preserved in Britain's National Archives. So are his censures and suspensions. In 1798, Jacob, who had started as a lowly writer, had achieved the status of governor of the company. Nevertheless, the effects of excessive drinking had changed the eager boy into a bullying, irresponsible man whose careless actions almost resulted in a war with the locals. Jacob Mould was removed first from governing responsibilities and then from the company's service for his alcohol-fueled mistakes and insubordinate behavior. After sixteen years in Africa, he left for home in disgrace in 1804.

The discredited governor, however, did not live to see England and Ebrington again, for he died aboard ship during the transatlantic voyage. Nonetheless, he left an important legacy, a son who bore his name, Jacob. In his better days, Governor Mould had married a local woman, Sarah Miles. She was the daughter of Richard Miles, a former governor of the company. Her mother had been a daughter of a Fante native, the Reverend Philip Quaque (1741–1816), probably from his second marriage. As a young man, Quaque had gone to England to be educated, and after completing his studies in theology at Oxford became the first Black African ordained to the ministry by the Church of England. He was a tragic figure caught between his native origins and loyalty to the British crown and church. Modern historians maintain the critical view that "he interacted far more closely with the African producers and European consumers of enslaved Africans than with the enslaved themselves."[3] As a cleric, Quaque was especially vehement on the subject of the sanctity of Christian matrimony, a sacrament into which he entered multiple instances. Twice a widower, he married three times. Quaque's first wife had been an Englishwoman; after her death he had married her African maidservant, the apparent mother of Sarah Miles.

One assumes that given Sarah's status as a daughter of the venerated Anglican priest, she would have been legally married to Jacob Mould. Nonetheless, imitating the regional custom of polygamy was not unusual among the English, as Quaque admitted. Among the foreigners, he complained, that there was "no real marriage, except that which they term consorting,"[4] which meant concubinage. Many of the men had "country wives" (the polite term the British used to describe native concubines) and families wherever their work assignments took them. By 1789, for example, Mould was posted to Anamabu; in 1790 to Accra; in 1791 to Seccomdu, and in 1792 to Pram-Pram. As he moved from one outpost to another, steadily rising in the ranks of the company, he may have become attached to local women. During his sixteen years on the Gold Coast, he could have left progeny in several villages. Indeed, there are many Moulds today in Ghana holding positions in business, government, science, and education who trace their ancestry back to Jacob Mould whom they refer to simply as "the Governor." When Jacob returned to England, it appears that Sarah remained in the castle. After Jacob Mould's death, she remarried a man named Dawson. He went back to England in 1816, but Sarah remained in Ghana. Her tombstone has been found in the castle—she died in 1839—where it bears the inscription "Mrs. Sarah Dawson/Late Sarah Mould." "Sarah may have been unusual in being accorded the rank of 'Mrs.' on her tomb," observes William St. Clair, historian of the Gold Coast slave trade, "but not in remaining in the Castle when her men left."

Young Jacob, Anglo-African mulatto son of Sarah Miles and Governor Mould and the future father of the architect, spent his first years in Ghana. He probably received his earliest education in the school for mixed-race children that Philip Quaque, who is regarded as the founder of the modern educational system in Ghana, maintained at the castle. At some early point in his life, the youngster, perhaps accompanying his father onboard ship in 1802, went to live with his grandparents in Ebrington. We do not know how the Gloucester family felt about their son's association with the slave trade—the Church of England was divided over the morality of the practice—nor how they first received their exotic grandson. He apparently was sufficiently fair-skinned to be taken for white. But how he himself regarded his situation is unknown. As historian of the Ghana slave trade Rachel A. A. Engmann has pointed out: "Further sustained research is required to theorize the European-African entanglement in and around the coastal fortifications, as well as to increase our understanding of the role of material culture in the articulation and maintenance of Euro-African identity and social relations, particularly how Euro-Africans viewed themselves in relation to others, African and European, free and unfree."[5]

In Ebrington, the family apparently regarded Jacob as an English grandchild who just happened to have been born in Africa. Jacob had an unexceptional English upbringing, and ironically, grew up to become a member of the bar, practicing the legal profession that his errant father had staunchly refused to pursue. Apparently, the son had not inherited his father's adventurous character—nor his quixotic temperament. To all appearances, his was a quiet, uneventful life. Africa, the land of his birth, appears to have held no attraction for him; as an adult, he probably never went there. Jacob Mould, Esq., first appears in the "London Attorney" section of the Law Lists in 1821. He had an office at 3 Field Court, Grey's Inn at the Inns of Court. Mould's days revolved around drawing wills, leases, mortgages, patent applications, and documents for sale of real estate. His practice was successful enough for him to be able to marry Miss Mary Ann Oakley (1794–1875) on May 15, 1823. The wedding took place in Shepperton, just outside of London, where the couple chose to reside.[6] Jacob's great uncle, the Reverend William Mould, performed the ceremony.

Mary Ann was born in 1794, one of eleven children, nine of whom survived into adulthood. Her parents, William and Mary Oakley, lived in the parish of St Johns Horselydowns in the south London neighborhood of Bermondsey in the borough of Southwark. In Chaucer's day, Southwark had been a place where pilgrims found rest and lodging in many inns and hostels located at the gates of London. In the sixteenth century, it was home to Shakespeare's Globe Theatre. In Mary Ann's youth, however, Southwark was a sprawling network of neighborhoods and a busy center of manufacturing and commercial activities, notably leather tanning and wool processing. It was in the later industry that William Oakley, Mary Ann's father, was engaged. The convenience of the docks helped his wool stapling (the weaving together of single strands of wool to form a string fiber) trade to thrive. In 1790, the travel writer Thomas Pennant commented, "Bermondsey Street (in Southwark) may at present be called the great Wool-Staple of our kingdom. Here reside numbers of merchants who supply Rochdale, Leicester, Derby, Exeter, and most other weaving counties."[7]

At twenty-nine, Mary Ann entered married life a bit later than usual for those days. At the time of her marriage, her father was struggling to reestablish his bankrupt business in distant America on money borrowed from a brother. Jacob Mould could well have been able to afford a dowerless but well-educated and accomplished wife. To his in-laws, the Oakleys, a middle-class merchant family, he was more than acceptable. He was a professional man, his father had held a well-regarded post as a governor of the Company of Traders to Africa, a prestigious royal charter company, and his grandfather was a beloved clergyman in Gloucester.

William Oakley's family home on Church Street, where Mary Ann grew up, was in an enclave of comfortable middle-class life. Though warehouses and small manufacturing premises stood nearby, in the years the Oakleys resided there, they could still enjoy spring walks along lanes lined by blossoming trees and hunt for mushrooms in the nearby grassy fields. As faithful churchgoers, the family probably took part in the ancient custom of the "Perambulation of the Boundaries." An annual event held on Holy Thursday, the ceremony consisted of clergy, officials, and parishioners solemnly walking the boundaries of the parish.

Together with commerce, the Oakley family included accomplished artisans and artists among its members. Mary Ann's father's younger brother, George Oakley (1773–1840), conducted a thriving business in fine furniture in Bond Street. As early as 1799, following a visit by Queen Charlotte and other members of the royal family, he had received the Royal Warrant. His reputation flourished after that. In 1801, the *Journal des Luxus und der Moden* of Weimar (a popular periodical on the subject of fashion in Germany) noted that "'everyone of taste and discernment' is 'making purchases at Oakley's, the most tasteful of London's cabinet-makers."[8] George Oakley's list of distinguished clients was headed by the Prince Regent, who fitted out Carlton House, his elegant London residence, with Oakley pieces. The prince delighted in collecting magnificent furniture and put George Oakley's work among the famous names in the decorative arts of the Regency era.

Others of Mary Ann's family were associated with the arts. Another uncle,

Benjamin Oakley (b. 1792), was both a successful stockbroker and a talented portrait painter. Mary Ann's brother, Octavius Oakley (1800–1867), the eighth child, rejected his father's ambition to have him follow him in the wool business and instead became a successful painter. He achieved a considerable reputation for his images of gypsies and London street scenes. Among his portrait clients were luminaries such as the botanist and architect Joseph Paxton, designer of the Crystal Palace, and the anthropologist and explorer Francis Galton, the inventor of fingerprint identification. Today, the National Portrait Gallery in London counts among its collection numerous pieces by Octavius Oakley.

All of the Oakley children were encouraged to pursue drawing and music together with the traditional subjects considered essential to be well educated. Mary Ann herself was particularly devoted to music. At a young age, she learned to play the recently improved pianoforte with its rich and varied sound. With her accompaniment, her younger siblings sang the latest songs that were available in growing numbers through popular sheet music sales. Among these new publications were opera scores "reduced" to piano arrangements with libretti translated into English. This musical form was to play a significant role in the life of Mary Ann's yet undreamed-of child, Jacob Wrey Mould.

When Mary Ann was in her early twenties, William Oakley suffered serious financial setbacks. Together with loss of some risky speculations, the lifting of wartime commercial restrictions had compromised her father's once prosperous wool business. The French blockade imposed during the Napoleonic wars that had inflated the demand for domestic wool in England and had made the Oakley family financially comfortable ended in 1816. Former shipping lanes reopened, making raw materials available from outside of England.

With the precipitous decline in the family's business prospects, their lives underwent dramatic changes. In 1815, William Jr., George, and Alexander accompanied their father to America with the hope of reviving their prosperity. Mary Ann's brother Cyrus, the youngest, went to seek his fortune in Calcutta, where he died unexpectedly in 1819. Mary Ann and her younger sisters Louisa, Decima, and Arabella remained in England for the time being. They may have lived with the family of Uncle Benjamin and Aunt Hannah in Tavistock Square, London.

Eventually, Mary Ann had the good fortune to meet a suitor, a solicitor practicing in London. The slightly exotic Jacob was a fine catch for a woman already in her late twenties. In 1823, she married the African-born Jacob Mould. The newlyweds settled into a comfortable house in Bloomsbury near the border with the neighborhood of St. Giles-in-the-Fields. If it had not been for marriage, surely Mary Ann would have joined her sisters Louisa, Charlotte, and Decima when, in May 1825, they sailed aboard the fast packet ship Acasta to join their father and brothers in New York. By then, Mary Ann had already begun a journey of another sort; within four months, she was to become a mother.

Having borrowed one thousand dollars from his financially successful younger brother Benjamin, William, with his sons and Alexander,[9] reestablished their wool trade business in New York's busy dock area on the East River. They started on Water Street, not far from the old Tontine Coffee House at the juncture with Wall Street. By 1826, *Longworth's Business Directory* listed William Oakley & Sons at 3 Phoenix Building. The family resided in a house on Varick Street, a stone's throw from St. John's Chapel and its private park. The tranquil neighborhood a block from the Hudson River was the most fashionable in the city. In addition to William Sr., the household included his son George and his new American wife, Elizabeth (his first wife had died in England in 1807). Also living there were the American widow of William Jr., Susan, and her two daughters. William Jr. had died of a fever in Kentucky, where he had gone presumably to establish a link with the merino sheep farmers.

While the Oakley men worked hard to make a good living in business, the women of the family devoted themselves to education. In 1836, Louisa, the oldest of the sisters who had left England in 1825, had charge of the Young Ladies' Academy on Park Place. When she retired in 1845, her younger sisters took over running of the exclusive finishing school for girls of good family and rechristened it the Oakley Misses School.

Attention to the arts characterized life in the Oakley home on Varick Street. When George was not busy earning a living in the wool trade, he devoted himself to painting and drawing. In 1826, he became an associate member of the National Academy of Design, which his friend Samuel F. B. Morse had inaugurated the year before and which George was keen to see succeed. The academy's annual exhibition of members' work introduced its artists to a growing New York art scene, and its classes put art education on a firm institutional foundation in America. The collection of engravings and mezzotints and skillful copies of masterpieces that George had made in the galleries of Europe were a part of his own talented daughters' education in the fine arts. Georgiana, Isabel, and Juliana were all sent to Europe to study and visit museums and monuments.[10] His granddaughter, Violet Oakley (1874–1961), America's first important female muralist—and second cousin to architect Jacob Wrey Mould—would also benefit from studying his collections of prints and the copies made from them by Juliana. As a child, Violet remembered that she could sit for hours, "gaze, and study . . . before my Aunt Juliana's copy of the portrait of Sarah Siddons, by Gainsborough."[11]

Around 1830, George took his family, now four little ones, to spend three years in England where two more daughters were born. The reason for his return was most likely to be the agent for the American business. How happy Mary Ann must have been for three years to have her beloved older brother once more within visiting distance. Her only child, five-year-old Jacob Wrey, came to know his transatlantic family. Arthur, three years his junior, seems to have been a favorite. In 1833, George returned to New York. By then, his father had taken the fruits of his labors and gone to live out his days in England, near Bath, with his daughter-in-law Susan and her two children. Though Mary Ann could occasionally visit them there, it was to be almost twenty years before she would see her brothers and sisters again.

2

Youthful Years in London

Architecture and Music

> His intellectual interests were, and remained to the end of his life, architecture and music, and they amounted to passions.
>
> —Montgomery Schuyler, "Jacob Wrey Mould"

THE BIRTH OF THE ONLY CHILD of Mary Ann Oakley and Jacob Mould, Esq., took place on August 7, 1825. Jacob Wrey Mould was registered into the parish records of St. Giles-in-the-Fields, London, their municipal administrative district.[1] Mary Ann and Jacob lived in the Bloomsbury neighborhood at 12 Keppel Street in the combined parishes of St. Giles-in-the-Fields and St. George's. In later life, their son claimed the suburb of Chislehurst as his birthplace. Since Mary Ann had Oakley relatives living there, it is possible that she had stayed with them during her pregnancy.

While St. Giles was associated with the disreputable area that Charles Dickens portrayed often and graphically as a nest of disease and crime-ridden "rookeries," Bloomsbury, next door, with its green squares and well-kept houses, offered a gracious place for the newly married couple to raise their child. The area had been distinctly aristocratic in the eighteenth century and in their day accommodated people in the rising middle class seeking respectable homes to rent. The neighborhood was close to much and offered many advantages to the young couple. It put them close to Mary Ann's Uncle Benjamin and Aunt Hannah Oakley who were then living nearby at Tavistock Place. Moreover, it was an easy trip for Jacob to his solicitor's office at nearby Gray's Inn.

Keppel was a very short street, only one block long. In the early nineteenth century, a surprising number of well-known people lived there or in the immediate vicinity. Augustus W. N. Pugin, "God's Architect," who elevated the Gothic style to be synonymous with Christian piety, was born at number 39 in 1812. Anthony Trollope, the prolific novelist, was born at number 6 in 1815 and baptized at St. George's, as would be young Jacob. In 1817, the artist John Constable set up housekeeping with his new bride on Keppel Street. Just around the corner, at 6 Gower Street, Lord Eldon, the longest-reigning Lord Chancellor of England, resided in splendor in an elegant Greek Revival mansion. In 1839, Charles Darwin brought his bride Emma Wedgwood to live nearby on Gower Street, where they occupied a small, furnished house that he dubbed "Macaw Cottage" for its red and yellow décor.

The Moulds enjoyed a good life in Keppel Street. Young Jacob's father pursued a successful law practice, busy with wills, estates, real estate sales and land disputes. Such perennial work could make a good income for a diligent man. Young Jacob seems to have been a clever lad, the cherished center of his little domestic world. His father was pleased to pay Henry Howard (1769–1847), a fashionable London artist, to paint a portrait of his young son (fig. 3). The boy, whose family nickname was "Lovely-go-Bubbins," appears charmingly curly-haired, bright-eyed, and endowed with a peaches-and-cream complexion. There is no hint of the Black African blood he would have inherited from his grandmother Sarah Miles. The hoop and stick he holds, however, might be an oblique reference to her place of birth. The game hoop-and-pole, while known everywhere, was especially popular throughout Africa.

We know relatively little about Jacob Wrey Mould's earliest education. At first, his mother, with the help of two tutors, schooled him herself at home. It is easy to picture mother and toddler as he learned his alphabet and numbers. Later, she would have taught him English history and geography. Young Jacob would have memorized all the kings and queens of England and the names of the battles that had been fought and won for England, especially the most recent against Napoleon. The Oakleys were a well-educated family and stressed languages, especially for boys because they would find them useful in careers in the international wool trade. It is possible that Jacob began at an early age to master German, French, and Italian, knowledge of which would be essential to him in later life. It would also be nice to know if after lessons he might have constructed fictive buildings using the popular "The Young Builder" game.

Nor would Mary Ann have neglected her son's outdoor recreation. As a

Figure 3. Henry Howard, pastel portrait of the young Jacob Wrey Mould, ca. 1835.

small child, Jacob surely enjoyed all the play of any boy of his class. From Howard's portrait, one can guess that running with the hoop was a favorite pastime. As an adult, he would advocate fresh air for growing children. He once recommended to a client that he encourage his young son to enjoy outdoor exercise every day for robust health.

Since it was fashionable at this time for well-bred boys and girls to learn to draw and paint, there is a good chance that Mary Ann's home curriculum included art. If young Jacob showed any signs of talent in this direction, surely his mother would have been pleased and encouraged him. Jacob's great passion for music also must have begun at his mother's knee. She possessed an intense interest in music and considerable amateur talent. He remembered that his mother had convinced his father to buy a fortepiano, a sizeable investment at the time. On many a rainy London afternoons, his mother would play the piano for him—Mozart's "Turkish March" was his favorite. The precocious Jacob wrote poetry set to music composed by his friend William Rockstro. As an adult, his love of music was a constant source of pleasure, comfort, and income.

He maintained an especial fondness for opera, with its dramatic stories and lyrical music. When Mould was barely out of his teens, he translated opera librettos for publication.[2] In his introduction to Thomas Boosey's score of Carl Maria von Weber's 1821 opera *Der Freischütz* (*The Marksman*), which he considered "one of the most beautiful, striking, and original productions of Musical Art," Mould described his first reactions as a fourteen-year-old to the highly charged story:

> Most vividly did this tale of horrors seize upon our youthful imagination; and most clearly do we remember the period when we were allowed to go to the play alone for the first time, and, procuring pocket-money, ran off to the pit of Drury Lane to witness the performance of this Work, in 1839. A sleepless night was the result, and a confused terror of Samuel and the Wolf's Glen monsters intruded upon our Homer and Virgil lessons at school, bringing us, too, into sad disgrace with the Mathematical master for (as may be guessed) inattention. Well did the constant relation of its wonders to gaping schoolfellows change our patronymic to the soubriquet of "Der Freischütz."[3]

In March 1830, Jacob Mould dissolved his barrister partnership at Gray's Inn. After 1832, his name and office address disappear from the London lists of solicitors. For reasons unknown, Jacob chose to move himself and his family to the southern Irish city of Cork. He would practice law there until his death in 1841. Though Cork was a thriving commercial port and the second largest city in Ireland, it offered limited cultural attractions. Mary Ann would have been far from remaining family and old friends and London's familiar places. To her, Cork must have seemed a place deficient in the cultural pleasures she so loved. Indeed, in later life Mould described the years in Cork as "a childhood spent for the most part in seclusion from all the things of Art."[4]

By the time young Jacob was thirteen, his parents decided it was time to send him to attend school in London. Both Moulds were faithful communicants of the Anglican Church, so they favored a Church of England institution. They enrolled Jacob in the recently established King's College in London where he would study in the Lower Department.

King's College, now part of London University, was one of two new schools founded in response to the call for reforms in the British educational system. Traditional instruction limited to the study of theology and the classics no longer seemed to meet the requirements of modern life. Widespread industrialization, overseas empire, and the growth of new occupations had brought about many social and economic changes. The times demanded an expanded educational curriculum. In 1828, a group of eminent politicians, churchmen, and educators envisioned a university that would provide middle-class students with a pragmatic education. Formerly, education beyond basics had been primarily for those going to enter the church, government, the legal profession, or medicine. Now there was a need to train scientists, engineers, architects, and businessmen. King's College came into being to meet those needs. In August 1829, King George IV granted the institution a royal charter.

Leading Anglicans among the reformers also suggested that in contrast to Oxford and Cambridge, the moral and spiritual welfare of students of the new college would best be served if they continued to live at home under the guidance of their parents and local religious leaders. The new college acquired property in central London adjacent to Somerset House at the Strand. Its "middling rich" students could greatly benefit financially from living at home. The student body represented a great change from aristocracy to meritocracy and included members of all religious persuasions. (Faculty, however, were generally required to be members of the Church of England.) In a further departure from tradition, the directors banned corporal punishment.

In order to become a pupil it was desirable to have a sponsor. A Bloomsbury neighbor and friend, William Rothery (1775–1864), who was a proprietor of King's College, supported Jacob's candidacy.[5] Rothery was a churchwarden at St. George, Bloomsbury, where the Moulds had been congregants. He was also the chief of the office of the King's Proctor at the Doctors' Commons at the Inns of Court where he had known Jacob's father. Coincidentally, Rothery, who embraced liberal social and political causes, had, in 1821, been the admiralty's mediator on slave trade issues under the Act for the Abolition of the Slave Trade. Enacted in 1807, the act eventually led to the peaceful abolition of slavery throughout the empire in 1833. A few years after that, Rothery actively supported the Society for the Extinction of the Slave Trade and for the Civilization of Africa. Founded in 1839, the society aimed "to make the Africans acquainted with the inexhaustible riches of their own soil." One wonders if he ever discussed with his friend Jacob Mould Sr. his Gold Coast origins or mentioned to him the irony of a man so active in the eradication of slave trading sponsoring the grandson of a slave trader. Rothery was a pivotal figure in Mould's young life. His help and connections were later were going to be important in opening the way to Jacob's career in architecture.

Though the founders of King's College planned it primarily for local young men, they also made provision for a small number of boarding students. The student body included boys from as far away as the West Indies, Ceylon, and Spain. Jacob left Ireland and the year after Victoria ascended the throne, became a boarder staying with the assistant headmaster of the lower school. At the time Jacob entered there were more than 350 boys enrolled. The school fees of £9.8 and 6 shillings for a half year were paid on August 11, 1838. "I have followed the profession of architecture since 1838,"[6] Mould would declare many years later in New York.

The "lower department" in which Jacob was enrolled occupied the basement of the college in a building erected in 1831 to designs by Robert Smirke. It was attached to the east side of the Somerset House, which Smirke had also designed. Sabine Baring-Gould, the author of the hymn "Onward Christian Soldiers," who attended the college somewhat later, found the building "depressing." He condemned Smirke's work as "fossilized ugliness." Charles Fell, who entered twenty years after Mould, remembered that the courtyard received no sun in winter and no breeze in summer.[7] We have no record of Mould's impression of the place, but it is possible that he shared these negative views of his alma mater.

The King's College curriculum covered a broad range of subjects: arithmetic, history, religion, grammar and composition, natural philosophy, algebra, modern geography, and the classics. It embraced studies from classical Greek and Latin to modern European languages. Drawing lessons were also available at no extra fee from John Sell Cotman (1782–1842), whom the school had hired in 1834 on the recommendation of J. M. W. Turner. Cotman was an accomplished landscape painter, illustrator, watercolorist, and etcher whose pupils remembered him as a generous teacher. His sensitive representations of architecture had won him honorary membership in the Royal Institute of British Architects. Later critics recognized two distinct sides of his artistic nature: "As an architectural draughtsman and illustrator he was skillful, but sometimes dull. As a 'fantasist' in colour and design he produced work of unique quality and character and he used nature for those purposes rather than for its own sake."[8] Dante Gabriel Rossetti, a fellow student of Mould's at King's College, was one of his

Figure 4. John Sell Cotman: *Doorway, Heckingham Church,* graphite and wash, 1838.

pupils. One would like to think that Mould also sought Cotman's mentoring, and that perhaps the origins of Mould's later handsome architectural drawings and remarkable mastery of color rested with Cotman's instruction (fig. 4).

Gregarious by nature, Mould doubtlessly enjoyed being in the company of the high-spirited and creative boys who were his companions. Several who were there during Mould's time achieved notable careers in the arts. Outstanding among them was Dante Gabriel Rossetti, the future founder of the Pre-Raphaelite Brotherhood. His brother, William Michael Rossetti, who became a writer and critic, was also a classmate of Mould. Their father, Gabriel Rossetti, poet and Dante scholar, was the school's Italian master and surely counted Mould among his pupils. A fervent Italian patriot in exile, Rossetti was a man who had fought for his country's freedom with the weapons of words. The Austrian government viewed his writings as so powerful a threat that he had been forced to flee for his life from Italy. In England, he continued to support constitutional government for his homeland and waited for the unification he would not live long enough to see. One surmises that Mould first learned to love the language, art, and music of Italy from his contact with this extraordinary family. Not long after leaving the college, Mould would demonstrate perceptive command of the language in his translations of opera librettos.

Other boys at King's College would go on to become successful architects. William Burges (1827–1881) entered the school in 1839. He later became one of England's leading High Victorian designers. Mould would have taken pleasure in remembering him when he would have learned that, in 1863, Burges won the commission to design the new cathedral in Cork. In 1872, he convinced the trustees of Trinity College in Hartford, Connecticut, to accept his elaborate plans for their new campus. Henry Bayley Garling (1822–1904), recipient of both silver and gold medals from the Royal Institute of British Architects, later became the partner of Edward Middleton Barry (1830–1880), another King's College student. The son of Sir Charles Barry, the designer of the new Houses of Parliament, Edward made his reputation in 1857 when the directors of Convent Garden Theatre chose him to design a replacement for the building that fire had destroyed. Gervase Wheeler (1815–1889) would proceed Mould in immigrating to the United States where, for over a decade, he enjoyed a successful architectural career. His 1855 book *Homes for the People in Suburb and Country* was a significant contribution to the growing body of literature in America devoted to domestic architecture.

Just before Jacob completed the lower classes set of courses in 1841, and a few months before his sixteenth birthday, his father died in Cork. Soon after, Mary Ann returned to London and resumed residence with her son in the house on Keppel Street. The widow, however, had evidently been left with little money. In Keppel Street, she took in lodgers to help meet expenses.[9] Her Kentucky-born niece, Charlotte Oakley, daughter of deceased half-brother William Jr., joined her and contributed materially to the household. She and her sister Louisa had an inheritance from relatives that made them financially independent.

No longer a boarder at King's College, Jacob Mould continued as a nonmatriculated or "occasional" student. In April 1841, he enrolled in the "Natural Philosophy" department, for which he paid fees of three pounds as well as three shillings for stationery and one pound for workroom fees. Natural Philosophy was a broad rubric encompassing a range of subjects in the growing areas of science and practice. Courses such as mathematics and measurement would have served him well for a future career in architecture, upon which he had evidently set his heart. His record at King's College ends after 1841.

At age sixteen, Jacob Mould, was at a critical point in choosing a path to his future. There can be little doubt that his mother's ambitions for him played a significant role in the decision to pursue an architectural career. She had married up, out of the trades, to a professional man, and she nurtured love for the arts. The counting houses of the Oakley family wool stapling business would have seemed a dreary life's sentence for Mary Ann's son.

Outside the little family circle, other factors encouraged the young Jacob Mould to become an architect. His interest may have been stirred in his school days. The Reverend Edward Hayes, a well-liked classics master at King's College School, maintained an avid interest in architecture and may have inspired the artistic youth. Moreover, architects in general were no longer thought of as mere mallet and chisel wielding stonemasons or callous-handed master carpenters. The rise of professionalism and the evolution of new and larger building types had opened the door for many middle-class men to pursue a career in design.

By the early 1840s in England, architecture was well on the way to achieving the rank and respect of the traditional professions, such as law and medicine. Academies and societies formed to satisfy these new conditions and expanded the role of architects. The Royal Academy of the Arts, founded in 1768, had for its purpose to foster all the visual arts. It provided for the appointment of a professor of architecture, who, according to its charter, "shall read annually six public lectures, calculated to form the taste of the Students." Another early bud among the branches of professionalism was the Architects' Club in London, which came into existence in 1791. Its purpose was to encourage discussion of professional concerns such as the qualifications of architects and technical matters such as fireproof construction. In 1835, the Institute of British Architects formed with the intent of establishing "uniformity and respectability of practice in the profession." Two years later, the crown granted it a royal charter, and the organization assumed the name the Royal Institute of British Architects.

Its aims had powerful appeal to practitioners who regarded membership as a way to consolidate their social stature. The organization is still a key player in Britain's architectural profession.

A later addition to the architectural scene was the Architectural Association, which organized in 1847. Its members, usually younger aspiring designers, fostered independent inquiry. From early on, it invited illustrious avant-garde thinkers such as John Ruskin to speak. It is still a driving force in forward-looking design and use of new techniques and technology.

New building types were also coming into being to meet the needs of an increasingly complex, urbanized society. The American architect Henry Van Brunt enumerated "railway buildings of all sorts, churches with parlors, kitchens and society rooms, hotels on a scale never before dreamt of, public libraries the service of which is fundamentally different from any of their predecessors, office and mercantile structures such as no preexisting conditions of professional and commercial life have ever required."[10] The patrons of architecture were also changing and expanding beyond the church and nobility. In the mid-nineteenth century, clients included businesses, merchants, bankers, and the ever-increasing middle-class homebuyers who wanted residences that both provided substantial comfort and displayed their worldly success.

This was an exciting time for architecture, a time of experiment and transformation. Architecture was being examined, discussed, and argued avidly in professional and academic circles and in the press. The predominance of the Neo-Classical style based on the architecture of ancient Greece and Rome was being disputed by proponents of picturesque expression. Gothic, English vernacular, and even non-Western traditions, were finding a place in British architecture. In London, the general interest in architecture increased with the massive work of reconstructing the Houses of Parliament. The disastrous fire of 1834 had destroyed most of those hallowed medieval buildings. A competition conducted for their replacement resulted in the choice of a Gothic Revival design. When the construction work actually began in 1840, Jacob was a student at nearby King's College. He could easily have walked the short distance along the Thames and out on Westminster Bridge to watch its progress. One could image him together with his classmate Edward Barry whose father, Charles, was the architect of the great pile. No Mould diary survives to reveal to us an epiphany as he watched the majestic rising of Westminster Palace, but perhaps seeing the extraordinary building take form and discovering the debates that surrounded its design influenced young Jacob to pursue a career in architecture.

After a single term in Natural Philosophy at King's College, Jacob Mould took a decisive step toward becoming an architect. With academic instruction in architecture in its infancy—King's College and the University of London offered courses but no degree—apprenticeship was still the preferred mode of training. In addition, for a student in strapped financial circumstances, it was the most economical way to enter the profession. Down through the ages architects had learned their craft by working for master builders. Apprenticeship was fine if the master was devoted and capable, but many a would-be architect found himself tied helplessly to an institutionalized form of slavery that taught little.

It is likely that William Rothery, the family friend who had sponsored Jacob's application to King's College, also played a key role in securing for him a good apprenticeship situation. Rothery knew Owen Jones (1809–1874), a rising star in the British architectural profession whose design interests ranged across many Western and non-Western traditions. Jones's love for history and learning may have been a heritage from his father who had been active in saving the Welsh language and literature. The elder Jones preserved over thirty-five thousand manuscripts of Welsh prose and poetry, some of which he published at his own expense. The son's own historic research, together with color theory and speculative thinking, would have a potent influence internationally on architecture and design in the last half of nineteenth century.

Rothery and Jones shared a common interest in Middle Eastern civilizations. They were among the group that in December 1844 founded the Syro-Egyptian Society of London. Rothery's acquaintance with Jones, however, may have started as early as 1835 when Jones read a controversial paper at the Architectural Society. This paper, entitled "On the Influence of Religion upon Art," discussed the lack of compelling modern English architecture. Jones decried the fact that architects continued to design buildings ignoring the factors that dominated everyday society: modern science, industry, and commerce. He put forward his credo that the present required a new architecture, one that rejected imitation of styles of another, more primitive time. He had sensed the enduring vitality present in the ancient ruins of Greece, Italy, Sicily, Egypt, Constantinople, and Mozarabic Spain. What was missing in contemporary architecture in England, he theorized, was the connection to religious beliefs and cultural habits. The power of ancient buildings lay in giving expression to their society's convictions. The lifeless state of English architecture was due to the absence of powerful belief, the kind of ardor rooted in religious faith that was evident in earlier civilizations. Architects of the day were also criticized for ignoring new materials, which offered the possibility of innovative ways of designing. He castigated them for lagging behind engineers who were cleverly employing iron in the construction of bridges and other utilitarian structures. Jones expressed his faith in the power of science and industry in the post-agrarian, industrial society of the nineteenth century. Rothery, his fellow-traveler, was the suitable intermediary to arrange for the would-be architect to study with Jones. It proved to be an admirable match for Jacob Mould. He was to become Jones's pupil, assistant, and friend.

Following his primary education, Owen Jones, at fifteen, had articled himself to the rising London architect Lewis Vulliamy (1791–1871). Under Vulliamy's tutelage, Jones came to know both current practices and the architecture of past ages. Vulliamy's apprentices also taught Jones to draw with speed and precision. This handy skill Jones would also pass on to Mould.

When Jones had finished his apprenticeship with Vulliamy, he set out abroad to study buildings, past and present. These post-apprenticeship journeys, which many young men made, enhanced lessons learned from the master and from books. Publishing one's own book might also be a desirable result of such travels. In 1823, Vulliamy had used his experiences to compile *Examples of Ornamental Sculpture in Architecture, drawn from the originals in Greece, Asia Minor, and Italy*.

In 1831, Jones started on a three-year-long, eventful journey that would influence the course of modern British architecture. As Vulliamy had done, he traveled far afield, through Italy, Sicily, Greece, Egypt, Turkey, and Spain. In Greece, he teamed up with the young French architect and artist Jules Goury (1803–1834) who had been investigating how ancient architects had used color on their buildings. Jones and Goury formed a friendship and together traveled to Cairo and Constantinople to study Islamic architecture. Then, in Granada, they became enthralled with the ruins of the mid-thirteenth-century Arab palace known as the Alhambra, one of the high water marks of medieval Islamic civilization. They spent six months in the warm Andalusian sun in 1834, measuring and sketching in an attempt to understand the organizational secrets of the intricate designs that bedecked the interior and exterior walls of the extraordinary palace complex that took one century to complete. Tragically, in August, Goury contracted cholera and died. After that, Jones returned home to London where he determined to publish their findings. His deep appreciation of the Alhambra's opulently ornamented halls and courtyards served to shape the philosophy and character of his architecture and decorative designs. It was also to have a lasting impact on the imagination of his pupil, Jacob Mould.

Color on ancient and medieval buildings and statuary was a newly current topic much debated among architects. While traces of color on temples and sculpture had been noted for some time, proof that color was commonplace on the buildings of antiquity was slow in coming. The given wisdom held that Greek architects had concerned themselves only with elegant forms and harmonious proportions. Neo-Classical designers preferred to see classic ruins glimmering pure white in the unclouded Greek sunlight. Nonetheless, already in the eighteenth century, James Stuart and Nicholas Revett, authors of *Antiquities of Athens* (1762), the Bible of the Greek Revival, had raised the possibility that Greek and Roman buildings and statuary had been painted with several colors. In the early nineteenth century, French architect Antoine-Chrysostome Quatremere de Quincy invented the term *polychromy* to describe the phenomenon. In 1812, the British architect C. R. Cockerell had uncovered sculpture from the pediment of the temple of Aphia on the Greek island of Aegina that displayed bright, deeply saturated color. Unfortunately, with exposure to the air after centuries of burial, the paint oxidized and rapidly disappeared. Slightly later, Frenchman Jacques Ignace Hittorf described ancient polychromy he found on Greek Sicilian temples. Hittorf presented a paper on the subject to the Académie des Beaux Arts in Paris in 1830. He had worked out a scheme to demonstrate how the ancient builders had employed color to highlight all parts of the temples at Selinunte and Agrigento. The notion that bright colors occurred on temples seemed to many preposterous; conventional opinion ascribed the fragmentary bits of paint found on them to be of medieval origin. Following Hittorf, the German architect Gottfried Semper set off to Greece to conduct his own serious research into ancient polychromy. Jules Goury was working with him when Jones met him.

It would take several years for Jones to complete the monumental task of publishing what he and Goury had learned from the Alhambra. The process of presenting drawings in rich color to do justice to the striking beauty and vitality of the Alhambra's craftsmen compelled Jones to perfect a new, improved printing method—chromolithography. This innovative technique would revolutionize the publication of architectural books. As architectural historian Nicklaus Adams observes, "Ruskin used color lithography to reproduce his watercolors in colors that would jump off the page. . . . So too the French architect and architectural critic Eugene Viollet-le-Duc for whom color and texture were essential."[11] Along the way,

Jones became an accomplished book designer and illustrator. Gift books were a specialty. He had his own printing press in his John Street studio and trained his apprentices in its use. Mould actually contributed some color-lithographed plates to Jones's 1849 edition of *The Musical Bijou, an Album of Music and Poetry*.

In 1836, Jones brought out the first part of his monumental two-volume *Plans, Elevations, Sections and Details of the Alhambra*, which he fittingly dedicated to his departed friend, Goury. Over the next nine years, he published the remaining eleven sections of detailed drawings, rubbings, and studies of traces of paint. Modern scholarship still recognizes that Jones and Goury had created "the most comprehensive visual and textual survey of the monument possible."[12] The completion of the Alhambra volumes was one of the projects on which Jacob Mould, with others, would assist during his tenure as Jones's apprentice. This work included transferring drawings to lithographic stones for printing. Thus, together with architectural design and decoration, Mould acquired from Jones considerable skill in the arts of graphic design and illustration.

Jones sold the Alhambra volumes by subscription, with sections distributed to patrons as they were ready. Among the subscribers were A. W. N. Pugin, whose influential Gothic-inspired design was then becoming widely known; Herbert Minton of the pottery family in Stoke-on-Trent; Thomas Cubitt, prolific London builder whose new methods brought all the trades of building into one office; Isambard Kingdom Brunel, the renowned engineer; and Jones's old master, Lewis Vulliamy. In addition, Jones proudly donated a copy of the first completed part, "printed in colours and with gold," to the new library of the Royal Institute of British Architects.

Together with his desire to seek professional advancement, Mould may have been drawn to Jones's studio by the seductive charm of the architect's high-minded devotion to theoretical thinking. What a pleasure it must have been for young Mould to listen to his employer hold forth on architecture and design. Jones's architectural work at the time may have been limited, but his perceptive and far-reaching theories were to be the foundation for much of Mould's future work. Notably, Mould's delight in color and his dazzling use of it would be the product of Jones's congenial instruction. Mould also came to value Jones's workshop for its extensive library of architectural books. These included both standard works and thought-provoking items of current interest, such as A. W. N. Pugin's *Contrasts*, a sharply aimed polemic indicting modern English architecture and society published in 1836, and the same author's *The True Principles of Pointed or Christian Architecture* (1841), the book that established the revival of faithfully rendered Gothic architecture as the proper setting for modern worship.

Much of Jones's attention during the time that Mould spent with him focused on the publication of the Alhambra project and other books. His great contribution to architectural decoration, his immortal *The Grammar of Ornament*, however, appeared in 1856, after Mould had left. Yet, it was such a comprehensive undertaking that we must assume that Jones began working on it when Mould was his pupil and assistant. This treasury of designs has been through numerous editions and remains in print. It is still consulted by architects and designers. Jones's expanding graphic design activities also produced magnificent gift books. The first of these came in 1841 when he fabricated *Ancient Spanish Ballads* for the publisher John Murray. Beginning in 1842, Jones designed book covers and title pages for the London publisher Longman, Green and Longman. Among other volumes were religious selections such as the *Sermon on the Mount* (1844) and *The Book of Common Prayer* (1848), and poetry, including a delightfully flower-and-vine-framed edition of Thomas Gray's beloved *Elegy in a Churchyard* (1846). Mould proudly claimed to have had a significant hand in the creation of the latter two books. Jones also worked for the upscale stationer and printer Thomas De la Rue.

In addition to advancing the art and craft of printing, Jones did much to stimulate the use of decorative tiles in architecture. This trend had been increasing with the advent of the Gothic Revival, and the search for permanent colored materials for buildings (as opposed to painted surfaces). Illustrations of the intricately patterned tiles and stone floors at the Alhambra inspired manufacturers to reinvent the ancient art of encaustic tile production. At the request of entrepreneur John Marriott Blashfield, an early manufacturer of encaustic tiles (and a subscriber to Jones's Alhambra), Jones published brilliantly colored chromolithographic plates of tile designs. "These designs," states Jones biographer Carol Flores, "demonstrated the potential for realizing new patterns by varying color and patterns."[13] In 1843, Jones published *Encaustic Tiles*, which contained over ninety illustrations of tiles and floors.

To contemporary American historians, Jones's contributions to the art of his time and the Victorian's general fondness for ornament may be seen has having broad social implications. "In seeking to understand the meaning of nineteenth-century historicism and eclecticism . . . for American architects" writes Joanna Merwood-Salisbury, "some scholars have argued that the Orientalized Gothic Revival style popularized by Ruskin was attractive because it suggested a privileged cultural and racial lineage of which they might claim to be descendants." According to this view, writes Merwood-Salisbury, many Americans saw Near Eastern references "as signs of the link between their cultural and religious heritage and an ancient Jewish past."[14] This interpretation seems most appropriate to the inclusive Christian spirit of Unitarianism espoused by Mould's future American client, the Reverend Henry Whitney Bellows.

Given what we know of Mould's personality and manner of living in later life, we can assume that he must have enjoyed instruction in the good life from the example of his genial master. Jones relished good food and drink, took frequent trips to Paris and elsewhere on the Continent, enjoyed lively conversation and the company of interesting people, especially those informed about matters dealing with art. "In his profession, as in private life, the singular sweetness and simplicity of his nature was as remarkable as the modesty of his genius, as his devotion to the art which he adorned, and as his large and various intellectual attainments," is how one contemporary remembered Jones.[15] Moreover, Jones's wife, Isabella Lucy Wild Jones (1817–1875), was an accomplished amateur musician. Mould would have felt at ease and at home hearing her play the piano, for pretty melodies could often be overheard in the atelier, which adjoined the Jones family home in Argyll Place. Without doubt, Mould learned from his cosmopolitan teacher an expanded view of life's pleasures and possibilities from what he would have known as the son of a solicitor and his well-ordered homelife. Mould would inherit many fond memories from his days with Owen Jones who would grow to count Mould among his wide circle of friends.

When Jacob began his apprenticeship in 1841, Jones was finishing his work on four Westbourne Terrace houses begun the previous year and completing the interior work at 22 Arlington Street. He was also decorating the interior of Lewis Vulliamy's Italian Romanesque–style All Saints Church, Ennismore Gardens, Knightsbrige, London (fig. 5), and he was planning the interior decorations—notably, colorful apse mosaics in the Byzantine style—of Christ Church (1840–1842), Streatham, for his architect brother-in-law James Wild (fig. 6).

In 1843, investor John Blachfield put Jones in charge of overall management of his Kensington Palace Gardens, a residential street that assumed the reputation of London's most exclusive address. The plan, with its large-sized lots and costly houses, assured that only the most select householders could invest. The mansions were placed along a wide private road, gated at each end, and watched over by liveried attendants. Today, Londoners refer to it as Millionaire's Row, and most of its residences serve as embassies and

Figure 5. Lewis Vulliamy: All Saints Church, Ennismore, 1846–1849.

ambassadorial residences. Jones himself drew up plans for the residences at 8 and 24 Queens Road. For 8 Queens Road, designed in 1843, he introduced colorful tiles as flooring for the entrance hall, the central stairs, and an outside terrace.

Throughout the period that Mould worked with him, Owen Jones entered architectural competitions. His proposals usually displayed unmistakable Moorish details. This was certainly true of the most important of the competitions he entered, the 1844 contest for the decoration of the new Houses of Parliament. Jones submitted plans for patterned floors throughout the vast building. His design encompassed a variety of materials, including tile, marble, porcelain mosaic, and inlaid wood. One reviewer called his detailed drawings (on which Mould surely worked) "very beautiful and the colours extremely gorgeous."[16] Despite many

Figure 6. Owen Jones: Apse decoration, Christ Church, Streatham, 1851.

appreciative comments, however, Jones lost the competition. Ironically, this may have been due to the resemblance of his designs to the Alhambra, a subject too foreign for many cautious and traditional English clients. In conservative circles, Jones was even mockingly referred to as "Alhambra Jones." Tongues stopped wagging, however, a few years later when the directors of London's Great Exhibition announced that Jones would direct the elaborate color scheme for the enormous iron and glass structure that Joseph Paxton had designed to house the 1851 international fair. Although Mould by then had left Jones's office, he said that his former mentor had asked his aid with that formidable task. The vast and subtle medley of tints stood among the major achievements of Victorian polychromatic interior decoration.

Outside his work in Jones's design atelier, Mould actively cultivated his love of music. Among Jones's friends was William Chappell, a major London music publisher. Chappell was a witness to Jones's marriage, and when his wife died he turned to Jones for the design of a monument for her. He must also have eased Mould's entry into the world of musical publishing. While with Jones, Mould had embarked on a lifelong avocation writing original lyrics to songs composed by others. Earlier, as a student at King's College, Mould had struck up a friendship with the young musician named William Rockstro (1823–1895) whom he met at an opera.[17] Rockstro, who studied piano and composition at Leipzig with Felix Mendelssohn, was to become a notable musician and musicologist as well as a friend and biographer of the great diva, Jenny Lind (1820–1887). Rockstro's and Mould's friendship soon became a collaboration. Together with Rockstro, who wrote the music, Mould composed the words to "Faery Power," a canzonet published in 1845, and, a year later, he supplied the lyrics for Rockstro's duet "Evening."

Mould's first known libretto translation appeared in 1844 when he was nineteen. The publisher was Louis Antoine Jullien (1812–1860), an eccentric French impresario, composer, and conductor. Jullien, who had fled his native country to escape his creditors, had recently started a publishing company in London. He was also well-known to English audiences for his popular "promenade" concerts. These events, where the flamboyant conductor dressed in a striking white waistcoat and waved a sparkling, bejeweled baton, featured outsized orchestras and often hundreds of choral singers. For Jullien, Mould first translated the poem by Le Comte H. de Viel Castel, "The Dying Soldier," that was set to music by the German composer Robert Stoepel. Additional work for Jullien included the 1847 translation of the French tenor Gilbert Louis Duprez's manual for singers, *Treatise on the Art of Singing*. In 1847, Jullien published Mould and Rockstro's collection of Jenny Lind's songs. Of these, Mould supplied the lyrics to "The Sea King's Bride," "The Stars of Heave'n Are Gleaming," and "Pasture or the Herdsman's Echo Song." These were among the favorites sung by the famous vocalist who was known everywhere as the "Swedish Nightingale."

Mould's work for Jullien continued with several translations of German lieder which were fashionable with mid-nineteenth-century British audiences. Ever market-wise, Jullien put out a series of German love songs that he entitled *Deutsche Lyra*. They were songs of passion and longing that had been performed in concert in London by popular artists. Mould's translations included Gustav Hoelzel's "Song of the Chimes," Beethoven's "Thus or Thus, Adelaide," and "The May Song," Spohr's "Tears of Affection," Dessauer's "The Minstrel's Solace," Reissiger's "The Wanderer's Evening Lay," and Von Lindpainter's "The Song of Spring."

Above all, it was as a translator of opera librettos that Mould would become best known in London musical circles. In July 1847, Thomas Boosey (1794–1871), a prominent English music publisher and instrument maker who catered to the Victorian demand for parlor music scores and affordable editions of the classics, announced that he would be issuing *The Standard Lyric Drama*, a serial publication of operas in multiple parts. Rockstro and Mould edited this inexpensive monthly sequence of vocal scores and memoirs of composers. An advertisement announced that each consisted of fifty to sixty pages of the "most favorite Operas of MOZART, GLUCK, SPOHR, ROSSINI, MEYERBEER, BELLINI, DONIZETTI, VERDI, etc."[18] J. W. Mould translated all of the librettos into English and also provided Boosey with some cover illustrations.[19].

Between 1847 and his departure for America in 1852, Mould published many libretto translations. These included Weber's *Der Freischütz* (the opera that had made Jenny Lind famous); Donizetti's *Lucrezia Borgia*, *Lucia di Lammermoor*, and *Daughter of the Regiment*; Rossini's *Barber of Seville*; Bellini's *Norma*; Gluck's *Iphigenia in Taurus*; Bellini's *Norma and La Sonnambula*; Verdi's *Hermani*; Mozart's *Don Giovanni*, *Magic Flute*, *Marriage of Figaro*, and *Don Juan*; Beethoven's *Fidelio*; and Spohr's *Faust*. Critics praised Mould for the special talent he displayed in retaining the original rhythmic relationship between the music and the lyrics when he rendered them into English. The *Spectator* remarked in an extended review of the Boosey series,

> The task of adapting an English version to a foreign libretto to the original music is at all times a difficult one, and Mr. Mould has increased the difficulty by imposing on himself an unusual restriction. It is the custom, in adapting English words to foreign music, to use a good deal of freedom with the original notes,—to multiply syllables, and consequently to split one note into two or more of shorter duration, or, vise versa, to slur together several notes, each of which in this original is articulated to a separate syllable. These liberties are injurious to the melody and the expression of the music; and, besides, when the two versions are printed together, the musical notation, adapted to both is rendered confused and embarrassing. Mr. Mould has avoided both of these evils by making his version *totidem syllibis* with the original; and the advantages of his plan counterbalance the occasional awkwardness of phraseology, and even the deviations of the sense of the original, which it renders unavoidable. But Mr. Mould is gaining skill by practice; and his versions of all the opera before us are on the whole much superior in spirit and idiomatic

> freedom of expression, to any others that have appeared. The recitatives go trippingly on the tongue, and the melodies lose very little of their Italian flow and smoothness.[20]

Indeed, Mould could take exceptional measures to maintain sympathy between word and melody. For the libretto accompanying Rockstro's reduced vocal score of Beethoven's *Fidelio*, Mould apologized to the user for preserving the deliberately archaic language, "having been hampered and tied in," he said, "by ungainly meters and irregular lines in many places."[21] Modern judgment of Mould's contributions has sustained his reputation. Commenting on Mould's "long and learned introduction" to *La sonnambula*, musicologist Emanuele Senici declares it "a volume for the library shelf even more than for the piano, an extraordinary example of philological intentions applied to a repertory that would have to wait for more than a century to be taken seriously from a textual, and therefore, aesthetic, point of view."[22]

After completing his apprenticeship, Mould worked for Owen Jones for about a year as a paid draftsman. He soon came to realize, however, that Jones's atelier was failing to provide him with enough experience in real-world architectural work.[23] Jones had too few actual architectural projects to provide Mould with the understanding of day-to-day doings of a practicing architect. Indeed, contemporaries of Owen Jones faulted him for his lack of construction knowledge. Apparently, Jones himself acknowledged the deficiency, for he advised Mould to seek more actual architectural experience beyond his own atelier. Since Jones enjoyed an ongoing professional relationship with Lewis Vulliamy (Jones had provided interior design work for Vulliamy church commissions), he recommended Mould to him as an office assistant. Vulliamy's busy office was a most suitable place for Mould to advance his knowledge of the profession. The fifty-seven-year-old architect had a thriving practice. His office would offer Mould exposure to the actual business of architecture. Mould's personal relationship with Jones, however, continued after he left his mentor's employment.

Lewis Vulliamy followed quite a different path in his architectural career from that of Owen Jones. He had been born into a family of celebrated clock makers, whose fine pieces, large and small, sold to nobility and the moneyed gentry. His father, Benjamin, managed the family business from their home at 68 Pall Mall. Lewis, however, did not wish to be in trade but to apply his talent to architecture. He articled to the noted architect Robert Smirke and, in 1809, went on to be a student at the Royal Academy, winning the Silver Medal in 1810 and the Gold Medal in 1813. In 1818, he obtained the Academy's traveling fellowship, which enabled him to spend four years abroad, including the Middle East.

Vulliamy schooled himself to become capable at every aspect, esthetic and functional, of the business of architecture. His studies made him fluent in many styles, including Classical or Romanesque and Gothic. The extensive list of his works includes houses, churches, public buildings, farm buildings, and even grandstands for a racetrack. Three of the ten churches built in London's Bethnal Green district during a period of growth for ecclesiastical building were his. Vulliamy ran an efficient office and prided himself on his keen ability to estimate accurately material and building costs. Judging from the voluminous office papers preserved at the Royal Institute of British Architects, he stayed in close contact with projects from design through construction. There could have been no better teacher with whom Mould could have studied. Vulliamy could also have nurtured Mould's passion for ornament. His impressive 1823 volume, *Examples of Ornamental Sculpture in Architecture*, consisted of clearly drawn details Vulliamy had gleaned on his travels through Greece, Italy and Asia Minor.

At the time Mould joined his office, Vulliamy had recently secured a valuable commission for a large new dwelling for Robert Staynor Holford, reputed to have been the richest man in England. Holford came from an old and wealthy family whose money derived from their holdings in the New River Company. In the eighteenth and early nineteenth centuries, this company had constructed the canal system that supplied most of London's drinkable water. For Holford, who could have purchased whatever made people happy in that pre-consumer age, the measure of his wealth was in his art collection. He owned paintings by Titian, Velasquez, Rubens, and Murillo. He also possessed a large collection of rare books. When it came to building, Holford need not allow cost to impede his goal of living in a house worthy of his elevated stature in British society. It is likely that Vulliamy hired Mould because he needed another architect in his office to accommodate the enormous work that the London residence would require.

For his grand new dwelling (fig. 7), Holford had selected a site facing Hyde Park on Park Lane, a highly fashionable address, and determined to name his place Dorchester House. (The Dorchester Hotel occupies the spot today.) A close neighbor was the Duke of Wellington, whose Apsley

Figure 7. Lewis Vulliamy: Holford House (aka Dorchester House), London 1840s.

House stood at the other end of Park Lane. It took from 1850 to1863 to complete the vast Italian Renaissance style mansion that Vulliamy designed (and which Mould would never see completed). Vulliamy's office had to deal with excavators, materials suppliers (bricks, timber, cement, plaster, tiles, drainpipes, iron, slate, ornamental ironwork, heating systems), tradesmen, and workers of every description. The architect chose many of the costly furnishings as well. All of this activity would have provided young Mould with a thorough education in the matter-of-fact requirements an architect needed to master in order to carry a project through to success. He gained the technical experience that he had missed in the more rarified artistic atmosphere of Owen Jones's establishment. Holford was the very model of an educated, exacting, micromanaging client. Almost daily letters and notes from Holford to Vulliamy gave expression to the client's opinions on bids and tenders, aesthetics, and materials. Numerous letters on matters such as the "chimney question" are preserved. Holford required ever more sketches for each detail.

Jacob Wrey Mould was the perfect office assistant for Vulliamy. With his swift and proficient hand, he could turn out the sketches that the demanding Holford wanted immediately. Did the patron desire alternative ideas for the framing of a doorway? Mould could provide them almost instantaneously. By 1851, Mould was sufficiently senior to deal directly on small matters with this supremely important client. In a letter of August 23, 1851, Holford wrote to Mould to discuss a sketch of an entablature over some windows. Holford required a redesign because he had decided that more space was needed to allow for a shutter. There are also a few words

Figure 8. Grand staircase, Holford House, London.

on a second back staircase that Mould had designed and which was far less impressive than the main stairs that were a marvel of grandeur (fig. 8).[24]

Mould surely gained valuable practical experience as Vulliamy's trusted assistant, but the emotional tenor of life in the Vulliamy office overshadowed what he had known with the easy-going Owen Jones. Vulliamy was known for the intransigence of his beliefs, an extremely short temper, and, especially as he grew older, his eccentric ways. His father had displayed the same prickly temperament. When the elder Vulliamy, for example, had lost the competition to design the clock for the tower of the Houses of Parliament (known today as Big Ben), he spent several years attacking the character of the winner, E. J. Dent, and harassing his supporters in a vain attempt to reverse the decision. Lewis Vulliamy himself frequently quarreled acrimoniously with his employees, even those who were family members. His nephew, George John Vulliamy, quit his uncle's office after an angry quarrel, and his son, also an architect, refused to work with his father.

After laboring with the cantankerous Vulliamy, Mould must have found evenings spent at the opera and in the London concert halls and theaters even more appealing than before. Mould took to frequenting the nearby Marylebone neighborhood where he could readily attend a play or musical performance. He continued living with his mother on Keppel Street and providing translations of librettos for Thomas Boosey. He must have felt that his life had settled on a steady course, with the prospect of a promising future in architecture.

In the early spring of 1851, Mould met in Marylebone a young widow who introduced herself as Mrs. Boynton. A relationship blossomed quickly, and on August 16, 1851, at Christ Church, a parish church near Regent's Park on Redhill Street, the two were married. The license registered the bride's name as Emelie Annie Davies; there was no longer mention of the name Boynton. Apparently, no relatives of the bride were present, not even her father who she said was Ambrose Henry Davies, a professor of botany.[25] A brief day in the country is all that Mould could accommodate from his busy schedule in Vulliamy's office for a honeymoon. A couple of days after the marriage, he sent a note to "Emmy" that he would be working late but that she should get ready for the picnic and boating excursion he had arranged for the next day. Signing himself "your affectionate hubby, Jake," he asked her to bake a pie for the occasion.[26]

Whatever happiness Mould experienced, however, was soon to be exchanged for trouble that would shadow him for much of his life. A few days after the wedding, there was a knock at the door. An unexpected caller announced herself as Rosalind, Emelie's sister. Holding her hand and half-hidden by her skirts was a timid little girl about two years old. The toddler, said Rosalind, was Alice, Emelie's daughter, who her mother had kept secret from her new husband until now.[27] Despite Mould's amazement and dismay at sudden fatherhood, he seems to have attempted to accept the situation. In February 1852, he rented a property in suburban Chislehurst more suitable for a family. It consisted of a "dwelling house, wash house, scullery and a garden for 32£ a year," payable quarterly, a large sum for the times.[28]

Rapidly, however, the lies and omissions Emelie had maintained during their brief courtship began to unravel marital bliss. Mould then sought legal counsel to rid himself of Emelie. The only grounds for divorce in an English court, however, were adultery. He had no evidence to support such a claim because Alice had been born long before their marriage. (Her paternity was never made clear.) In July of 1852, in an attempt to find Emelie's alleged father, he and his mother made their way to Richmond, just outside of Kew, where Ambrose Davies supposedly lived. Nonetheless, they failed to find any trace of him.[29] After that, they went seeking Emelie's mother, whom they eventually found to be a pauper in the Marylebone workhouse. This woman, Mould bitterly recalled, "gave her daughter a bad reputation" and said that her true name was Sarah Quinn. It was evident now that Emelie was not the daughter of a professor of botany working at Kew Gardens, as she had claimed.

The marriage became a battleground, and their relationship more and more tempestuous. Emelie's behavior became erratic. Her furious outbursts forced them out of rooming houses several times, and their attempt to live with Mould's mother in her Keppel Street home became a frightful experience for Mary Ann. As Mould learned Emelie's real character, he and his mother experienced the full fury of her violent temper. She destroyed his property and treated his mother with "insolence and violence," to the point that Emelie "willfully smashed his mother's furniture in his mother's house." Worst of all, uproars in public settings probably led to Mould losing his position with Lewis Vulliamy, an old-fashioned man cautious of his contacts with influential clients. Mould soon went from chief assistant to unemployed nobody. Without a regular income, Mould fell back on his relationship with Owen Jones for odd jobs and on his musical talent and translation facility for work from Boosey. For her part, Emelie, living in a society with no social safety nets and no sympathy for single mothers, must have been deeply disappointed to learn that the well-spoken gentleman she presumed to be a prosperous architect was, in fact, a person of modest means. (Indeed, conflict between limited resources and refined taste would be a trial for Mould for most of his life.)

Before July, the couple had ceased living together, though Mould continued to support Emelie and her daughter. In a note dated July 26, 1852, Mould, sent her forty pounds, and asked her to explain "what you really want?"[30] He refused to see her in person without a reliable witness to their discussion. He could no longer afford the rent for the Chislehurst house. Instead, he rented rooms for Emelie and Alice in London.[31] He wrote Emelie a coldly worded missive informing her that he was sending someone with money to pay for moving expenses and instructing her to finish packing to be ready by noon for the return to London. Above all, he told her, not to forget the two zinc plates he prepared for printing as the cover of some music for Boosey. The signatory is no longer "loving Jake" but simply Jacob.

The stress of events evidently took a heavy toll on Mould's well-being. He reported suffering from a serious, unnamed illness that caused him to lose a quart of blood. His loss of position in Vulliamy's office had cost Mould both current income and dimmed his future prospects. Moreover, commissions for young architects were scarce at that time. Years later, Mould's American attorney would observe that from Emelie (Mrs. Boynton? Miss Davies? Sarah Quinn?) his client "never received any dowry . . . except lasting disgrace, somebody else's child whose paternity was and is unknown, the ruin of all his hopes and fortunes in England."[32]

Adrift in his profession, aggrieved and bruised by a disastrous marriage, and burdened with financial obligations, Mould determined on a drastic remedy for his situation. Others of Mould's generation—such as Calvert Vaux, Frederick Clarke Withers, and Latrobe Bateman, another Owen Jones protégé—had immigrated to America or elsewhere to seek their fortunes. Hoping to put martial misfortune behind him, Mould determined to flee Emelie and London for a new life in the United States. When he revealed his scheme to Owen Jones, his old employer sought to discourage him from going. Jones warned Mould that he would not survive in the capricious arena of American competitiveness. Placing his hand on the young man's shoulder, Jones declared, "Jacob, the Americans will wring you out like a wet rag, then drop you like a hot potato."[33] Unpersuaded by his mentor's awkward metaphor—that would surely return to haunt him later—in August 1852, Jacob Mould, with his mother, stood on the deck of a steamship bound for New York. Perhaps he expressed to himself the sense of relief he must have felt leaving his troubles behind with lyrics he knew so well: "the stars of heav'n are gleaming, above the world at rest." At twenty-eight, the major narrative of his life was about to begin.

3

Fresh Prospects in New York

We at one time understood that a gentleman from England, Mr. Mould, a pupil of Mr. Owen Jones, offered some meritorious designs for the decoration of the building.

—George Carstenen and Georg Gildermeister, *The New York Crystal Palace*

IT WAS THE LATE SUMMER of 1852 when Jacob Wrey Mould and his mother arrived in New York to be greeted warmly by their Oakley relatives. It had been arranged for Jacob to live with his uncle Alexander, his wife, Susan, and two young daughters, Decima and Louisa, in their home on East Seventeenth Street. Perhaps wanting to underscore his intention to make a fresh start in his new country, Mould henceforth preferred to be known to American colleagues and friends by his middle name, Wrey.

Surely his American relatives would have brought him up to snuff on developments in the New York architectural scene. Foremost would have been the tragic news of the death in a steamboat accident in July of Andrew Jackson Downing, the man who through his books and articles had been leading a reform of American domestic architecture and landscape gardening. It had been a great loss for the progress of American architecture and culture in general. King's College alumni Gervase Wheeler had known him and contributed designs to Downing's publications. Mould may even have known Calvert Vaux, Downing's partner in the architectural practice he had formed at Newburgh, sixty miles north of New York on the Hudson River. A former member, like Mould, of the Architectural

Association in London, Vaux had immigrated to America in 1850. In fact, Mould and Vaux both had shown drawings in the association's 1850 summer exhibition that Downing had attended and where he had met Vaux. Mould had displayed a drawing of a large medieval barn at Thornhill Hall in Yorkshire—perhaps in the manner of his King's College drawing master, John Sell Cotman—and Vaux had submitted a drawing of a turret. The *Morning Post* had singled out both works for special praise.[1]

Other big news in New York at the time of the Moulds' arrival was the announcement that the city had settled upon a plan to erect a large glass and iron pavilion to house the Exhibition of the Industry of All Nations. On August 26, the directors had chosen the winner of a design competition that had included submissions by Vaux and Downing as well as Joseph Paxton, designer of the Crystal Palace for London's Great Exhibition of 1851. The judges had passed over both of these proposals in favor of one by Georg Carstensen (1812–1857), a Danish military engineer, and Charles Gildemeister (1820–1869), a German architect. The New York Crystal Palace, as it came to be known, was to be erected within a few months on Reservoir Square, the present Bryant Park. When it opened in July 1853, it would be the largest structure in the city's history.

The Crystal Palace would draw the world's attention to both commerce and art in New York. Those who wished to establish their city as the premier New World cultural metropolis could be proud of the thriving musical scene that Mould would have encountered upon his arrival. Much good instrumental and vocal music could be heard, for a host of European and native talents had found enthusiastic audiences in the polyglot city. The incomparable Jenny Lind, managed by promoter P. T. Barnum, had dazzled audiences with her singing at Castle Garden in 1850. Undoubtedly, she sang some of the songs that Mould and Rockstro had published. Likewise, Elizabeth Taylor Greenfield, a popular African American singer, may also have used Mould's scores. Called the "Black Swan," she was best known for her repertoire of the music of Handel, Bellini, and Donizetti. She made her New York City debut at Metropolitan Hall, in March 1853, not long after Mould arrived.

Mould would soon develop friendships and acquaintances among New York's music publishers, impresarios, composers, conductors, singers, and instrumentalists. Among them were the French musician Emile Millet and the German composer Robert Stoepel. Millet had been a professor of singing at the Paris Conservatory before coming to New York in 1849. Here he had found employment as chorus master at the Astor Place Opera House. He also composed popular songs and frequently accompanied soloists in concert. Moreover, he surely would have discussed with Mould the trip he had made as a young man with his friend Eugene Viollet-le-Duc to study mediaeval churches in Southern France.

Robert Stoepel had come to New York from Berlin in 1850, after living for a time in London (where, in 1844, Mould had translated the words of Stoepel's song, "The Dying Soldier.") Stoepel quickly established himself as the popular orchestra conductor at Wallack's Theater on Broadway. He also played some of his own compositions to accompany the comedies and melodramas for which the house was primarily known. In the mid-1850s, the *New York Times* called him "one of the best informed musicians in the country."[2] In 1859, he had created his most famous work, the Hiawatha symphony. Based on Longfellow's poem, *The Song of Hiawatha*, the lavish score called for several soloists, chorus, and orchestra. He later inscribed a copy of the ambitious piece of music to Mould.

New York was also well provided with grand opera, the performing art especially dear to Mould. By the early 1850s, the *New York Times* remarked on opera's growing popularity and identified New York City as the center of the art form in America.[3] The Astor Place Opera House, designed by the Greek Revival architect Isiah Rogers, opened in 1847 with a performance of Verdi's *Ernani*. With its dress code stipulating that men have newly shaven faces and wear evening dress with fresh waistcoat and kid gloves, it was plain that the elite were to be in the ascendance as opera spectators. Women in the audience prided themselves for being decked out with brilliant jewels and silk and satin gowns.

As opera attendance grew, other theaters profited from the developing fashion. Niblo's Garden, a popular downtown Broadway venue for plays and music, offered Friedrich von Flotow's *Martha* during the 1852 fall season that also included Donizetti's *La Fille du Régiment* and *Lucia de Lammermoor*. Both performances were in English, using librettos that Mould had translated.[4] In 1854, with a significant audience attending grand opera, the Academy of Music opened its doors uptown at Irving Place and Fourteenth Street. Renowned for its splendid acoustics, it was designed by German-born Alexander Saeltzer (1814–1883), who was also planning the Astor Place Library concurrently. He had studied in Berlin with Karl Friedrich Schinkel before immigrating to New York in 1849. With seating for four thousand, Saeltzer's academy touted itself as the largest opera house in the world. The opening night selection was Bellini's *Norma*, another work with which Mould was thoroughly familiar from having translated the libretto during his days in London. The mammoth Rundbogenstil hall reigned as *the* place for society and the public alike to enjoy the pleasures of opera until the Metropolitan Opera House in 1886. It would have been especially convenient for Mould to attend performances at the Academy of Music, for in the early years after his arrival he lived with his uncle Alexander on nearby East Seventeenth Street.

Mary Ann's family in New York helped her and her son immensely. Mould's uncle George Oakley, the oldest of William's children, was now the *pater familias*. George remembered leaving London almost penniless with his father and brother Alexander thirty years before when London was bursting with a population of 1,378,947. In contrast, New York, though the largest city in America, was a small town with a population of only 125,000. The Oakleys struggled through difficult and uncertain times there. Only Uncle Benjamin's one-thousand-dollar letter of credit sent in 1820 had enabled them to keep their fledgling wool business afloat.[5] Now, thirty years later, they were well established in New York, which had become the country's financial capital, and were happy to take care of Mary Ann and to help their gifted nephew get a fresh start. Without this loving family, the Moulds' transatlantic move would have been far more difficult than it was. London had proved to be a burial ground for all Wrey Mould's hopes and ambition. New York now offered him a sense of endless possibilities. Here in America, he would have the chance to use the talents he had cultivated in England and earn recognition on his own. In a favorite phrase of his, he was ready to "work like a beaver."[6]

It may be that his uncle Alexander first encouraged his nephew to speak up about the new Crystal Palace that was to house New York's answer to London's Great Exhibition (fig. 9). Alexander was a juror for the chemical and pharmaceutical products section. Clearly, an important public building commission would make his talented nephew known and would help him attract future clients. Sometime in the fall of 1852, when construction had begun on the building, Mould offered unsolicited suggestions to the directors concerning the future interior decoration of the vast glass-and-iron

Figure 9. New York Crystal Palace, illustration, 1853.

building, Mould's impeccable credentials as the pupil and confidant of Owen Jones—the author of the much-admired coloration of the London Crystal Palace—certainly entitled him to be heard on the subject. Nonetheless, the organizers summarily dismissed Mould's ideas. Instead, they chose Henry Greenough, an artist from New Bedford, Massachusetts, and the brother of the sculptor Horatio Greenough, to do the work. Greenough was also a close friend of the exposition's superintending engineer. Greenough's scheme involved a general tone of yellow-orange. For the great dome that covered the crossing of the Greek Cross plan structure, Greenough proposed that it be tinted blue around the periphery and yellow in the center with strips of yellow descending to the base.

When their building was finished, the architects, who had not been consulted on the subject of color, expressed dismay over the appearance of their majestic cupola, which was the centerpiece of their design. "The yellow brings the top nearer to the spectators," they observed, "while the blue gives the effect of distance, and the vault which should have looked light, aerial, and expansive has now been flattened down." They were extremely disappointed that the "dome has lost a third of its apparent size by this distribution of colors."[7] They were even more upset when they learned that Mould had proposed a better solution. "We at one time understood that a gentleman from England, Mr. Mould, a pupil of Mr. Owen Jones, offered some meritorious designs for the decoration of the building which were not accepted. We had not the pleasure to see these designs until seven months after the Crystal Palace had opened [viz. January 1854], but we think in a matter so important as the decoration of a building which we designed it was the duty of the Executive to permit us to have a voice in the affair; a just courtesy which was never granted."

They had had the opportunity, however, of seeing on display in the exhibition some of the De la Rue products on which Mould had worked back in London. "They are specimens of exquisite tooling, and the designs are of the most chaste and elegant nature," stated Horace Greeley, editor of the *New-York Tribune* and one of the foremost promoters of the exhibition. "We fancy we can recognize the pencil of Owen Jones in these beautiful lines."[8] Mould could have reassured him that he was correct in his judgment.

Mould's drawings for the Crystal Palace are lost to posterity; however, in December 1853, five months after the Crystal Palace opened its doors, the English architectural journal *The Builder* published an account that purported to describe the interior color scheme.[9] The unidentified writer began by stating several guiding propositions in the manner of Owen Jones. One of these proclaims that "the prevailing colour of the ceilings should be sky-blue, thus borrowing from nature the colouring she has placed over our heads." Color lithographs of the actual interior of the Crystal Palace, however, indicate that ceilings were painted a yellowish color, not sky blue. Other descriptions of Henry Greenough's colors deviate from the program outlined in the *Builder*. For example, an article published in the *New York Times* described Greenough's scheme as having a "prevailing tone of buff or rich-cream color,"[10] whereas the *Builder* author said they were a "harmony composed in the key of orange and blue." The *Builder* also mentioned the prevalence of Moorish decorations, a feature with which Mould would have been intimately familiar. In the author's opinion, it is highly likely that the color scheme of the Crystal Palace described in the British journal was the one that Mould had proposed.

The Crystal Palace architects had other conflicts with the directors of the exhibition. The organizers had blamed the foreign architects both for shortcomings in the building's design and for delays in its construction. Carstenen and Gildermeister refuted these accusations in their 1854 book, *The New York Crystal Palace: Illustrated Description of the Building*. Angered and hurt by treatment they thought was unjust, both men eventually turned their backs on New York. Within two years of the opening of the exhibition, Carstensen had gone home to his native Denmark; Gildermeister followed his lead in 1857 repatriating to Germany. If Mould might have gotten to know them, he surely would have commiserated with them and could have repeated what Owen Jones had told him: "The Americans will wring you out like a wet rag, then drop you like a hot potato."[11]

Despite the rebuff from the Crystal Palace organizers, Mould remained confident that he could win a major commission that would allow him to demonstrate his full powers in his new homeland. Another opportunity came in early 1853 when the recently appointed Episcopal bishop of Illinois, Henry John Whitehouse (1803–1874), agreed to hire Mould to design the new cathedral he wished to erect as the seat of the diocese. Whitehouse was an avid follower of the Oxford Movement within the Church of England that preached a return to medieval liturgy in church services and to Gothic forms and precedents in the design of modern churches. He also was one of the early advocates for the adoption of the centralized cathedral system of administration, which threatened to overturn the parish-centered organization that prevailed heretofore. Both of these would find resistance in his new diocese where some accused him of "un-protestantizing" the faith.

By all accounts, Whitehouse was a difficult man. He was, observed Samuel Kerfoot, a congregant, "the prime cause or source of the constant and unceasing difficulties of one kind or another; one scarcely being settled before a new one would spring up."[12] At the time he met Mould, Whitehouse was living in New York, having refused to take up his Mid-West post until his salary and other demands were met. The dispute would take nine years to resolve

How Mould became acquainted with Whitehouse is unclear. Perhaps the Oakleys had introduced the two men. Mould was himself an Anglican and through his association with Vulliamy and James Wild, familiar with the prescriptions of ecclesiology. He readily agreed to carry out the bishop's Anglo-Catholic vision of modern religion, "in the true spirit of the Anglican Church." Echoing the language of Pugin, he would avoid all "sham" architecture in his plans. Moreover, he would do the job free of charge. This was not, however, purely an act of Christian charity, for Mould asked his client to agree, "to seek as much as possible to bring my name in connection with your plan before the Christian and Protestant public of

[your] vast community." Furthermore, Mould specified that the design was to be his and his alone. No changes were to be made by other architects. All of this was to remain cloaked in secrecy, for Mould demanded that the bishop would "let the arrangements as to my services be kept quite as a private matter, known to none save our two selves."[13]

Perhaps Mould had Jones's admonition in mind when he made these unusual requests to Whitehouse. On the other hand, the bishop himself may have actually tutored him, for Whitehouse was prone to suspicious and conspiratorial thinking. "The peculiar turn of his mind," reported Samuel Kerfoot, "the tendency to close framing of bargains and contracts—the mind at all times leaning toward the accumulation of money, the peculiar interpretation of language when embodied in secular or pecuniary bargains, an acuteness in framing agreements as touching the subsequent circumstances under which those agreements will be used, unfilled or carried out, mark the man."[14] In any event, Whitehouse agreed to Mould's terms and, in March 1854, signed a letter of intent.[15] In spite of this accord, however, a complex set of circumstances tied the cranky bishop's hands, and he was never able to obtain the funds to erect his grand new building.

While this potentially prestigious commission simmered, Mould gained a valuable social connection through Bishop Whitehouse, whose family continued to make their lives in New York. Whitehouse's sons, among them Francis, who later became a distinguished Egyptologist, would visit Mould's home and be guests at some of his festive boating parties. Whitehouse himself gave Mould express permission to list him (but by title only) as one of the architect's premier references. One wonders if the relationship would have flourished if the minister, a pro-Confederate sympathizer during the Civil War, had known that Mould had Black African blood and could have legally been categorized as a hexadecaroon.

All Souls Unitarian Church

In the summer of 1853, Jacob Wrey Mould obtained the great commission he was seeking. It was for a church headed by quite a different man of the cloth from the eccentric Henry John Whitehouse. The Reverend Henry Whitney Bellows (1814–1882) was an outspoken abolitionist minister, orator, and editor, and pastor of the First Congregationalist Church in New York. The congregation itself was one of the most progressive and influential in the city. Founded in 1821 as the "First Congregational Church in the City of New York," it saw itself as a "refuge from the intolerance, which then existed in this community toward all freedom of individual opinion in matters of religious faith."[16] Among knowledgeable contemporaries, the church enjoyed a reputation for "the cultivation, solid worth, and for the social and moral influence it has possessed; also for stability, amity and peace." All Souls, noted the *New York Times*, attracted "an array of literary, artistic, philanthropic, and patriotic men and women in its ranks of political, social and literary leaders, cautious reformers and guides in new forms of charity." This broad array of individuals raised it "among the foremost churches in this community, especially as regards the larger and broader applications of Christianity to public interests."[17] The congregation numbered among its members the poet and editor William Cullen Bryant, popular novelist Catharine Sedgwick, industrialist and philanthropist Peter Cooper, pioneering nurse educator Louisa Lee Schuyler, and well-known attorney Joseph Hodges Choate. On Sundays, All Souls parishioners, in the words of architectural historian David Van Zanten, "sought a religious philosophy more direct and elemental than tradition and ritual."[18] Because his client was not Episcopal, the architect was free from having to obey the strictures of ecclesiology—that arcane study of traditional medieval church observances—and was open to choose a mode of expression even entirely outside the limits of the Gothic Revival. Mould could not have hoped for a better audience for his premier creation in the United States.

By mid-century, Dr. Bellows had become acutely aware of the need for a new church in a new location. In the words of church historian Victor Fidel, "All Souls Church's relocations reflect the development patterns and architecture of New York City itself. The city's population centered at the southernmost tip of Manhattan island at the turn of the eighteenth century and spread northward as the century progressed."[19] Largely because of its address on Broadway at Crosby Street in Lower Manhattan, the church was losing parishioners. Members were moving away from the downtown area, which had once been a pleasant residential district. Commercial growth and tenements had transformed it into a noisy neighborhood of crowded, ill-sorted streets. On Sundays, the stench of rotting garbage and the presence of many beggars dismayed churchgoers. Uptown pew holders were growing more and more reluctant to go back to Crosby Street to attend services. Both the loss of members and the constant need for expensive repairs to the existing structure made action necessary. In October 1852, the congregation sold the Gothic style building, which had been built in 1845 to plans by Minard LaFever, and purchased a highly desirable new site at the southeast corner of Twentieth Street and Fourth Avenue (the present Park Avenue South).[20] Worship would henceforth take place around the corner from Gramercy Park, one of the city's most distinguished residential squares. Bayard Taylor, Horace Greeley, Peter Cooper, and William Cullen Bryant were among the congregants who lived in the neighborhood. While a new church was being erected, the congregation attended services in a variety of rented spaces. Even Niblo's Theater, a place of popular entertainment more accustomed to the reverberating musical showmanship of Louis Jullien than the spiritual strains of liturgical music, housed Sunday worshipers.

For Mould, the road to success was not an easy one. Unlike Whitehouse, Bellows, a Unitarian known as "a defender, preacher and minister of rational religion," cared little for elaborate ritual.[21] A seasoned orator with the ambition of increasing his flock, he desired a house of worship suited to preaching the word of God and to enhancing the stature of his congregation. Nonetheless, he undertook the project with some apprehension remembering how Lafever had miscalculated the strength of the walls to support the roof of the Crosby Street church, causing no end of trouble. Moreover, the quaint design had failed to do justice to the congregation. George Templeton Strong, a staunch Episcopalian and member of Trinity Church on Wall Street—the premier parish in the city—had demeaned the Church of the Unity, as the building was known, calling it a "deplorable example of infatuated vulgarity trying to look venerable and medieval." Bellows had learned from the experience and now felt wiser and more confident in dealing with architects and builders. On the eve of the new venture, he mused on the "chastened expectations, the sobered interest, the prudent economy of power and strength, which later years have necessarily brought with them."[22]

Moreover, Bellows, who longed for acceptance of his ministry by New York society, aspired to put the Unitarians, and in particular his own congregation, on the same social footing as the Episcopalians and Presbyterians, the dominant denominations in the city. Yet, Bellows was a revisionist who spoke out against the traditional Protestant suspicion of worldly luxuries. New York's inrushing wealth had begun to erode the conservatism that had dominated the city's elite culture. In a long sermon devoted to praising the marvels from around the world on display at the New York Crystal Palace, Bellows asserted that "as a simple matter of fact, in proportion to moral and intellectual refinement, does the taste for comfort and elegance increase; and, reflexly, comfort and elegance, instead of brutifying man, have a tendency to soften his heart, open his conscience, and refine his soul."[23] What better way to achieve favorable acceptance among uptown society than to erect a splendid new church in a prominent location and to choose an up-and-coming British new arrival who had the entire credentials one could want, including a connection to a prominent family in the city? Bellows might well have dreamed of upstaging venerable Trinity Episcopal Church and its renowned architect, Richard Upjohn. Even in choosing to rename his new church building "All Souls," Bellows displayed a desire to have his progressive congregation assume a more mainstream social position. The title echoed esteemed institutors in England and America and far outshone the former "Church of the Divine Unity," which hinted at downtown tract societies and backstreet missionaries.

In early December 1852, Mould submitted his first drawing of the design to the building committee.[24] Others apparently soon followed. Early in the new year, however, Mould's hopes for a commission seemed to fade. For reasons unknown, but perhaps because they were uneasy with Mould's inexperience and ambitious ideas and apprehensive over the fanciness of his drawings, the cautious members of the committee turned to a plain-spoken veteran engineer, C. F. Anderson, for an alternative plan. On April 10, 1853, the committee approved Anderson's design. When Bellow's saw it, however, he was deeply dismayed. To his eyes, it was too unimaginative for the splendid new location and for the prominence he wished his church to occupy in the community. "I felt it impolitic, unwise, and certain to injure the Society," he thought.[25] Bellows rejected the decision and dismissed the building committee. He reconstituted it to include himself and his friend and church benefactor, Moses Hicks Grinnell (1803–1877), a wealthy merchant and philanthropist. At this point, Mould's star began to rise again.

On July 8, 1853, after a period of lively debate, the new committee finally approved Mould's expanded plan that included a parsonage adjacent to the rear of the church. He immediately undertook to prepare working drawings, a task that required him to hire assistants beginning in August 1853 and lasting until September 1854. During this time, he himself worked feverishly to complete the undertaking, despite suffering from a serious but unspecified illness. (Mould had periods of precarious health throughout his life.) When his work was done, Sarony & Co, the well-known New York printing and engraving firm, published a handsome lithograph of Mould's striking perspective drawing for the future All Souls (fig. 10).

Construction of the new church was an expensive undertaking for the congregation. Several well-to-do parishioners helped with the financing. Peter Cooper, one of America's wealthiest men, stepped forward, but primary among them was Moses Hicks Grinnell. A trustee of the church and a member of the building committee, Grinnell was a native of New Bedford,

Figure 10. Jacob Wrey Mould: *All Souls Church*. Lithograph of the architect's drawing published by Sarony & Co., ca. 1855.

Massachusetts, whose mother's family had come over on the Mayflower. Grinnell's position on the upper rung of New York society resulted from his extensive shipping interests. He also numbered bank executive, congressional representative, and president of the Chamber of Commerce among entries on his extensive resume. As a philanthropist, Grinnell committed himself to advancing projects that promised to raise the stature of his adopted city in the eyes of the world. Socially, Grinnell had the reputation for giving lavish parties at his brownstone mansion on Fifth Avenue where he welcomed a wide range of interesting people. Perhaps Mould saw in Grinnell something of Lord Holford with whom he had negotiated on behalf of Vulliamy. Grinnell was exactly the sort of expansive, make-no-little-plans personage Mould would gravitate to all his life. Moreover, at the time, Grinnell was leading fund-raising efforts to construct Alexander Saeltzer's Academy of Music building. Certainly, Grinnell and Mould found common bond in the love they shared for opera and church music. Moreover, both men found pleasure in sailing.

Grinnell came to play a significant role in Mould's association with the All Souls commission. When the man of affairs turned his eyes away from ledgers to the beautiful drawings that Mould had prepared, he was utterly seduced by them. As Mould began proposing ever-improved designs for the church, he gained Grinnell's ardent support. He repeatedly gave from his own pocket to further the success of the remarkable building.

Financing the project had proved difficult for the church, especially during the 1854–1855 recession that followed the investment market panic of 1853—a financial catastrophe brought on in part by the action of Robert Schuyler, a member of the original building committee. (As president of the New York & New Haven Railroad, Schuyler had issued two million dollars of fraudulent stock certificates.) Once the new building committee had been formed (Schuyler escaped justice by absconding to Italy), a group of members donated ten thousand dollars to get the construction of the new church started. Yet, it was still not easy going. With the recession dragging on, the building committee, to Mould's consternation, became economy-minded. "That impossible committee," Mould is said to have remarked, "they even wanted to cut down my rose window." Nevertheless, Mould was adamant; "I made 'em keep it just as I drew it." Although he admitted that it was "too large for their gable, but it was made for mine, not theirs." He insisted that he "wouldn't pare it down an inch."[26] In the summer of 1855, as the financial system picked up, Grinnell donated the princely sum of twenty-three thousand dollars. The building now began to reveal itself to the congregation and the public. In June, Bellows wrote,

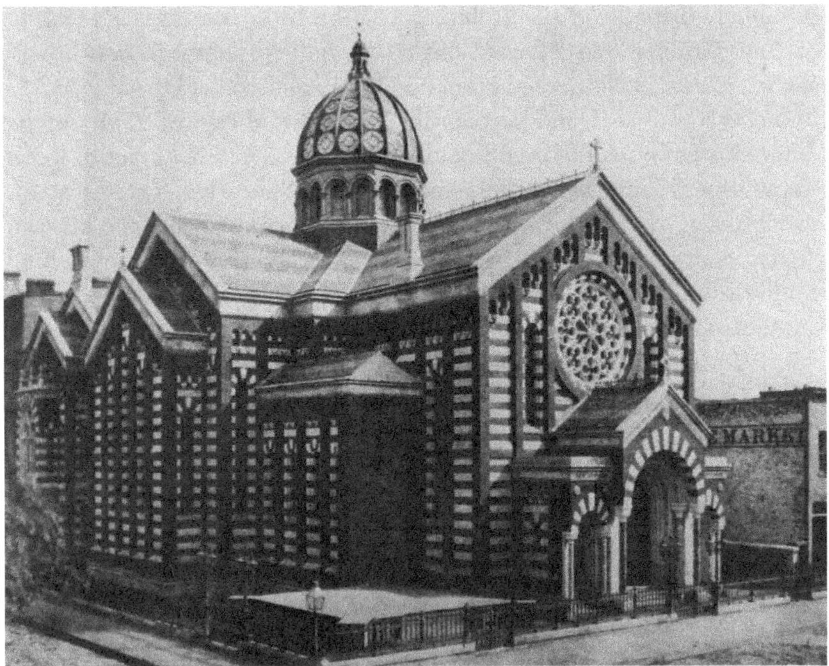

Figure 11. All Souls Unitarian Church, ca. 1855.

"the outside is mostly cleaned and looks like a quite different building. You can hardly conceive how much the cleaning has done to bring out the beauty of the materials. People begin to talk in a very changed tone about it."[27] By September, workers had nearly completed the interior plastering. Grinnell's gift, together with those of others, carried the work to the finish line by the end of the year.

On Christmas Day 1855, Bellows stood before the congregation to dedicate the completed building (fig. 11). Joining him were the pastor of Boston's Brattle Square Church, Samuel Kirkland Lothrop, who in the following decade would have H. H. Richardson design his congregation's new building, and Octavius B. Frothingham, later historian of transcendentalism in America. Bellows praised Mould as "the modest architect of this Christian temple" who displayed "a consummate skill, an unfailing taste, an unsparing devotion, a self-possession which neither ridicule nor blame could disturb, and a zeal which neither sickness nor pain could impair."[28]

Despite his kind words spoken at the dedication of the church, Bellows harbored ill feelings toward Mould. A number of years later, in an address to the congregation on the fortieth anniversary of his pastorship, he publicly disparaged the architect. (At the time, Mould was living in Peru and Grinnell was dead.) Taking a tone quite different from his dedicatory remarks, Bellows recounted how "our architect had bewitched Mr. Grinnell with his plan and his plausible estimates of expense." Mould, he admitted, was "a man of genius and taste," but he had been out to make a reputation for himself at the expense of All Souls. He "cared less for our interests," said Bellows, "than for an opportunity of showing his own talents."[29] After numerous skirmishes, Grinnell had succeeded in pushing Mould's submission; "weariness and suspense finally had too much to do with allowing the plan we adopted to prevail," conceded Bellows. Bellows had wanted a church that would seat 1,200 and cost no more than $120,000. Instead, Mould's building seated only 750, added a parsonage attached to the rear that reduced the size of the auditorium, and ended up costing $168,000. Bellows, a thrifty New Englander who probably equated "architecture" with "building," succeeded in trimming some of the expense by forcing Mould to reduce the height of the church several feet. Even more disturbing to the success of Mould's conception was the failure of the congregation to erect Mould's magnificent tower, which would have added another $40,000 or more to the total cost. As it was, the congregation, Bellows complained, had "incurred a debt far beyond any original purpose or expectation." It took many years of tough finances to pay off the loan. Bellows's daughter, commenting on Mould's demise in the same month that Augustus Saint-Gaudens placed an impressive bronze portrait of her father in All Souls, was even more blunt in her opinion: Mould, she said, was "what one might call a talented spendthrift. Peace be to his remains."[30] These were harsh words spoken with unchristian charity toward a man who had given his all to create a masterpiece.

Mould's spendthrift ways would never change; other clients would find that his designs often came with huge price tags. In his defense, one can speculate that his years with Owen Jones, at heart a Romantic devoted to art and beauty above all else, conditioned him to regard the economic requirements that constrained his clients as secondary. Moreover, his one patron before All Souls, Robert Holford, had found money no object when it came to erecting the sort of building he desired. Owen Jones had called for a glorious new architectural statement, a statement that would renew English architecture and connect it with modern times. With passion and artistry, Mould's All Souls had proclaimed his mentor's heartfelt motto: *pulchritudo vincit omnia*—beauty conquers all. Whatsoever the consequences for Bellows and his congregation, Mould had realized his dream—he had won a prestigious commission after only a year in residence at New York.

Mould's love for color in architecture—polychromy—found fully evolved expression in this, the first original building that he had entirely designed. Mould's creation consisted of three major parts: the Latin Cross plan church proper, a 230-foot bell tower at the northwest corner, and a parsonage at the rear of the church facing onto Twentieth Street. All Souls solidified in three-dimensional form the ideals of color and pattern that Mould had perfected working on the pages of Owen Jones's books and absorbing the theories and subtleties of his thinking. With only monochrome lithographs of Mould's perspective drawing and historic black-and-white photographs to go on, we can, nonetheless, appreciate that the exterior of All Souls was a carefully orchestrated assemblage—one is tempted to use the musical term *composition*—of color harmonies. Neither was the effect as brash as implied by the nickname that many gave it of "Church of the Holy Zebra." The walls consisted of alternating twelve-inch bands of cream-colored stone imported from Normandy and courses of "a deep Indian red" Philadelphia brick. Limestone quarried in Indiana was used for trim elements. Mould mitigated the design's insistent horizontality by articulating the walls with tall arched windows and blind arcades that paced a lively rhythm all around the building.

The spirited ensemble struck a note of welcoming gaiety to all those who came to worship there. The triple arches of the deep entrance porch consisted of so-called Florentine arches of alternating dark and light voussoirs resting on slender polished granite columns (fig. 12). Dominating the façade, the great rose window (which Mould had sworn to preserve from the building committee's economizing), with its circles of quatrefoil tracery orbiting the central rosette, eased the insistent grid of the walls and resonated the sprightly rhythm of the entrance arches. Recessed surfaces, molded openings, corbel tables, and banded arches kept up the lively pace and vibrant texture all around the building (fig. 13). Color patterns continued into the roof where the slate formed long dark and light bands. The dome of the crossing cupola, which rose some 130 feet above the street, was resplendent with bright mosaic designs; "an airy, spirited dome, almost afloat overhead," was a contemporary's response.[31]

Another current description reflected that the "chromatic combination" included "the blue of the sky."[32] This recalls remarks made concerning the Crystal Palace color scheme: "the prevailing colour of the ceilings should be sky-blue, thus borrowing from nature the colouring she has placed over our heads."[33] Mould's choice of colors, like those he had proposed for New York's Crystal Palace, echoed Owen Jones's endorsement of the supremacy of the primaries. As David Van Zanten pointed out, the suggestion of the

Figure 12. All Souls, main entrance.

sky also recalls contemporary French architect Jacques Ignace Hittorff's explanation of why the ancient Greeks had painted their temples the way they did. Moreover, it is not inconceivable that Mould in his choice of sky-topped colors might have had in mind a reference to the red-white-and-blue of his new homeland, an affirmation of the preservation of national Union that Bellows ardently advocated.

Only a master could have integrated so many colors and varied forms in such perfect equilibrium. Viewed from the corner, especially, the multihued façade and long north elevation formed a lively arrangement of projecting and receding components and rising and falling rooflines. With only the testimony of black-and-white historic photographs to go on, one

Figure 13. All Souls, side entrance.

can sense how vivid and mirthful the picturesque building must have appeared when newly completed. The striking impression the church made on passersby would have been compounded by the contrast with monotonous brownstone row houses that lined neighborhood streets.

From contemporary accounts, one can cobble together a general impression of what surrounded worshippers inside this extraordinary building (fig. 14). The spaciousness of the cruciform interior created a

Figure 14. All Souls, interior at the time of the funeral of William Cullen Bryant, 1874.

memorable first impression. Instead of the long narrow nave-and-aisles space that greeted George Templeton Strong and others as they entered Upjohn's Trinity Church, All Souls congregants viewed a wide and broad, all-embracing inscape. (Persnickety Strong dismissed Mould's All Souls as "pied variety" Hagia Sophia.) Inside the entrance from Fourth Avenue was a deep gallery "that was not sufficiently upraised to interrupt the singular dignity and spaciousness of the interior," noted a sympathetic visitor—likely art critic Clarence Cook.[34] Carefully decorated structural elements played a significant role in the impression of loftiness. Four impressive trusses bearing patterns of Gothic tracery (and possibly made of iron[35]) spanned the square central area that rose to a dome seventy-five feet above the floor. The cupola shed tinted light from stained glass windows into the high-ceilinged space. The dominant rotunda area, fifty-five-feet square, expanded on either side into forty-feet-wide, shallow transepts of unequal depth. Noting "Mr. Mould delights in sweeping arches," an eyewitness explained that he had enhanced the scale of the north and south transepts by framing them with tall round arches. Another discerned "its perfect dome resting as airily and as gracefully as a bubble of light above the nave and transept intersection."[36] Among the rows of pews in the deeper north transept, slender iron columns supported the loft that displayed the great organ that nearly touched the ceiling. The southern transept responded with "an unbroken wall surface pierced by five slender windows," that, like the rising and falling notes of a musical composition, exalted the height of the wall by "following the curvature of the great arch in their varying lengths." To many, it must have seemed that the generous, unrestrained interior of All Souls reflected the open-arms spirit of Henry Bellows who had chosen the name "All Souls" for the new building.[37]

With floors that sloped slightly upward toward the outer walls, the interior space summoned all to attend the words of the speaker who delivered his sermons from a large carved pulpit in an apse-like niche in the center of the eastern wall. The recess served a ceremonial rather than liturgical function, for since the earliest days of New England meetinghouses, Congregationalists came to hear the word, not to participate in liturgy. The church admirably fulfilled the purpose of housing a large number of people who would have a clear view of the spokesperson.

The elaborate throne-like pulpit exemplified the true focal point of this inner spiritual world. It occupied the center of the richly decorated apse recess. Framed by Corinthian pilasters, this alcove brought to mind Owen Jones's apse decoration in James Wild's Christ Church, Streatham (see fig. 6, ch. 2). An inscription proclaimed "The Temple of God is Holy, Which Temple You Are" (1 Corinthians 3:17). Here, each Sunday, wearing his clerical robes, Bellows would mount the rostrum to address his flock standing in front of a large shell-shaped sounding board. Mould must have known from his long experience with music and musicians that the concave shape would best project voice toward the audience. Perhaps it was also Mould's intention that when Bellows stood before the dark brown billowing shape, the gilded edge, as one observer noticed, made "one dream of a halo."[38]

Lost to us are Mould's instructions for how he planned to transform the interior into a universe of color harmonies. It appears that whatever Mould intended for the interior color scheme was never carried out. In 1858, when architect Richard Morris Hunt, who had recently established his office in New York after years of study and work in Paris, stepped inside All Souls he lamented that "what is not done leaves a painful nakedness." His practiced eye appreciated the pressing need for the church to be painted. "Without this, the interior is unfinished," he declared, "and while the architect can see that it is merely prepared for painting, the more superficial observer thinks of it as completed."[39] Later contemporary descriptions suggest that the walls were eventually "tinted mauve with the woodwork finished in a golden brown and gilt."[40] Red and black carpets covered the floor, and slender crimson columns with gilt capitals sustained the cantilevered organ loft.[41] Mould had planned to carry the color into the ceiling by painting and gilding the exposed trusses.[42]

Yet, those who came to listen and to pray never enjoyed the fulsome visual feast that Mould had planned for them. At the time of Mould's death in 1886, his friend Clarence Cook wrote that "the interior of the church, designed expressly to receive a rich decoration—the exposed rafters and beams painted and gilded—the large wall spaces enriched with frescoes (to be painted by an artist evolved for the occasion!)—all this was frankly abandoned by the Trustees for lack of money, and the building remains today a cheerless blank within."[43] Another informed visitor at the time also reflected on the unrealized interior decoration, "The Byzantine invites and almost demands lavish mural decoration in gold and glowing harmonies of colors," he told readers of the *Tribune*. "With this addition, and some really good stained-glass of the later English makers for the morbidly toned windows, the intention of the architect would be fully ripened into an ensemble of marvelous beauty and symmetry."[44] By then, H. H. Richardson and painter John LaFarge had fulfilled All Souls' prophesy on the richly embellished interior of Boston's Trinity Church.

For sure, to Mould, the lover of musical pageantry, the heart of the edifice was the impressive Ferris and Stuart organ. Hymn singing and uplifting music had been a significant part of Unitarian worship services for many decades. One would not be surprised to find that Mould had had a hand in choosing the organ builder and even in designing its cabinetry and decoration, which he did for other organs by the same firm. While working on All Souls, for example, Mould had on display for sale in his office in the Morgan Bank building on Bowling Green a Ferris and Stuart organ that he had decorated. He would later have one of their organs in his own home.

All Soul's impressive three-manual instrument was a masterwork of Richard M. Ferris (1818–1858), an expert New York organ builder. Described as a "nervous, precise and exceedingly irritable" perfectionist, Ferris enjoyed a special reputation for his acute sensitivity to the tone and resonance of his organs. "In finishing the organ at All Souls Church," recalled a contemporary who knew Ferris, "he was so over-particular about the tuning, being several months about it, that it was thought he would never get through."[45] In fact, Ferris failed to complete his work by the time of the dedication, so its full power could not be heard during the selections from Handel's *Messiah* that figured prominently in the choir's program.

The dithering senior organ tuner and the visionary young architect must have truly tried poor Bellows's Christian patience.

By all measures, All Souls was a remarkable building. Embodying the colorful principles that Mould had learned in Owen Jones's atelier, it brought to the sidewalks of New York a brilliant example of the polychrome synthesis that Jones and his circle had pioneered in England. Mould had seized the opportunity to introduce this polychromy phenomenon to his new world compatriots. All Souls fully justified Mould's contention, "I'm Hell on Color"; it established his reputation as a "master of color" in architecture.

The reality of Mould's conception lay back in the 1840s with the British forebears of architectural polychromy. His building brought to America another tradition from England different from that of the Gothic Revival of Richard Upjohn's Trinity Church. Only a few years earlier, Upjohn had opened the eyes of New York and the nation to the English medieval parish church model of Christian architecture. Mould, instead, turned his eyes southward to a more distant and more colorful architectural past. He drew upon his fondness for the medieval architecture of Italy, the Italo-Byzantine style that had welcomed influences from the Eastern Roman Empire and even the Arabic world. His fascination with Italy had more in common with Romantic poets Keats and Shelley and Mould's former classmate, artist Dante Gabriel Rossetti and the Pre-Raphaelite Brotherhood, than it did with Pugin's *The True Principles of Pointed or Christian Architecture* and Anglican ecclesiology.

German architects had also pioneered the return to Italy for inspiration. Notable was Munich's Court Church of All Souls designed in 1828 by Leo Von Klenze. Von Klenze drew upon the example of Palermo's beautiful Arab-Norman Palatine Chapel.[46] Karl Ludwig Von Zanth, a Germanic associate of Hittorf's, had been among the first to explore the colorful Arab-Byzantine architecture of Sicily. In the 1820s, he and Hittorf visited the island and from 1826 to 1835 published a series of studies of Arab, Norman, and Byzantine architecture there.

In 1838, Zanth, who in France went by the name Louis de Zanth, conceived the most audacious application of exotic sources to date for modern buildings. When King Wilhelm I put him in charge of planning his extensive royal suburban villa retreat near Stuttgart, Zanth based his designs on the Alhambra. The Wilhelma, as the park is known, brought forth the pages of Owen Jones's great book into the world of living architecture. When completed in 1846, the Wilhelma became known beyond Germany from ten beautiful chromolithographs that Zanth published of it (fig. 15). Zanth, said Thomas L. Donaldson, the British architect who knew his work well, "did not fetter himself by slavish adherence to precedent, nor neglected any means of success; and he employed stone of various colors from the adjoining quarries for the principal buildings, rich colored brick for the office, and cast iron for various details."[47] Surely Mould knew of the Wilhelma—which no one ever seems to have ridiculed as "Die Zebravilla"—and its architect, for Zanth had spent time in England to learn about conservatory design and was an honorary member of the Royal Institute of British Architects where he had exhibited some of his Sicilian drawings.

An esoteric movement, the polychromy that the Mediterranean world inspired remained a lesser current in the larger flow of British architecture in the 1840s and 1850s. James William Wild, Owen Jones's brother-in-law, cautiously introduced materials of mixed color inspired by Italy into Anglican ecclesiastical architecture with his Christ Church, Streatham of 1841 (fig. 16). Wild had been impressed by the twelfth-century church of San Zeno in Verona, which Christ Church resembled in general outline. Moreover, like Italian churches of that distant period, the bell tower or campanile stood independent from the church, rising sheer from the ground and

Figure 15. Karl Ludwig van Zanth: Die Wilhelma villa and garden, Württemberg, chromolithograph, 1855.

Figure 16. James Wild, Christ Church, Streatham, 1841.

might be placed at either the front or the back of the church. It had made no difference to Italian medieval designers where it went. At the three entrance portals, Wild had introduced voussoirs of alternating light and dark stone—precursors of the "banded arches" that would appear on All Souls and which became identified with much High Victorian Gothic architecture. Mould certainly knew Wild's church, for while he was in Jones's atelier, Jones had furnished plans for the colorful Byzantine style mosaic decoration of the interior. Nevertheless, it is amazing that such a masterful expression of these forward-thinking ideas should suddenly manifest itself in such an unlikely place as New York.

As an apprentice in Jones's studio, Mould had many other opportunities to learn about the beauties of Italian art and architecture. It is easy to picture him poring over the two folio volumes of Henry Gally Knight's *The Ecclesiastical Architecture of Italy from the Time of Constantine to the Fifteenth Century* (1842–1844), for which Jones had provided the chromolithograph title page (fig. 17). He may also have supervised the monochrome lithography. From these gray-toned atmospheric illustrations, Mould could have cultivated his South-facing imagination and stored up

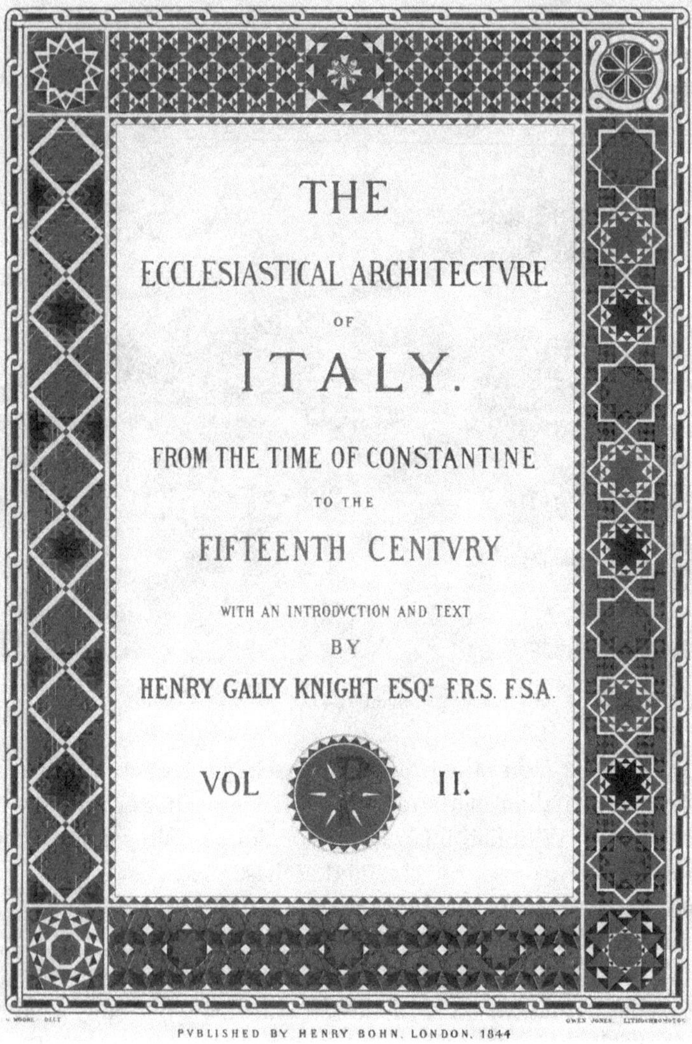

THE

ECCLESIASTICAL ARCHITECTVRE

OF

ITALY.

FROM THE TIME OF CONSTANTINE

TO THE

FIFTEENTH CENTVRY

WITH AN INTRODVCTION AND TEXT

BY

HENRY GALLY KNIGHT ESQ[r] F.R.S. F.S.A.

VOL II.

MOORE DELT — OWEN JONES LITHOCHROMOTOG

PVBLISHED BY HENRY BOHN. LONDON. 1844

Figure 17. Owen Jones, title page to Knight's *The Ecclesiastical Architecture of Italy* (1842–1844).

images in his mind for future reference. Indeed, the lithograph of Mould's perspective drawing for All Souls published by Sarony shows the architect imitating Knight's style of representation (fig. 18). Given his close relationship with Jones, it is even possible that Mould might have met Knight. Whether or not Mould actually ever visited Italy, however, either with Owen Jones or on his own, is an open question. Knowing Mould's love for Italian art, architecture, and music, the author is inclined to believe that he

Figure 18. Torre del Mangia on the Palazzo Pubblico, Siena, from Knight's *The Ecclesiastical Architecture of Italy.*

did. Books alone surely would have failed to instill in his imagination the profound understanding of color, form, texture, and detail that manifests itself in Mould's architecture. And given what we understand of his life-embracing personality, we can assume that he would have felt a perfect sympathy for the land of Donizetti, Bellini, and other composers whose operas he knew and loved.

Moreover, architectural references Mould made in All Souls are present in Knight's book, which illustrated all the major monuments of medieval architecture throughout the Italian peninsula. Included were San Zeno in Verona, the cathedrals in Modena and Monza, and Siena's town hall. Together with Wild's Christ Church, Mould used San Zeno as a starting point for his design of All Souls (fig. 19). But he went further afield for inspiration for his wholly original design. The distinctive red and white layers laddering up the exterior had precedent in the Palazzo del Comune and the church of San Fermo Maggiore (fig. 20), both twelfth-century structures in Verona that feature alternating courses of red brick and

Figure 19. San Zeno, Verona, twelfth century.

white stone. More subtle banding is also present on the cathedrals of Pisa—Ruskin's fondest Italian Romanesque buildings—Siena, Orvieto, and other monuments of Italian Gothic. He could have learned from San Zeno, Pisa, and elsewhere how the early architects used blind round-arched arcading to articulate exterior walls, as he did at All Souls. Likewise, examples of church fronts featuring a rose window and deep porch occurred in the pages of Knight, especially the cathedrals of Monza and Modena. A likely ancestor to the ribbed dome on a drum of round arched openings was Brunelleschi's famous dome on the Florentine cathedral. The cross-shaped plan with nave leading to a central rotunda could be found in many instances following the fountainhead of Byzantine church architecture, the sixth-century church of Hagia Sophia in Istanbul. Nonetheless, All Souls

Figure 20. San Fermo Maggiore, Verona, twelfth century.

was more festive than any single church Mould could have encountered back in his days of apprenticeship.

The most dramatic feature of Mould's All Souls design was the great tower he projected for the corner of Twentieth Street and Fourth Avenue. Mould's bell tower, which dwarfed the church, bore no resemblance to the Gothic Revival or earlier church towers and belfries that existed in New York. Specifically, its appearance harked back to the fourteenth-century secular campanile known as the Torre del Mangia on the Palazzo Pubblico in Siena (see fig. 18). Mould surely recalled that Wild had referred to the same source for both the tower for the Church of St. Mark in Alexandria, Egypt (ca. 1846) and his more recent colossal three-hundred-foot-tall water tower (1851) at Grimsby in Lincolnshire that provided water pressure for the harbor's hydraulic dock equipment (fig. 21).

The tower of All Souls, which stood independent of the church, would have been as much a civic monument as a religious one. At the intersection of the avenue and street, the 230-foot soaring marker would have been visible from a great distance in all directions. A clock face twenty-two-feet in diameter would have informed people of all faiths of the time, the day of the month, and the direction of the wind. Inviting the public to linger

Figure 21. James Wild, Harbor Water Tower, Grimsby, Lincolnshire, 1851.

on the church property, Mould foresaw a ground-level sheltered space for rest and contemplation at the base of the tower. Pedestrians gained access to this little outdoor room through four arches that daringly shouldered the structure's mounting stages. Like visitors to the Torre del Mangia, New Yorkers might have climbed the shaft to gain a splendid view of the city from an open-air balcony far above the street. On the way up, one would have been able to stop at a small library and to look into a chamber that held an organ, presumably for public concerts. The uppermost level was a polygonal belfry crowned with a steeply tapering conical spire. Sadly, for all those who loved architecture and were enthralled by the urban spectacle, only the bare twenty-four-foot square launch pad base of this heaven-directing projectile was ever built. Two decades after the dedication of the church, the *Tribune* spoke for many when it wrote: "There is little question to-day as to the brilliancy of Mr. Mould's design, which, however, sorely needs for its vindication the erection of the tower at the northwest corner."[48]

It would be another twenty years before New York saw a tower of comparable beauty and elegance actually erected. In 1874, Frederick Clarke Withers, another talented English immigrant architect, graced the angle of Sixth Avenue and West Tenth Street with a picturesque High Victorian Gothic fire tower attached to the Jefferson Market Courthouse. Before that, Mould's later colleague Calvert Vaux, had honored the All Souls tower with the affirmation of imitation in the design for his quaint "observatory" that he proposed to erect in Hillside Cemetery, a rural burial ground that he laid out in the early 1860s in Middletown, New York (fig. 22). And surely young H. H. Richardson, the rising luminary in the American architectural profession, took some lessons from Mould's All Souls when, in 1869, he designed the soaring 176-foot corner bell tower resting on ground-level arches for the Brattle Square Church on Commonwealth Avenue in Boston (fig. 23). Taking his cue from Mould's ecclesiastical landmark, Richardson fashioned his own interpretation of a medieval Italian belfry. "Richardson's campanile," notes author Hugh Howard, "which stood almost apart from the main nave, was unexpected in a city of churches with steeples that tended to sprout symmetrically from their roofs."[49]

In their original discussions with Mould, the members of the All Souls building committee had not planned to include a rectory as part of the church complex. But in July 1853, the board of trustees approved "the modified plan now submitted including a dwelling house in the rear of the church."[50] This was a significant development because it reduced the seating capacity of the church, to which the parsonage was attached. It added, however, another piece of exceptional design to the street architecture of New York, for the facade of the rectory completely rearranged the front of the conventional New York City brownstone dwelling (fig. 24).

Rather than the usual elevation of layered floors of evenly spaced pedimented windows terminating in a roof hidden behind a horizontal cornice,

Figure 22. Calvert Vaux, design for an observatory, Hillside Cemetery, Middletown, New York.

Mould's vivacious three-story façade featured tall, round-arched openings beneath a steeply-pitched peaked roof, a design that brought it into harmony with the adjacent north transept elevation of the church. Dominating the façade was an oversized bifora bay window—a type of medieval window composed of two arched openings divided by a column—inscribed within a banded round arch. It provided abundant daylight to the large first floor drawing room. The gaping window jutted boldly forward from the façade and rested on twin arches that had their origin in the long corbel

Figure 23. H. H. Richardson, Brattle Square Church (First Baptist Church), Boston, 1869–1871.

Figure 24. All Souls Church parsonage.

table supporting the uppermost level of the fourteenth-century town hall in Florence, the Palazzo Vecchio. The rudimentary props appear on other Italian masonry buildings in the Middle Ages, but never in this way at ground level. The exaggerated size of the eccentric bay window imparted brute drama to the façade and presaged the quirky details and abrupt changes in scale that would characterize some of Mould's later architectural designs. (Richardson's introduction of similar stone corbeling on the tower of his Brattle Square Church surely was another debt he owed to Mould.) Additional tall, narrow openings and portholes at close intervals minimized solid walls and brightened the other inside chambers. Architecturally, observed David Van Zanten, "this varied treatment must have produced striking effects of enclosure or exposure on the interior of the house."[51]

In the opinion of architectural historian James O'Gorman, the parsonage must have made a strong impression on the developing imagination of the young Frank Furness who was studying architecture with Richard Morris Hunt in New York at the time. O'Gorman recognized in the unusual façade "the first flickering of the kind of architectural design that Furness would produce after the war."[52] Nothing so bold and original had been seen in New York street architecture. Its unconventional character would find its reflection in later buildings Furness designed in his native Philadelphia. All who walked by, architects and casual strollers alike, must have intuitively been impressed by the powerful sense of materiality the little building conveyed (fig. 25).

Once the parsonage was finished in the spring of 1856, the congregation rented it to Bellows for one thousand dollars per year, a sum that he could now easily afford since his wife's uncle had died and left them a small fortune. The basement level accommodated the Sunday school and other church-related functions. The upper three floors were for the Bellows' private use. The church reserved the right to employ the bright and spacious first-floor drawing room, said by the *Journal of Commerce* to be one of the finest in the city, for meetings and lectures. It apparently also housed Bellows's extensive library.[53]

Bellows and his family passed their life comfortably within the parsonage. Eliza, Bellows second wife, a woman of delicate health, is said to have taken pleasure in the large, airy rooms. Nonetheless, she found the house, especially because of the corridors leading to and from the church, difficult to keep tidy. Her daughter Anna, who grew up in the rectory, thought the "complicated and somewhat mysterious and inconvenient parsonage

Figure 25. All Souls Church parsonage, detail of central bay.

delightful."[54] For Bellows, passage from the "complicated" internal arrangements of the parsonage into the unimpeded space of the church must have been an exhilarating experience, emblematic of the private and public sides of his energetic life. In fact, the boundary between these two spheres was rather porous. The drawing room became the scene of historic meetings. It was here that he encouraged Peter Cooper with his plan to found an educational institution. At the outbreak of the Civil War, Bellows convened in this room early discussions concerning the creation of United States Sanitary Commission (of which he became president and Olmsted the secretary).

Reception of All Souls

Within a couple of years of arriving unbidden, Mould had the good fortune to find his All Souls church become the talk of New York. Unsettled ground of possibilities now gave way to a firm footing in the profession of his adopted country. The vibrantly colored church awoke Americans to the new High Victorian esthetic. The church raised many eyebrows among the public, which was stunned by the audacity and energy of Mould's creation. "Wrey Mould, the architect, was soundly berated or gently commiserated, as a man quite beside himself, or one who had affronted and scandalized not only the venerable traditions, but even the religious sensibilities of all church-going people. It was not quite clear . . . whether his genius had become frenzied or crazed," wrote the *Tribune*.[55] Newspapers and scornful locals, even architects, were quick to dub All Souls the "Church of the Holy Zebra" for its contrasting stripes. Others compared the exterior to streaky bacon, fat-and-lean meat ("the Beefsteak Church"), and "Joseph's coat." "The grave and puritanical shook their heads with much doubting," reported Peter Bonnet Wight in the *New Path*, the journal of the Pre-Raphaelite movement in America, "said it was frivolous and gaudy, and that it spoke badly for our times that our churches should deck themselves in such gorgeous array. The *orthodox* affected to be not surprised, and declared it to be the natural result of *liberal* doctrines."[56] Already in 1854, certain "orthodox" members of the building committee had expressed reservations when they first saw Mould's drawings. "The only questionable point presented to my mind is the alteration of color in the materials of its exterior walls," wrote Nicholas Dean, a prominent and generous congregant and member of the building committee, to Henry Bellows. "Is there no danger that a display so new may miss the beautiful, and hit the ridiculous?"[57]

Mould need only to have read the article in *Putnam's Monthly* for September 1853, "New-York Church Architecture," to see how fully All Souls departed from the ecclesiastical architecture that New York churchgoers knew. The anonymous author noted that the city possessed some 230 houses of worship, "the majority of which are merely convenient houses for public assemblages, respectable enough in appearance, but making no pretentions to architectural splendor or to ecclesiastical symbolism."[58] The author describe the church that Bellows's congregation had occupied previous to Mould's building (and known as the First Congregational Church and later as the Church of the Divine Unity) as "a very large building, full of pretense and cheap expedients." The façade was "a series of unpainted brick walls, innocent of all deception." Thanks to the Episcopal and Presbyterian denominations, the writer acknowledged, "the renaissance, progress, and culmination of Gothic architecture in the New World, may be here seen in the course of a morning's walk." Handsome illustrations celebrated fine buildings that enhanced the standard Sunday fare, principally

Upjohn's Trinity Church, Renwick's Grace Church, and Joseph-Francois Mangin's St. Patrick's Cathedral. With these in mind, it was not surprising that Mould's All Souls elicited the shock of the new. Yet, Mould remained unflappable in face of negative criticism. "Never for one instant [had it] disturbed the self-possession of the architect," remarked a contemporary. Mould had faith throughout the process that "cultivated and true artistic taste and feeling for the picturesque effect and decorative color, would carry him triumphantly through the daring innovation."[59]

While the public might have found the new edifice bizarre and perplexing, knowledgeable observers recognized Mould's positive contribution to the city's architecture. The *Churchman* confessed that Mould's All Souls had "effectively revolutionized our religious architecture. . . . To his resolute persistence we owe the growth of color, light and flexibility in architectural expression."[60] Those who had access to the recent report of the Congregational church leaders on architecture, *A Book of Plans for Churches and Parsonages*,[61] would have realized that knowledge of Mould's drawings for All Souls had swayed Richard Upjohn in his design for a city church. It featured walls of horizontal bands of red-and-white brick, a clear sign that the architect had seen Mould's drawings. The rising art critic Clarence Cook, told the readers of the weekly *Independent* that All Souls proclaimed a new architectural truth, "the Gospel of beauty, derived from color."[62] The *Journal of Commerce*, recognizing the Italian and Byzantine origins of Mould's design, noted that the "style of architecture in this edifice, being entirely unknown and novel in this Hemisphere, has attracted much public attention, and given rise to many flippant criticisms; which the Intrinsic merits and beauties of the building will silently and satisfactorily rebuke and refute." The journal praised the "original and beautiful designs for the building and all its appropriate and harmonious details—so replete with evidence of genius and taste" of the architect.[63] The writer added that when viewed by moonlight, with the church interior illuminated, "the effect of color is truly rich and charming." Mould himself was especially fond of relating how when the British novelist William Makepeace Thackeray visited America and strolled by the church one moonlit evening, he declared the freshly minted exterior the finest example of polychromy he had encounter in the New World; it made him think for a moment, he said, that he had been transported to Italy.

A more nuanced review of the building appeared in 1858 in the *Crayon*, the most serious art journal America had yet produced. The extensive critique was written by Richard Morris Hunt, the first American to have received his architectural credentials at the Ecole des Beaux-Arts in Paris.[64]

Hunt acknowledged that the church appeared unusual to most people but was "by no means new or strange to the amateur, the architect, or those who have travelled abroad." (Also in this group would have been Leopold Eidlitz who, architectural historian Kathryn Holliday reminds us, had designed the interior of the little known Shaaray Tefila synagogue in New York in 1846 to evoke the polychromy and ornamentation of Moorish, Saracenic, and Byzantine architecture.[65]) Together with praising the church's color scheme, the review concentrated on the form of the building. "The whole church," noted Hunt, "has evidently been designed with reference to its purpose, its materials, and location." The writer complimented Mould for the way he had developed his plan to make the best of its corner site and for the originality of its decorative elements. "The general grouping of the church, with respect to its location, economy of space, and effect of light and shade, is as successful as the efforts to produce it must have been persevering and laborious," stated the magazine. Moreover, Mould had succeeded in making the church appear monumental, despite the relatively small size of the lot, 80 by 120 feet. On the latter point, Hunt asserted that the tower was the "base-note necessary to complete the harmonious chord." In its individual elements, All Souls was "the unmistakable off-spring of the architect's brain, carried out in all its details with the greatest care and judgment." Notably, both the trusses that sustained the dome above the crossing and the rose window on the facade "were nothing less that works of Art." Young Edward T. Potter, an admirer of Mould's work who began his architectural practice in New York in 1856, surely agreed, for he often repeated his own variation of All Souls' rose window in many of his church designs, notably Beth Eden Baptist Church in Philadelphia of 1864–1867.

To the readers of the *Crayon*, Hunt affirmed that, in short, All Souls was "a work of merit and genius, second to none in our city." With the aplomb of a savant, the writer predicted that while it was "premature for our present tastes," it pointed the way to a future time when "it will be abundantly appreciated by the next generation." This turned out to be true. Mould himself confirmed the progress American architecture had made in the years following All Souls. Writing in the *New-York Tribune* in 1880, he affirmed that "the 'doctrine of color' in architecture, which I preached when building All Souls Church twenty-seven years ago . . . has indeed flourished. . . . The architect who would discard the use of colored stone, encaustic tile, polished granite and moulded brick (for the employment of all of which I was then severely ridiculed) would not get salt to his porridge."[66] Years later, the *New York Herald* remembered how Mould "had been laughed at by his fellow workers, but soon the conviction dawned on them that he was right and the knell had been tolled of the poor, old, ordinary looking brownstone edifices."[67]

The *New Path*, the publication edited by Mould's admirers Peter B. Wight and William Sturgis for the Society for the Advancement of Truth in Art, generally seconded Hunt's appraisal when it published a review of the building in its first volume, which came out in 1863. Together with praising the architect for his bold use of color, the journal told its readers to pay close attention to the "ornamentation in stone" that was "cut with great care and expense and is moreover novel and ingenious in design." Specifically, the journal liked the Byzantine style floral capitals of the imported polished columns that graced the entrance, although it wished the designs had been more true to nature than stylized. In any event, the carvings on the church presaged Mould's designs for carved decoration in Central Park.

By 1870, a critic reviewing the progress of polychrome movement in American architecture could write that before 1860, "decoration in color was practically unknown in this country. White, glaring white paint, was the sole coloring of the interior of churches, court-rooms, theaters and banks, as well as of private dwellings." But a deep-rooted prejudice against sensual appeal of color had been gradually overcome, and, in the past decade, American public and private buildings had blossomed with an array of tints and patterns so much so that "it may be safely asserted, that in proportion to the population we exceed even England and France in the number of well decorated buildings." And why should this not be true? "Nor is it at all surprising that our people should love color in a country where nature has produced a most brilliant display of it, illuminated by a tropical sun, and reflected and varied by an almost constantly clear sky."[68] Mould's All Souls could lay claim to having been largely responsible for awakening America to this new way of embracing color in its architecture. "To his resolute persistence we owe our growth of color, light and flexibility in architectural expression," declared the *Churchman* at the time of his death in 1886.[69]

The most personal testimonial to All Souls came many years later, from the distinguished architectural critic Russell Sturgis and his friend Peter Bonnet Wight. They had been students at the Free Academy (forerunner to City College) in New York when All Souls was being built. Each day after their drawing class, they would pass by to view the progress of the work. Mould's ongoing creation made a strong impression on both of them. As young art students, they were even more impressed by Mould's drawings (sadly, now lost), which they were able to see. "And such drawings!"

proclaimed Wight. "I have never seen better ones since. Everything was drawn in ink and colored on fine white drawing paper, backed with muslin. It became our habit every day to study those plans and to compare them with the work being executed. We were fascinated, and I may say both were impressed for the first time with the desire to become architects."[70] Inspired by Mould's example, both of them determined to read Ruskin, Henry Cole, Owen Jones, and Christopher Dresser. Later, both men would design important buildings: Wight's National Academy of Design was, together with Mould's All Souls, one of the major monuments of High Victorian architecture in America; Sturgis is remembered for Yale University's Farnam Hall but mostly for his many books and articles on art and architecture.

Although Mould's magnificent building may have been the answer to his prayers for a commission that would generate much excitement among the public and profession, it failed to produce the amount of compensation for his efforts that he thought he had earned. Without an established schedule of charges for architectural services, Mould relied for reimbursement on the disposition of Bellows and the building committee. When Mould began his work on All Souls, he was living with the family of his uncle, Alexander Oakley. With no room for an office there, Mould rented space at 4 Bowling Green over the offices of the Belfast & Mersey Steamship company. (He began to list himself as an architect in the 1854 city directory.) He remained there during the two years he worked on All Souls. His dear aunt, Louisa Oakley, who was especially close with her older sister by one year, generously lent him two thousand dollars to tide him over until the building committee started to pay him.[71] Her school on Park Place, the Academy for Young Ladies, had been quite successful, plus Louisa had invested her earnings wisely.

The church began by paying Mould in small sums, but disagreed with him about the full amount he should receive. In February 1856, soon after the dedication ceremony, Mould wrote a letter to the committee detailing his claim for augmented payments. Mould itemized expenses, including the salary of two temporary draughtsman he had hired for the project, and claimed a fee of 5 percent of the cost of the building. After pointing out that he had devoted himself solely to the church and was not yet profiting from the fame the church had brought him, he closed his letter with an appeal to both the building committee and to the trustees "that both as Christians and Gentlemen and in the name of Honesty, Justice, and Humanity, they will now give the proper consideration to my long unremunerated Service."[72] Sometime later, Mould reiterated his contention that "the customary charge for designing, drawing working plans and superintending the erection of a building in the city is 5 per cent on the cost of the work,"[73] Eventually, Grinnell proposed giving him one thousand dollars in addition to the one thousand dollars Mould had already received. That would represent the church's final payment for its masterpiece.[74]

Little wonder that a short time later Mould responded to a call to discuss the formation of an official association of architects. In February 1857, a small group met in Richard Upjohn's office to plan a society to "promote the scientific and practical perfection of its members" and "elevate the standing of the profession." Mould's inclusion in this groundbreaking encounter signified that others now regarded him as a full-fledged colleague in the fellowship of thoughtful architectural practitioners. Others soon joined them. The first meetings highlighted how much the nation owed to immigrants and foreign instruction for its architectural development. Of the thirty or so founding Fellows, Richard Upjohn, Calvert Vaux, Frederick Withers, George Snell, Frank Wills, Joseph C. Wells, and Henry Dudley came from England. Mould was the latest addition to this veritable Sons of Albion coterie. Detlief Lienau had emigrated from Denmark after studying in Germany and Paris. John Rudolph Niernsee and Leopold Eidlitz had come from Vienna. Among the native-born minority, Richard Morris Hunt would have contributed ideas from his experience studying at the École des Beaux-Arts and working in Paris—he was the first American to do so. By April 1857, this pluralistic group drafted by-laws and adopted the name American Institute of Architects. When, fifty years later, the organization placed a plaque commemorating its founders at Octagon House, its national headquarters in Washington, DC, Mould's name was on it.

The issue of adequate payment for creative work was foremost among Mould's professional concerns. At the initial meeting, Mould had called attention "to the dignity and stability it would give to the profession, a position which it enjoyed abroad but not in this country."[75] He had also advocated for a standard 5 percent fee for architectural services.[76] Calvert Vaux stated the same figure in the business notice that appeared at the back of his book *Villas and Cottages* that came out at the same time. In 1866, the American Institute of Architects issued the document, "Schedule of Charges," which formalized Mould and Vaux's call for a 5 percent fee to include design and site visits.

Mould also campaigned for the right of architects to place their monogram on the exterior of buildings they had designed. Colleagues recalled that in support of this practice, which was common in Europe, Mould "used to sign his churches with his monogram wrought into a pretty finial, or panel ornament."[77] Many years after Mould's death, the AIA accepted a report from the committee appointed to examine the matter of building signature and recommended the practice. It added that such autographs append the AIA initials as well.[78]

In later years, Mould's masterpiece fared poorly in Manhattan's ever-changing cityscape. Later custodians of the church even had the temerity to conceal its colors behind a veil of ivy. In 1927, as many taller buildings were encroaching on the venerable Gramercy Park neighborhood, a visitor to All Souls described it as "unfortunately hedged in and deprived of daylight," a fact that compromised one's appreciation of the interior. Moreover, "its stone work is scaling off, its garden is overgrown, and its gates padlocked and rusty." The rectory had been transformed into "a church house and a hive of useful activities."[79] The final service took place in the church on June 9, 1929. After that, the parishioners sold the property and moved uptown to their present location. Abandoned by its flock, Mould's church lay empty, whatever plans the new developer owner had for it were undoubtedly curtailed by the beginning of the Great Depression. On the morning of August 23, 1931, firefighters were called to put out a fire in the abandoned church. Smoke streaming from several windows signaled a conflagration that had engulfed the entire interior (which had already been stripped of its finish). The formidable blaze took eighteen fire companies to put it out. One fireman suffered injury and several others narrowly escaped suffocation in the parsonage. When it was over two hours later, the church was destroyed. "We are all or most of us creatures endowed with an instinct for the accustomed place of things," mused a local newspaper reporter, "and the fire that achieves the ruin of this old place of worship leaves us with a sense of something lost."[80] What had been the impetus for a new era of "Ruskinian" design in America had vanished. Along with the H. H. Richardson's Marshall Field Store; McKim, Mead & White's Pennsylvania Station; and Frank Lloyd Wright's Larkin Building, Jacob Wrey Mould's All Souls Unitarian Church ranks as one of the major lost monuments of American architecture.

4.

Embellishing Central Park

After what you and Vaux and myself have done on that Park, we might have spent the rest of our lives perfecting it.

—Mould to Olmsted, August 3, 1884

BECAUSE OF HIS ASSOCIATION WITH Calvert Vaux (1824–1895) and Frederick Law Olmsted (1822–1903), Jacob Wrey Mould became intimately involved from the earliest days with the creation of Central Park, the first significant municipal recreational landscape in the United States. The subject of a place for civic rest and renewal had been discussed long before Mould arrived in New York in August 1852. His ship docked one month after the death of Andrew Jackson Downing, the nation's longtime chief advocate for the regenerative power of nature and natural scenery. At his idyllic home overlooking the beautiful Hudson River Highlands at Newburgh, New York, some sixty miles north of New York City, Downing had written books and articles extoling the virtues of life lived in harmony with nature. He had also called for the creation of a large public "pleasure ground" in New York, warning its residents to do so now before all of the land had been built upon. In 1850, Downing had gone to England to find an assistant to work with him on the business venture he had launched designing private houses and the grounds around them. He had engaged Calvert Vaux, a fellow member with Mould of the Architectural Association, to be his architect assistant. When Downing died tragically in a steamboat accident in July 1852, Vaux continued to work in Newburgh.

In 1857, he published *Villas and Cottages* which summarized his career as a designer of well-planned modern dwellings.

By the time Vaux's book appeared, civic leaders had heeded the call of Downing and others and had purchased a large tract of land in the center of Manhattan Island for a new public park. Surely, if Downing had lived, he would have received the job of laying out the new park. During Millard Fillmore's presidency, he had already designed an extensive public landscape for the federal government in Washington. In Downing's absence, the city had hired a respected civil engineer, Egbert Viele, to plan the new park. In 1855, Viele, on his own initiative, had gone over every inch of the future park site and mapped all its existing structures, topographic features, and water sources. Vaux, who was now a resident of New York, however, regarded Viele's design ideas as uninspired and unworthy of the genius of his departed friend and colleague whose memory shadowed the endeavor. He began to work hard to convince public officials that a better scheme could be secured if the job were thrown open to many minds in a competition. Convinced of Vaux's reasoning, the board of commissioners announced a national competition for the design of Central Park, the name adopted for the 750-acre green space. Competitors had the fall and winter of 1857/58 to prepare their entries. The winner would be announced in April.

In 1857, Olmsted, whose name was to become identified with the profession of landscape architecture in America, had no clear sign as to where his future lay. During his childhood years, which had been marred by ill health, he had acquired a love for rural scenery. This taste had been molded by his doting father, who enjoyed taking his young son on leisurely tours through the beautiful Connecticut Valley and in the vicinity of his native Hartford. The eighteenth-century tradition of British landscape writing by such authors as Gilpen, Repton, Knight, and others also informed these excursions. Despite ample family resources that would have allowed him to pursue a professional career, Olmsted spent an aimless youth. An interest in farming eventually gave way to a thirst for travel and writing. In 1843, he signed on to a ship sailing to China; two years later he undertook a walking tour of England. The journey produced a volume of essays that were published in 1852 under the title *Walks and Talks of an American Farmer*. The trip through the English countryside was followed by an extensive tour through the Southern States. This tour resulted in articles that appeared in the *New York Times* and eventually in his book *Travels in the Slave States* (1856). Historians still consider it a major document for understanding life in the antebellum South. These endeavors confirmed Olmsted's love for landscape, writing, and social theorizing. They brought him little, however, in the way of compensation and prospects for permanent employment. So, in 1857, Olmsted applied for the job of superintending the large labor force that the city had assembled to prepare the ground for laying out the new Central Park. At the time, work was proceeding according to the plan the city had commissioned from Olmsted's boss, civil engineer Egbert Viele. This position gave Olmsted the solid feel of the pragmatic world and a growing understanding of how to manage men and resources.

Soon, Vaux approached Olmsted with the proposition to join him in the preparation of a competition entry. Olmsted agreed, and the two men set to work at night and in spare hours to create the design they would submit under the name "Greensward." Perhaps also at Vaux's suggestion, the two men asked Mould to assist them. "They frequently invited me to cooperate with them," recalled Mould who went on a weeklong camping trip in the Catskills with Olmsted, Vaux, and Ignatz Pilat, an Austrian gardener and "Forty-Eighter" who was destined to become Central Park's superintendent. Yet, Mould dismissed their offer to collaborate because, he said, he had little faith "in the success of any art competition on its true merits, where politics are in anyway called into question." This sounds a bit disingenuous coming from a young man who had been willing to insert himself in the Crystal Palace project, to form a behind-the-scenes alliance with the conniving Reverend Whitehouse, and to memorialize the trustees of All Souls. Surely, Mould was not the only one who during the winter of 1858 stopped by Vaux's house on Eighteenth Street to view the progress of the submission. Mould may have gone even further than taking up his pen, as others did, to add a few dots and dashes to the grassy areas of the nine-foot-long Greensward diagram. Art conservator Cynthia Brenwall states that Mould prepared the elaborate flower garden design that featured as Vaux and Olmsted's presentation board no. 11 of their submission (plate 1).[1] The complex design, which exhibits an artist's sense for primary colors and integrated patterns, had echoes of Owen Jones's Proposition Eighteen that stated "ornaments of any colour . . . may be separated from grounds or any other colour by edgings of white."[2] It certainly bears the impress of Mould's imagination. In any event, once events overtook predictions and Vaux and Olmsted found themselves winners, Mould lost his reluctance to participate in the historic undertaking. "When, however, to my great astonishment their admirable design was honestly accepted and was being honestly carried out, I desired to come aboard the ship."

Because of their victory at Central Park, Vaux and Olmsted also became the acknowledged leaders of the nascent American park movement.[3] "It is pleasant to reflect," wrote Downing's old confrere, the noted journalist George W. Curtis, "that through his former friend and partner, Mr. Vaux, Downing is connected with the Park."[4] Olmsted would go on to become America's most famous landscape architect and eventually leave New York to establish his office in Brookline, Massachusetts. Vaux would spend the remaining thirty-eight years of his life in New York where he often defended his and Olmsted's vision of Central Park.

With the sponsorship of John A. C. Gray, one of the park commissioners (best remembered for his donation of a Venetian gondola for the park lake), Mould became an assistant to Vaux.[5] Gray, who had gained his fortune from railroads and insurance and secured his position in society by marriage to Susan M. Zabriskie, also hired Mould to decorate the interior of the elegant new house that Vaux had designed for him at 40 Fifth Avenue. "We have seen nothing in the way of painting in this modern Gotham, which can compare with the detail of the painting in Mr. Gray's house," reported William Stillman, the disciple of Ruskin who had edited the influential art journal *The Crayon*. "Every line and every leaf betrays the spirit of a master hand, and reminds us of the best works of the Alhambra and Gartner's modern productions in Munich." Gray was no ordinary client. Stillman praised him for his "boldness in initiating polychromatic painting, from which most men are apt to shrink." His striking living quarters, the author hoped, "will prove the initiation of an era in the history of polychromatic decoration in this country."[6]

As park commission vice-president, Gray informed Mould that at the beginning of his job with the Department of Public Parks, he would collect "a mere nominal and utterly insufficient rate of payment." Nevertheless, Mould accepted his assurances that once he had proven himself to the commissioners they would see to it that he was "duly remunerated."[7] Mould received his first modest payment in December 1858, several months after construction had begun. He would stay involved with the park until his death in 1886, except for a hiatus of five years between 1875 and 1879 when he left New York for Lima.

One of the earliest people to inform the public in a serious way about Central Park's designers and their intentions was Clarence Cook, a former assistant to Downing and Vaux at Newburgh and art critic for the influential *New-York Tribune*. In his handsomely illustrated book, *A Description of the New York Central Park* (1869)—the first truly in-depth appreciation of the park—Cook extolled the triumvirate of Frederick Law Olmsted, Calvert Vaux, and Jacob Wrey Mould as the rare concurrence of artistic genius that had brought the great park into being. At the time of the park's creation, all three were at the beginning of careers that would make their names well-known to their contemporaries. To these names must be added many more who lent specialized skills in engineering, horticulture, architecture, and other disciplines to implementing the Greensward plan, together with various carvers, masons, and other artisans. Not least were the thousands of drovers and laborers who literally moved earth to make it a reality. (By 1861, they had completed most of the park below Seventy-Ninth Street.)

Unfortunately, later writers lost sight of Cook's sound assessment of the park as the result of this fruitful collaboration. History has been unkind to the memory of the latter two men, leaving the impression in many minds that Olmsted guided the job nearly single-handedly. Whitelaw Reid, editor of the *New-York Tribune* and a close follower of the developments surrounding Central Park, thought that Vaux deserved most of the credit for the landscape design. "For the design of the Central Park as a whole, and for many of the most useful and ingenious details of the plan, the public is indebted to Mr. Calvert Vaux," he wrote in the pages of the *Tribune* seventeen years after the park was begun. Olmsted, Reid acknowledged, "may claim the chief praise for the administrative system of the park, and for the thoroughness with which it was carried out, as for the absolute freedom of the government of the Park from all political interference—features which long made this the only public institution in the country in which the common-sense principles of what is known as Civil Service were ever faithfully and steadily carried out."[8] In their plans for Central Park, Vaux and Olmsted included many structures to promote visitors' pleasurable experience of the landscape. As a trained architect, Calvert Vaux took special pleasure in furnishing the park landscape with bridges, viaducts, summer houses, and large and small constructions for assorted functions. Adding a wealth of festive ornament, Mould sought to heighten the charm and beauty of these delightful creations.

The Mall

A major feature of the new park was to provide New Yorkers with a safe and pleasant place where they might see one another and be seen. The pleasure of promenading in the company of others was one that many European city dwellers treasured. But before Central Park existed, residents of America's grandest city had scant opportunity to enjoy this civilized pastime. To fill this communal void, Vaux and Olmsted included in the Greensward plan a spacious, tree-lined promenade they called the Avenue

Figure 26. The Mall in Central Park.

or the Promenade but that came to be known as the Mall (fig. 26). Here they envisioned all classes of citizens strolling freely along a broad avenue a quarter of a mile long—the length of six city blocks—and over two hundred feet wide. To shelter the throngs from the summer sun, Vaux and Olmsted lined the Mall with four parallel rows of native elms, America's most gracefully formed forest tree that Downing had extoled for urban planting. "Magical emissaries from the countryside," as historian Thomas Campanella has called them, for elms had long been associated with small-town life, especially in New England.[9] By 1895, the overarching branches of the Mall's matured trees created a magnificent leafy canopy that resembled New Haven's famed Temple Avenue and often evoked comparison with the vaulting of a Gothic cathedral. And even during the many leafless months, the sight of the bare upraised arms of these splendid trees drew admiring visitors to the Mall. "Do I love it more," wondered Annie Nathan Meyer in 1898, "when its high, vaulted roof is a soft, waving green of myriad shades, when the green velvet carpet is dappled with bright sunshine and black shadows, when a coolness meets me at the very threshold; or when the bare branches and twigs write their fairy traceries against the pale winter sky, when the hard surfaces of the leafless branches reflect on all sides the wonderful, diffused golden light of the winter twilight."[10] The

Mall was a gathering place for New Yorkers who wished to be seen by their fellows and for those who hoped to catch a glimpse of citizens higher up on the social scale. For Vaux and Olmsted, the Mall confirmed their vision of the park as a place where all people could feel to congregate as equals.

Easily reached by carriage or on foot from the main park entrance at Fifth Avenue and Fifty-Ninth Street, the Mall quickly became the most frequented spot within the park. It also became the venue for statues of famous literary figures. These include Fitz-Greene Halleck, Robert Burns, Sir Walter Scott, and William Shakespeare. Of these, Mould received much praise for his pedestal under John Quincy Adams Ward's bronze *Shakespeare*.[11]

Thanks to Jacob Mould, visitors from the earliest days of the park also enjoyed the pleasure of music in the new public setting. Concerts began to take place already in the summer of 1859. Mould personally raised money for the free open-air events by soliciting donations from friends and acquaintances. Benjamin and Edward Whitlock, grocery importers, gave the most; Henry Bellows and George Templeton Strong also contributed. Every Saturday afternoon, the "immortal" Harvey Dodworth led his fashionable orchestra in programs chosen by Mould. His selections, commented a critic, were "a proper mixture of an instructive and elevated class of music which might also be characterized as popular."[12] The first one on July 9, 1859, included works by Mendelsohn, Verdi, and Strauss. Next year, the overture from Mould's much-loved *Der Freischütz* featured in the program.

The lovely Ramble, the part of the park that Vaux and Olmsted conceived of as its most secluded and picturesque portion, welcomed the initial concerts (fig. 27). It was the only area of the park finished at that time. Few who came, however, could fully appreciate the music's luring strains in the tufted landscape setting of labyrinthine walks, dense foliage, and impressive boulders. "The musicians' stand was placed on a rock too elevated for the effective distribution of the sound through the adjacent portions of 'the Ramble,'" reported the *New York Herald*. Moreover, due to the picturesque terrain, concertgoers were "induced to cluster around in immobile groups of listeners, instead of promenading the contiguous walks whilst the music was playing," as Mould and the organizers wished them to do. Not only did the Ramble prove an unsuitable venue for listening to music, one can assume that Vaux and Olmsted objected to it being used in this way. Their vision for the Ramble was a secluded "wild garden" for quiet walks of small numbers of people. Large crowds here would damage the densely planted foliage and overwhelm the meandering path system.

Figure 27. The Ramble in Central Park.

The following year, the commissioners moved the concerts to the north end of the Mall where they constructed a temporary bandstand. Olmsted countered in 1861 with the novel suggestion that the orchestra be set adrift on a raft in the lake. Drawings indicating the arrangement of the musicians on a covered hexagonal barge and its possible position in the water were prepared, presumably by Mould, who would have known best how to group the performers (fig. 28).

In 1863, the commissioners erected a permanent terrestrial bandstand according to Mould's design near the north end of the Mall. This "Grand Music Pagoda," which, unfortunately, no longer exists, ranked as one of Mould's major contributions to the park (fig. 29). It introduced this new type of music venue to the United States. Only two years before, Francis

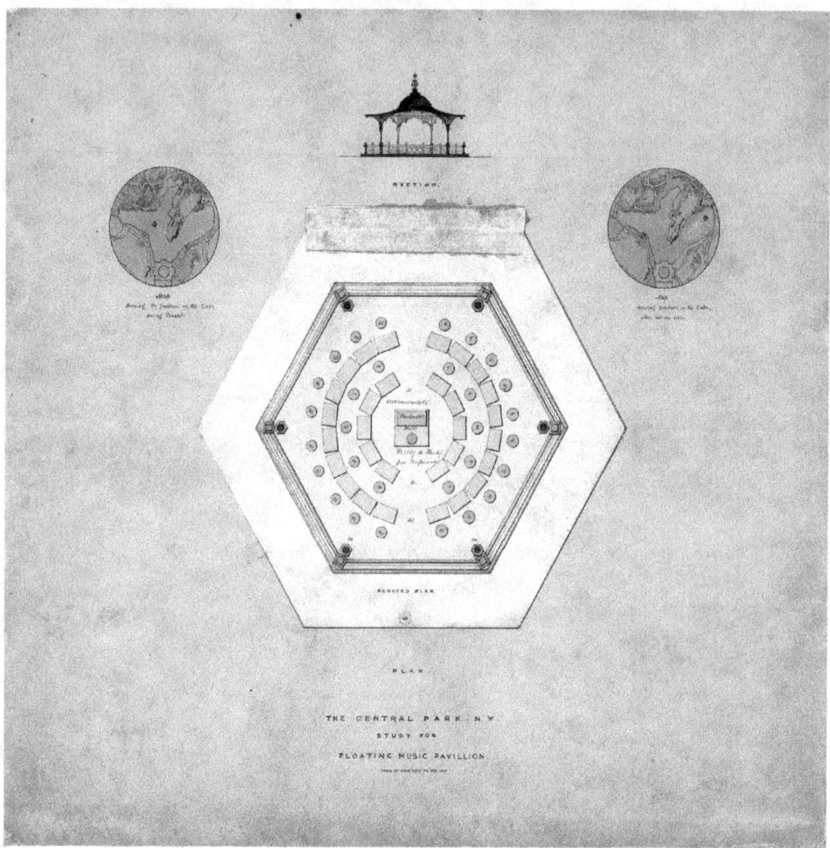

Figure 28. Design for a floating music pavilion in Central Park.

Fowke had designed the first bandstand—Fowke referred to the cast iron structure as a "band house"—at the Royal Horticultural Society's gardens at South Kensington in London.[13] Given Mould's love of music, he must have envied his homeland's introduction of concerts to the evolving park experience. His own version for America must have been very close to his heart.

Like his Medieval Moorish predecessors, Mould intensified the prominent design elements with vibrant hues. Unfortunately, today we know the bandstand only from a few of Mould's drawings and from black-and-white photographs. One of the best of these was taken by W. H. Guild Jr. and appears in Frederick Beecher Perkins's 1864 book on Central Park. Perkins featured a view of the bandstand looking along the Mall as the frontispiece of his book. It was the first book on landscape architecture

Figure 29. The Central Park music pavilion, from stereoscopic image, 1862–1863.

to use photographs as illustrations. (Vaux and Olmsted, who had nothing to do with the publication, must have been disappointed that Perkins, an aspiring journalist and novelist, had chosen to highlight an architectural feature rather than a landscape view.) With the help of the author's exuberant prose (a discourse one could imagine Mould himself voicing), we can see in our mind's eye the color lacking in the Guild's photograph.

> Count up the tiers of coloring from the foundation. Next the strong green of the grass is the gray stone water table, or base for the woodwork. Then come, a broad band of bluish gray; narrow line of olive green; red-brown moulding; broad band of yellow, with red and black ornamental decoration of pendent leaf forms, seen clearly in the picture; narrow black line; narrow red line; moulding in sky-blue; gilt line; ogee moulding in pea-green, with a leaf decoration in olive-green, each leaf having a little red heart; narrow red line; sky-blue moulding; gilt line; drab band with red-brown devices; red-brown line; indigo-blue moulding; gilt line; red-brown line; green line; and lastly, the ornamental rail-work of leaf designs and intermediate lotuses outlined strongly in white, with a blazing gilt outcry filling in each leaf; as if the predominating secondary colors and combinations of the strata below were to emblematize the successive strains and modulations of an overture or a sonata, while that terminal crash or blaze of color stands for *Tour fortissimo* measures in the last cadence of the grand finale. The colors of the roof, within and without, are far brighter, as they should be. It stands on six round red posts,

> with gilt bands and gay capitals. Inside are many fancifully outlined compartments, whose quaint arabesques, indeterminate in curve and combination, are proper to the obscure expressiveness of music. On escutcheons disposed among the gilding, are emblazoned the names of the great masters of music. The cupola, dark blue, sprinkled with gilt stars, is girdled with a coronet of larger stars and alternate trefoils, and one great gilded star crowns the tip of the finial, rising above a lyre, the only common-place device in the whole structure.[14]

Many of Mould's contemporaries considered the florid bandstand the third-most significant structure in the park, after the Terrace and the Bow Bridge—works Mould also enlivened with imaginative decorations. The sheet music cover that Harvey Dodworth published in 1863 for his "Central Park March" celebrated these popular attractions and highlighted Mould's bandstand. The performances, for which Mould took a measure of credit, proved a great success, and Dodworth returned summer after summer for over twenty years to lead his band in the popular concerts. "The effect of good music on the Park is to aid the mind in freeing itself from the irritating effect of urban conditions," asserted Vaux and Olmsted, "and by increasing the pleasure of a visit to the Park, it will tend to enlarge the number of visitors to it, and prolong the average period in which the special means of recreation afforded by its essential elements are active."[15] For half a century, Mould's colorful bandstand brightened the Central Park Mall. In 1923, the present monochromatic Neo-Classical Naumburg Bandshell replaced his joyous, fictively fluttering baldachin.

The Terrace

The Terrace, today commonly known as the Bethesda Terrace, is the grandest structure in Central Park. It was needed, said its designer, Calvert Vaux, because the overall landscape lacked any natural formation that would serve as a leading feature. In the architecture of large country houses in Britain and Europe, a terrace was a board platform at the rear of the mansion from which the owners could enjoy a panoramic view of the land beyond the house. Vaux was familiar with this tradition and adapted it to the conditions of the Central Park landscape, creating a terrace where there was no mansion. The Terrace itself consists of several distinct elements: three staircases, an upper landing, an underground hall known as the Arcade, and a broad lower terrace in the center of which is a large circular pool presided over by a bronze statue of the Bethesda

Angel. Vaux took justifiable pride in the success of this elaborate architectural statement that forms the transition from the lower park to the more natural landscape of the upper park. "So far as I am aware," he wrote, "it is new in composition and I feel justified that it makes in execution a central feature sufficiently ample and picturesque for the important position it occupies."[16] He considered it one of the most important works of his career (fig. 30). Strollers approaching from the Mall are rewarded with a striking panoramic view of the interior park landscape. "It was thought desirable; to insist as far as possible," asserted Vaux's friend, the Unitarian minister Henry Bellows, "upon a pause at the point where, to the visitor proceeding northward [along the Mall], the whole hillside and glen before Vista Rock first come under view."[17] Many regarded this prospect of the lake and the Ramble from the Terrace as the finest "picture" in the park.

From this open-air landing, two broad staircases lead visitors down to the Water Terrace, also referred to as the Esplanade, with its circular basin and statue fountain (fig. 31). Pedestrians coming along the Mall can avoid the Seventy-Second Street carriage drive by taking a third, central stairway that descends beneath the roadway. Either by design or coincidence, this approach recalls the ancient stepwells constructed along major routes in India, places where weary travelers descended elaborate staircases to reach a pool of cool water.

With Vaux's blessing, Mould took charge of creating designs for the relief carvings that adorn the Terrace's outdoor stairs, pillars, and railings. Vaux determined that the overall theme of these decorations would be the four seasons, with imagery dedicated to Spring and Summer allocated to

Figure 30. Bethesda Terrace (aka the Terrace).

Figure 31. Bethesda Terrace esplanade.

the eastern staircase and Autumn and Winter embellishing the western flight. Thick, rippling moldings cap railings, and curvilinear floral designs embrace capstones, many of which were intended to serve as pedestals for freestanding statuary that never materialized (fig. 32). Overflowing cornucopias, scrolls, twisting vines, and naturalistic flowers and plants complete the ensemble.

Mould drew amply from nature for his wide variety of relief carvings. Decorating the balustrades of the two main staircases, small panels realistically depict plants and flowers emblematic of the seasons (fig. 33). Spring and summer varieties appear on the eastern staircase, while fall and winter plants highlight the western stairs. For their design, Mould undoubtedly studied the chapter "Leaves and Flowers from Nature" in Owen Jones's *Grammar of Ornament*. All of Mould's naturalistically rendered vignettes conform with Owen Jones's observation on leaves found in nature that "the basis of all form is geometry, the impulse which forms the surface, starting from the center with equal force, necessarily stops at equal distances; the result is symmetry and regularity." All of these delightful little fragments snatched from nature seem to evoke Mould's teacher's inspirational pronouncement that "the Creator has not made all things beautiful, that we

Figure 32. Detail of railings in Central Park.

Figure 33. Detail of Bethesda Terrace balustrade, east flank of the east steps with spring flora.

Figure 34. Witch on a broomstick relief.

should thus set a limit to our admiration; on the contrary, as all His works are offered for our enjoyment, so are they offered for our study. They are there to awaken a natural instinct implanted in us—a desire to emulate in the works of our hands, the order, the symmetry, the grace, the fitness, which the Creator has sown broadcast over the earth."[18]

Mould furthered the tale of the seasons in a series of enchanting high relief trefoil rondels (truly small niches) that recalled the Labors of the Months scenes found on many Gothic cathedrals. These are accompanied with sprays of flowers or plants appropriate to the time of year evoked (figs. 34, 35, 36). He depicted such cameos as a witch flying on a broomstick, an open book the pages of which seem about to flutter in the wind, a rooster greeting the morning sun, an owl keeping watch in the night, and sheaves

Figure 35. Open Bible relief.

of wheat gathered at harvest time. All of these encyclopedic representations of nature, rural life, and the passage of time were intended to remind their viewers that the main purpose of the park was to afford city people the fleeting pleasure of a fictive country excursion. Mould's artful reliefs furnish illustrations to the book of nature that Olmsted and Vaux authored and enhanced the element of delight, especially for young park visitors. Stepping outside of grown-up convention, Mould evoked a world that anticipated the appealing children's stories of Kenneth Grahame. His reliefs are enchanting tokens of the Victorian ideals that shaped the Central Park landscape.

Work began early on this monumental project. By 1862, skilled carvers had completed many of the fine carvings that are still visible today

Figure 36. Rooster relief.

(many of which have been restored). The crescendo came in 1868 when the well-known German-born sculptor Karl L. H. Mueller (1820–1887) completed four large reliefs that Mould had drawn in 1866 and 1867 for the triangular "foliated ramp" panels on the outdoor staircase landings. Spring and Summer highlight the eastern landing; Autumn and Winter flank the western landing. These highly naturalistic arabesques—the drawings for which Mould proudly exhibited with the American Society of Painters in Water Color held at the National Academy of Design in the winter 1867/68—teem with bird life amid unfolding vines.[19] With wild profusion, Mould addressed the same seasonal themes illustrated more modestly on the balustrades. It was as if he had literally translated the observation of Owen Jones that "in the surface decoration of the Moors all lines flow out of a parent stem: every ornament, however distant, can be

Figure 37. Karl Muller, sculptor, autumn relief, after drawing by Mould, Bethesda Terrace.

traced to its branch and root; they have the happy art of so adapting the ornament to the surface decorated, that the ornament as often appears to have suggested the general form as to have been suggested by it."[20] In these marvelously rhythmic and fulsome visual compositions, birds flit and soar among entwining vines, buds pregnant with life appear about to open, and flowers in full bloom turn their faces to the sun (fig. 37). Mueller, who would be best remembered for the monument he created in 1870 for his father-in-law John Matthews in Green-Wood Cemetery, poured all of his skill into realizing Mould's conceptions. "A great advance will be secured if our best sculptors will execute works to be largely seen by the people of the present and the hereafter who are to frequent the Central Park," noted a contemporary journalist of Mueller's commission.[21] The abundant scenes seem conjured to illustrate one of the last passages in Darwin's *Origin of*

Species: "an entangled bank, clothed with many plants of many kinds, with birds singing on the bushes, with various insects flitting about, and with worms crawling through the damp earth . . . these elaborately constructed forms, so different from each other, and dependent on each other in so complex a manner, have all been produced by laws acting around us." They also evoke Ruskin describing carvings on St. Mark's in the *Stones of Venice*: "sculpture fantastic . . . of palm leaves and lilies, and grapes and pomegranates, and birds clinging and fluttering among the branches. All twined together into an endless network of buds and plumes."[22]

The Esplanade

The sweeping area known as the Water Terrace or Esplanade invited visitors to congregate at lakeside before choosing to go further into the park or to take a boat ride on the lake. A large circular basin occupied the center of the expanse, its generously molded rim designed to host leisurely dawdlers. In 1859, Mould made a plan that called for an elaborately inlaid pavement of colored tiles to surround the great basin (fig. 38). Unfortunately, Mould's design, which highlighted the various axes of the quatrefoil esplanade border, never left the paper on which he drew it. (The present surface of red and buff-colored pavers was installed in the 1920s.)

In the early days of the Terrace, several jets of water animated the center of the basin's placid surface. About a decade after the Terrace was constructed, the basin's rising water jets gave way to a monumental sculpture representing the biblical angel that cured the sick at the Bethesda pool in Jerusalem (fig. 39). The eight-foot-tall bronze sculpture of the *Angel of Waters* was the work of the American sculptor Emma Stebbins. Bearing a lily, the emblem of purity, in one hand, the angel (whose sex is still a source of puzzlement to viewers) "seems to hover over, as if just alighting on a mass of rock," wrote its creator. From beneath the figure's feet, Stebbins informs us, "water gushes in a natural manner, falling over the edge of the upper basin, slightly veiling, but not concealing, four smaller figures, emblematic of the blessing of Temperance, Purity, Health, and Peace."[23] The statue's pious imagery—Claus Sluter's famous fifteenth-century *Well of Moses* baptismal font may have informed Stebbins's conception—proved appealing to Victorian tastes but would probably be found unacceptable if proposed today. It was left to Mould to design the substructure for Stebbins's conception, in essence a new twenty-six-foot-high freestanding fountain within the original basin. At water level, a hexagonal bronze pad on which multiple stubby granite columns support a large flaring stone basin

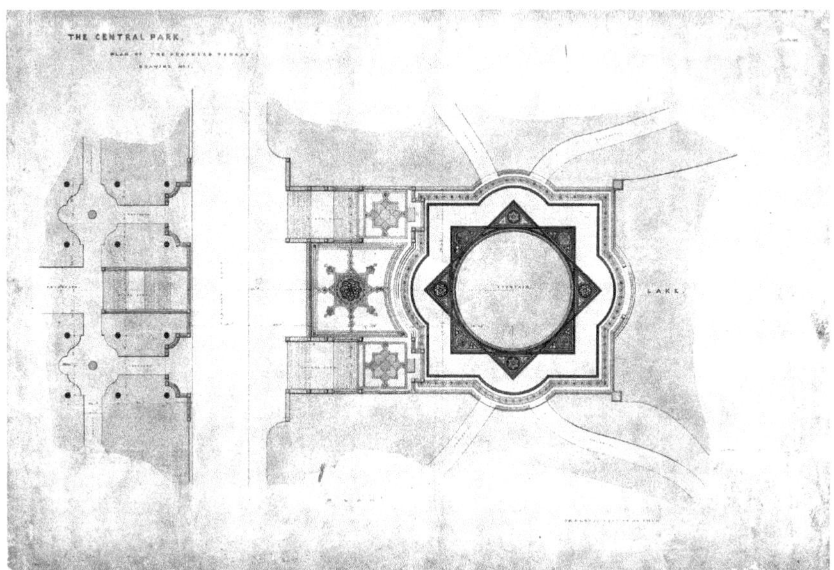

Figure 38. Design for floor of the esplanade, Bethesda Terrace, ca. 1859.

(fig. 40). Above that, the bronze allegorical figures and smaller circular basin serve as the statue's pedestal. Extending the earlier piping through the central spine, Mould raised water to spray the angel's feet. From there, it drips to the lower basin and then tumbles from six angle spouts into the original ground level pool. The Bethesda Fountain would be followed by other ornamental water displays from Mould's drawing board.

In later years, the image of the fountain became the catalyst for the renewed health of the entire park. In the 1970s, when the neglect of the park was at the worst it had ever been , Elizabeth Barlow Rogers undertook a campaign to restore the landscape to the days of Olmsted, Vaux, and Mould. Her efforts produced the Central Park Conservancy. "To repair the broken Terrace Fountain with its Angel of Bethesda sculptural centerpiece," Rogers said, "was for me . . . symbolic of our mission to heal the park. For this reason I chose as our young organization's logo an image of the fountain."[24] Over the ensuing decades, the Conservancy has accomplished what Rogers had envisioned. Moreover, as in the nineteenth century, when Central Park led the way in the American municipal park movement, the Conservancy spurred other cities to take note of and conserve their historic parks.

Figure 39. Emma Stebbins, sculptor, *Bethesda Angel.*

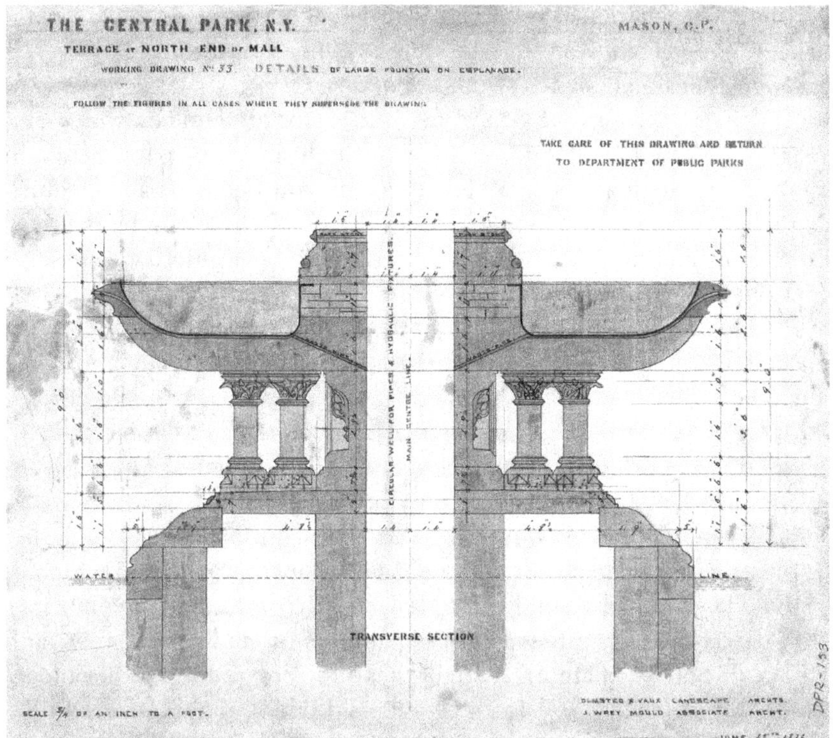

Figure 40. Bethesda terrace esplanade fountain, section drawing, 1872.

Terrace Arcade

Visitors descending the central staircase from the Mall arrive in a large underground hall that the designers referred to as the Terrace Arcade. Here, below the upper landing, two rows of arches divide the area into a long central section flanked by two shorter side aisles. Blind arcades on the walls repeat the seven Moorish-style arches at the end of the room that frame the view of the Esplanade and fountain. The soothing cadence of splashing water overheard from the Bethesda Fountain and the restful mood engendered by the indirect light made this semi-open space a favorite respite for Victorian visitors from the summertime heat. Additionally, for their comfort, six of the lateral niches were intended to have half-round recesses holding drinking fountains. (These were apparently never installed.) The other alternating bays were flat.

For the decoration of this unusual space, Vaux gave his collaborator Mould a free hand to dazzle the public with his skill as an ornamentalist.

Delving for inspiration into his vast knowledge of decorative motifs from his days in England, from the Alhambra volumes and from other works by Owen Jones, notably his *Grammar of Ornament*, Mould concocted a colorful array of designs that surround the visitor on the floor, walls, and ceiling. The result is a grand vestibule to the heart of the park. Beneath visitors' feet, Mould laid a floor of unglazed tiles divided into panels featuring repeated star designs in muted tones (fig. 41). (These tiles lie beneath the present flooring.) Mould would have surely been tutored by Jones's 1842 publication *Designs for Mosaic and Tessellated Pavements*. Jones, says architectural historian Kathryn Ferry, did not intend that his examples be copied; "rather Jones provided examples of how different traditions of mosaic composition could be integrated to produce something new."[25] Though not identical, the densely packed carpet-like fields also recall examples of repetitive patterns that figure in plate 30 of Jones's *Grammar of Ornament*, which he identified as of Byzantine origin.

Along the side walls, Mould drew varied designs for mosaics to fill the flat niches of the blind arcades. These panels of marble and granite Mould composed in patterns of subtly related shades. His drawing of September 4, 1865, depicts an elaborate gray diaper pattern surrounded by a green and red lattice border (plate 2). A somewhat later design for another niche charmed the eye with soft tones of rose and pink. Mould intended that brilliant bursts of color would emanate from the little gem-like rondels centered near the top of each niche (plate 3).

The biggest challenge for Mould was finding a way to transform the overhead brick vaulting into a firmament of vivid color. To do this, he decided on lining it with glazed tiles. These were laid up in forty-nine sections, each of which was comprised of 324 individual tiles (plates 4, 5, and 6). He centered a cross-shaped floral design in every other section. The overall ground is a delicate shade of yellow with the individual sections bordered in red, blue, and gold. It is a color scheme that recalls the formula Jones employed for the roof of London's 1851 Crystal Palace. Mould was also undoubtedly familiar with the intricate designs on a pale yellow background Jones created in 1843 for the ceilings of 8 Kensington Palace Gardens. (Jones had also coauthored a book on encaustic tiles.) In deliberate contrast to his darker and more solidly woven design for the floor, the ceiling appears open and bright. In this way, Mould freed the mind from the shuttering reality of the extended flat roof. It was as if he had unfolded a magic flying carpet above our heads (plate 7). The result asserts the ceiling's planarity while mitigating any feeling of oppressiveness in the low, slant-lighted space. When, on a lovely summer day in 1873,

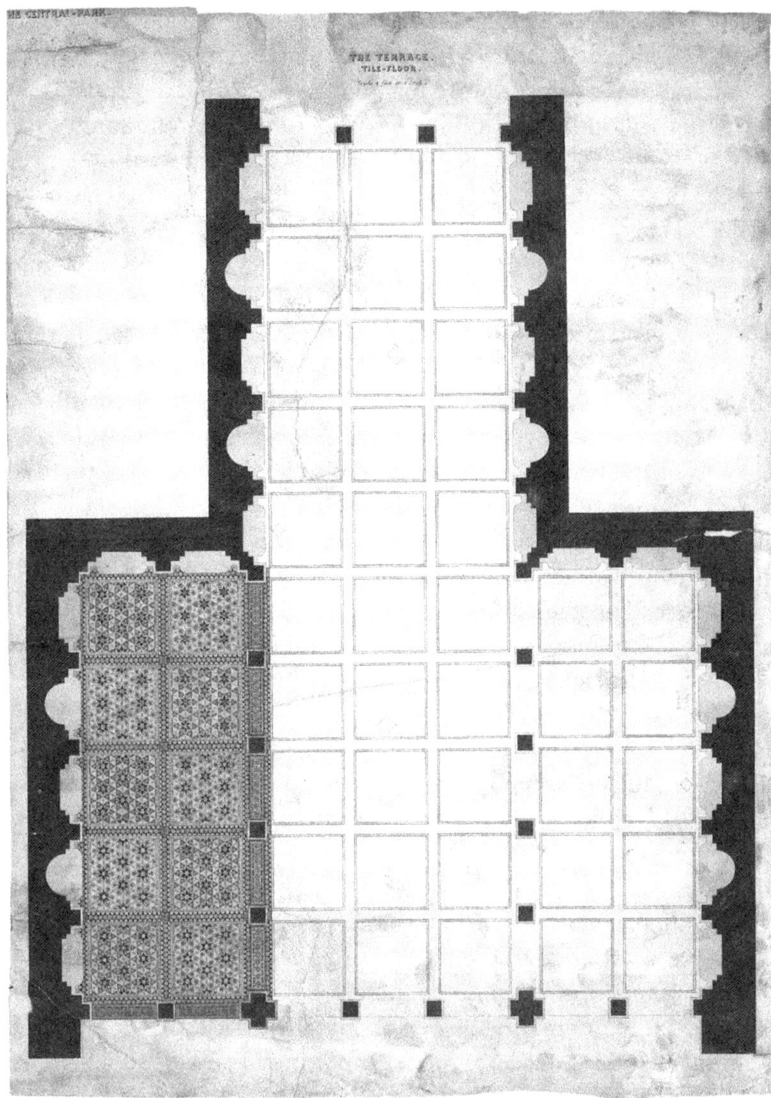

Figure 41. Design for floor tiles, Bethesda Terrace.

Little Peachblossom, Edwy, Oswald, Amy, and Uncle Nathan descended from the Mall to the Terrace Arcade, they marveled at the beautiful, exotic room, "richly ornamented on all sides with elegantly-colored tiles." It was, exclaimed one of the enchanted fictive siblings, a "Fairy Hall."[26]

In order to achieve this remarkable effect, however, Mould needed to invent a way to attach the tiles to the ceiling, a feat never before attempted. Working with the Minton tileworks in Stoke-on-Trent, where all the ceramics for the Terrace were manufactured, Mould devised a system whereby the 324 individual tiles were placed in forty-nine large square sections held together by iron frames (plate 8). Other features of the scheme involved wrought iron plates, iron scaffolding attached to the masonry ceiling, and brass keys or plugs incorporated into the back of every tile. Clarence Cook marveled at the ingenious method and recounted it in detail for his readers of his 1869 book on Central Park. "So neatly is the work done," he asserted, "that, to all appearance, the tiles are laid upon the ceiling as they are laid upon the floor."[27]

Thanks to Mould's skill and imagination, the Terrace is a masterpiece of High Victorian imagery and ornament. Finished in its basic elements by the end of the Civil War, it was the most elaborate piece of public art New York had yet seen. Following Vaux's directions, Mould consulted his fertile imagination for images that evoke rural life and the world of nature and for colorful abstract motifs that delight the eye. Collectively, the many and varied designs constituted for Mould a personal grammar of ornament. Some contemporary critics even found his exuberant decorations too rich for their taste. Clarence Cook, who first admired Mould's work, in later life thought the Terrace was "marred by the fault of excess, a fault which always appeared in his designs, when he found himself working for a client with a full purse; and at the time the Park Department had no lack of funds."[28] Peter B. Wight—now a convert to the doctrines of Ruskin, writing anonymously in the *New Path*—was scathing in his evaluation of Mould's designs. "All of the architect's work," he complained, "is not only very conventional but much of it borders on the grotesque; in some of it the conventional is mixed with the natural ornament and the result is simply ridiculous." (Mould might have countered by quoting Jones's proportion 13: "Flowers or other natural objects should not be used as ornament, but conventional representations founded upon them sufficiently suggestive to convey the intended image to the mind, without destroying the unity of the object they are intended to decorate."[29]) Citing Ruskin directly, Wight also objected to the practice of having Mould make drawings for hired sculptors to execute. "What we see," he said, "are merely clever copies of office drawings, by men who are degraded by being made the machines to carve other men's designs." On the pedestals at the base of the staircase, Wight reported, Mould freed the sculptors from premeditation and gave them license to carry out their own conceptions of nature. "Here, what was cold, contorted and conventional," Wight maintained, "is now easy,

Figure 42. Winter pillar at the base of the western stairway, Bethesda Terrace.

graceful and natural. We have fruits and flowers and berries which we know at first sight."[30] Perhaps the man standing next to the winter pier in Victor Provost's 1862 photograph of the Terrace was one of these artisans (fig. 42). His photo was paired with that of Mould on the opposite side of the Esplanade where the fashionable architect leans with proprietorship on the spring pier (see fig. 2, introduction). The bouquet of fruit there appears decidedly more "conventional" than the more naturalistic grape vine design that decorates the winter pier.

Calvert Vaux apparently gave no heed to the negative opinions of Cook and Wight. "The richest man in New York or elsewhere cannot spend as freely as is here spent" for the lounging spot dedicated to the use of ordinary citizens, said Vaux.[31] He regarded the Terrace as an example of enlightened public patronage of the arts, a testament to the democratic spirit. Reiterating that the Terrace was "an original conception of my own in its entirety" that was "carried out prior to any cooperation with Mr. Mould," Vaux nonetheless praised Mould's subsequent contributions to the project as "continuous, original and invaluable."[32] The two men of art were fortunate that the city was flush with funds and spent lavishly for the park's construction. Mould personally could have felt as he did working for Lord Holford on Dorchester House. His design work at the Bethesda Terrace still inspires admiration, still confers pleasure, and still proliferates beauty.

Architect-in-Chief

In 1870, New York adopted a new city charter that wrested control of Central Park from the state appointed commissioners who had overseen its construction and operation from the beginning. The new charter established the Department of Public Parks, a municipal agency that had jurisdiction over all of the city's public spaces. A board of locally nominated commissioners reflective of the populist Tammany Hall Democrats, under the control of William Magear "Boss" Tweed, assumed power. Generally unsympathetic to the Greensward ideals, they ignored Vaux and Olmsted who eventually quit in disgust. Finding the raffish Mould more to their liking, they installed him in their place. In May 1870, the new park board president, Peter B. Sweeny, one of the four members identified as the Tweed Ring, appointed Mould as architect-in-chief to the newly established the department. He held this post until November 1871 when the Tweed Ring and its commissioners were ousted and Vaux and Olmsted returned to service. Just how Mould had ingratiated himself with Tweed and Sweeney is not clear. Nonetheless, Mould had no qualms spending the open stream of taxpayers' money that flowed to the department, a major source of patronage favors. He also nursed a grievance against the original commissioners for never having loosened their purse to pay him what he thought he was worth. "As to my non-recognition and remuneration from 1858 to 1870," he complained, "it was shamefully inadequate, and remains to this day a standing blot on the escutcheon of the old Central Park Commission." To the commissioners' argument that he "need not to have taken the pay unless I had wanted it," he replied by citing the proverb: "Needs must when the devil drives."[33]

During the nineteen months of the Tweed-controlled board, Mould earned more and made extensive contributions to Central Park. Together with completing work already begun, he designed or proposed several new buildings that had not been part of the Greensward plan. These included the Sheepfold, stables and repair sheds, a menagerie building and other zoological structures, and incidental features. He also designed a large and lavish fountain to adorn the park in front of city hall. "In recapitulation," wrote Mould proudly of his initial year's tenure as architect-in-chief, "the sum total of the year's work foots up as forty-four (44) separate Structures and Items designed, in progress of construction, or constructed, for which three hundred and sixty-eight (368) Plans, Designs, or Working Drawings have been prepared, some of them exceedingly intricate and elaborate, and in all cases thoroughly well figured, and in addition to the drawings we have prepared thirty-two (32) specifications."[34] Moreover, Mould proved to have had a generous spirit when it came to acknowledging the contributions that others made to the park under his charge. These included contractors, workmen, and assistants, especially the German-born architect Julius Munckwitz who had worked with Vaux before.[35]

The Sheepfold

Mould had little trouble convincing his new bosses of the need to erect across from the meadow on the west side of the park a palatial home for sheep. It was their role to add a poignant note of bucolic charm to the park scenery (fig. 43). "At first a structure of wood was contemplated," wrote Mould, but then the commissioners decided on a building "constructed of hollow brick walls to exclude damp." Mould laid out the building on a symmetrical plan that consisted for four parts. Overlooking the fenced sheepfold itself was a group of connected structures that featured a central arched gatehouse with living quarters planned above for the shepherd and six assistants. This was flanked on either side by two double-story barns (the animals' winter quarters) and, at either end, twin arcaded "loggias." These loggias were to be the most colorful part of the composition. The ground level arches were to be trimmed and banded, said Mould, "with

Figure 43. Sheepfold, Central Park, 1871.

blue and gray Malden stone, further enhanced by small columns of polished Scotch red granite, to form an agreeable architectural relief to the otherwise somber and monotonous character of the building." Both loggias were to be open to the public so that visitors might watch the sheep "feeding or reposing" in the fold. Sightseers were also intended to view "oil paintings and photographs of all the various breeds of sheep; and on side tables, under the microscope, specimens of the various kinds and quality of wool, illustrating their texture, fiber, etc."[36] A visit to the Sheepfold, Mould asserted, would "thus not only interest the casual visitor to the Park, but prove a vehicle of education to the farmer and the student in industrial economy." In this sense, the Sheepfold may be said to have anticipated the "visitor centers" of our own day. Perhaps his kindly Oakley in-laws, who had made their wealth in the wool trade, had some hand in all of this.

Seizing the opportunity offered by a free-spending board, Mould demonstrated yet again his fondness for picturesque design and virtuoso command of multicolored materials. Radiating voussoirs, projecting and receding building units, and a rising and falling roofline impart a lively quality to the building's symmetrical architectural form. Today, the low, semicircular building preserves its colorful walls of bright red brick laid up in black mortar and larded with contrasting bands of gray and blue stone from Malden, Massachusetts (fig. 44). Rose granite colonettes, gilded ironwork, and decorative tiles completed the exterior polychrome palate. Looking at the Sheepfold today, one can, with modest effort, feel the glow of the rich and joyous polychromy of Mould's departed bandstand and the vibrancy of the exterior of All Souls. And even despite serious misgivings, Vaux and Olmsted grudgingly admired the building's beauty and charming appearance. When they returned to the park in 1872, they, like others, roundly criticized its near useless purpose. They also strongly objected to the fact that no provision had been made for people to reach the building from the Green or sheep meadow without crossing the busy carriage drive at grade. They fell short, however, of calling for the building's removal, as they did for other structures—including the recently rebuilt wooden canopy on the north side of the Belvedere—that Mould had erected during their absence.

The Sheepfold did provide shelter for the flock that sometimes pastured on the meadow during the day, but in what style and at what cost! It was "a singular extravagance to construct such a building for the accommodation of 108 sheep,"[37] ranted an irate citizen in the pages of the *Times*. (Mould himself had counted the flock at nearly three hundred.) Even its critics, however, had to admit that it was "unique in architectural design

Figure 44. Detail of Sheepfold exterior.

and splendidly finished."[38] The building was a costly boondoggle that suffered from poor ventilation and dampness. Within a few years after it was finished, the exhibits were dismantled and the loggias converted to storage. Nonetheless, the Sheepfold is the one of the few surviving examples of Mould's genius that we have, for history has not been kind to his independent works of architecture. In the 1930s, the jewel box building, which had undergone some changes since Mould's day, came to perform service as a full-scale restaurant, a feature that Vaux and Olmsted had envisioned for the park but never had the opportunity to build. Since 1934, the Sheepfold has served almost continuously as the major part of the popular Tavern on the Green restaurant.

Varied Structures and Objects

During his tenure as architect-in-chief, Mould drew plans for many small structures and objects designed to embellish the park landscape and add pleasure and convenience to visitors' experiences there. The Stables and Sheds that Mould designed for use by the Department of Public Parks is a long rectangular structure that hugs the southern side of the Eighty-Sixth Street transverse road (fig. 45). Largely completed by the fall of 1871, it

Figure 45. Stables and Shed, Central Park, 1870.

provided stabling for twenty-six cart horses, repair shops, and an ample amount of general storage space. This latter function, said Mould, was "a very great desideratum, taking into account the vast stock of plants needed, and that further will be needed, to fill the various requirements of the Central Park."[39] An attached residence for the park keeper was added and repair shops projected. Knowing that the building was not intended to be part of the public life of the park, Mould declined to lavish on it the colorful details and picturesque architectural forms he had invented for the Sheepfold and other park structures. Yet, the building is no makeshift affair. A masterwork of understatement among Mould's creations, the long, low brick and stone structure (the stone and brick, declared Mould, "is admirable in material and execution") bears the mark of architectural distinction. If Frank Furness had ever seen it, he would surely have felt a great affinity for it. Its appeal to modern taste surely lies in its compact massing, the loping rhythm of the dormers, and the high level of craftsmanship. In 2013, the city rescued this sterling building from dereliction and hired Karlsberger Architects to adapt it for use as the Central Park Precinct police station.

Mould also furnished the park with many fanciful designs for subsidiary features. These included lampposts, seats, benches, tree gratings, and a clock balanced on a tall ornate column for the south end of the Mall (plate

9). There were also two flagstaffs on massive stone bases that flank the water wall of the Esplanade where the flags of the city and state were displayed.

"The increased popularity of the Park carriage service," wrote Mould, led to the construction of "agreeable resting places" along Fifty-Ninth Street at the Seventh Avenue and Eighth Avenue entrances for people waiting for a carriage to take them on a ride through the park (fig. 46). These pleasant "ombras" were, in Mould's words, "light, ornamental structures of wood and iron. The roofs, which overhang considerably to afford shade, are supported by iron columns, the capitals of which are practicable flower-baskets, and will be kept supplied with an ever-varying series of cannae, and other pendulous and ornamental plants."[40] When the present Maine Monument was erected at Eighth Avenue in 1912, the novel cast iron amenity that had been there was moved inside the park. Since then, renamed the Ladies Pavilion and shorn of its flora, it has graced Hernshead, an arm of land extending into the west side of the lake where herons apparently once bred. Probably, Vaux and Olmsted would have found Mould's fabrication too ornate and urban in expression for such a location. But they could not have helped but admire how cleverly Mould exploited the qualities of cast and wrought iron which allowed him to build a sturdy structure that is nonetheless extremely light in appearance. In a

Figure 46. Shelter for passengers in waiting (present Ladies Pavilion), 1872.

more modest way, it calls to mind Hector Guimard's more renowned Art Nouveau essays in metal for the Paris metro system.

A related amenity was a restroom for women and children that Mould designed for a site near the Arsenal building. It was put there, he said, especially to accommodate visitors to the museum displays on view in the building. The structure has long disappeared, but contemporary illustrations show it sheltered by plantings to provide an appropriate degree of privacy. Mould drew plans for another, more elaborate Ladies Cottage, as these buildings were known, that was erected at the north entrance to the park near the present intersection of Central Park North and Malcolm X Boulevard. The octagonal wooden building—a *cottage ornée* Mould's contemporary French designers would have called it—featured a steeply pitched roof with a ventilating cupola flourishing a fifteen-foot-tall crown of filigree ironwork terminating in a weathervane balanced on a copper ball. In miniature, the little building represented the picturesque symmetry that characterized most of his architectural designs (fig. 47).

Many arches and bridges facilitated the "separation of ways" that was one of the chief features of Vaux and Olmsted's park design. Throughout

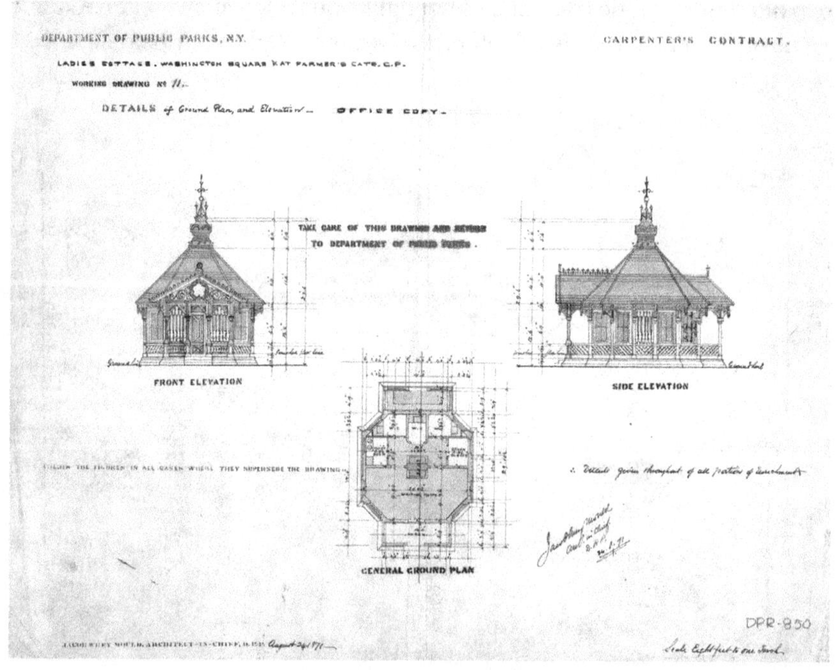

Figure 47. Design for Ladies Cottage near Farmer's Gate in Central Park, 1871.

the landscape, arches kept pedestrians safe from carriage drivers and horseback riders by taking their footpaths either over or under drives and bridle paths. Bridges made traversing the many water features in the landscape equally pleasant. Vaux created them diverse in design. He justified the added expense that this incurred on the principle that repetition would have dulled the park goer's imagination and, thus, worked against the fullest enjoyment of their outing. Henry Bellows agreed. In one of the earliest appraisals of the park, he declared that: "it was necessary to pay some attention to make them agreeable and unmonotonous objects, or the general impression of ease, freedom, and variety would be interfered with very materially."[41] To these, Mould often added handsome railings and other decorative details.

The low-slung, gently arching Bow Bridge is the best known of all these Central Park bridges. It leaps eighty-seven feet across the lake to the Ramble with apparent lightness and striking gracefulness. In order to accomplish this impressive feat, Vaux resorted to the use of the modern materials of cast and wrought iron. Traditional masonry construction would have required a much more solid and bulky structure. And by raising the center of the Bow Bridge, Vaux gave elegance to its flowing profile and assured skaters gliding below on the winter ice that they would have no need to duck their hatted heads when passing beneath the span. Vaux depended on Mould to beautify the elegantly flowing lines of the Bow Bridge, which was also known as the Flower Bridge because of the summertime arrangements that filled the vases Mould placed on the four abutments (fig. 48). For the side railings, Mould adapted the ancient guilloche, a design of continuous bands or ribbons embracing circular bosses or "buttons" to mirthfully impel the eye along the structure's softly swelling and falling lines. His and Vaux's invention was a masterful response to the challenge of creating a structure that would complement rather than compete with its lovely natural surroundings.

In addition to serving as an element of entertainment, water was offered freely for drinking throughout the park. The drinking fountain that Mould designed for the north end of the Mall often appeared in early photographs of the park. It was also published in England in the journal *The Garden* in which the editor, the well-known horticultural writer William Robinson, stated that such permanent features had been "developed with rare taste and ability" (fig. 49).[42] Its stout granite column supported a carved granite hood that sheltered a perpetually flowing jet of water. On hot summer days, many parched visitors accepted the invitation proffered by the little tin cup hanging from a chain and enjoyed a refreshing thirst-quencher.

Figure 48. Bow Bridge.

"But we may all drink our fill," wrote Clarence Cook, for beneath the roofed fountains were "deep pits filled with blocks of ice, over which the water flows before it falls into these cool basins."[43] Mould made designs for a number of drinking fountains in Central Park in forms reminiscent of ecclesiastical Baptismal fonts—perhaps to emphasize the sacredness of the gift of clean water (plate 10). Unfortunately, none of these gems has survived to the present day.

Nor were equine park goers forgotten. For those who would lead their horses to water, Mould completed the trough—euphemistically termed a "drinking fountain for horses"—on Cherry Hill by designing a terminal feature "in pure light bronze" for the center.[44] While drivers stopped their carriages here—the knoll received its name from the many flowering cherry trees that were planted in the vicinity—to admire the pretty view, their horses could drink from the large circular basin. Water descended into the center of the basin from a tall stone and metallic fixture capped with a crown, ball, and flora finial. Today, the liquid again spouts into cup-shaped holders before dripping into the trough below. Mould added the pleasurable sight and sound of moving water to the charm of this popular resting spot. The fountain attracted people and their steeds to what was one of Mould's most cheery park furnishings (fig. 50).

The nature-friendly authors of the Greensward plan wanted their park

Plate 1. Flower Garden design from "Greensward" entry for the Central Park competition, 1858.

Plate 2. Design for marble and granite niche panel, Bethesda Terrace arcade, 1865.

Plate 3. Design for marble and granite niche panel, Bethesda Terrace arcade, 1869.

Plate 4. Designs for encaustic tiles, Bethesda Terrace arcade, 1869.

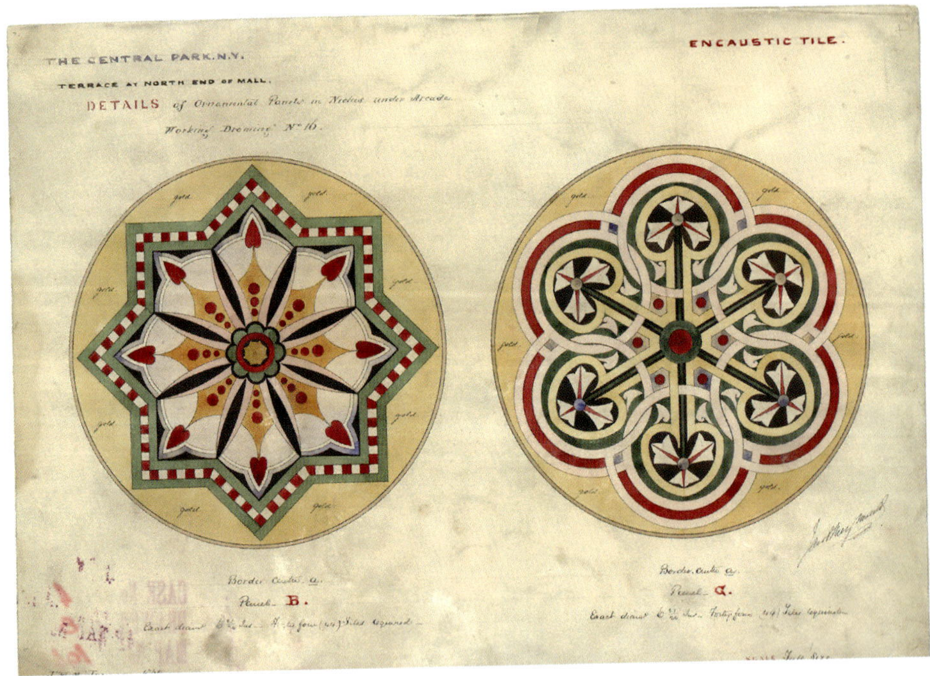

Plate 5. Designs for encaustic tiles, Bethesda Terrace arcade, 1869.

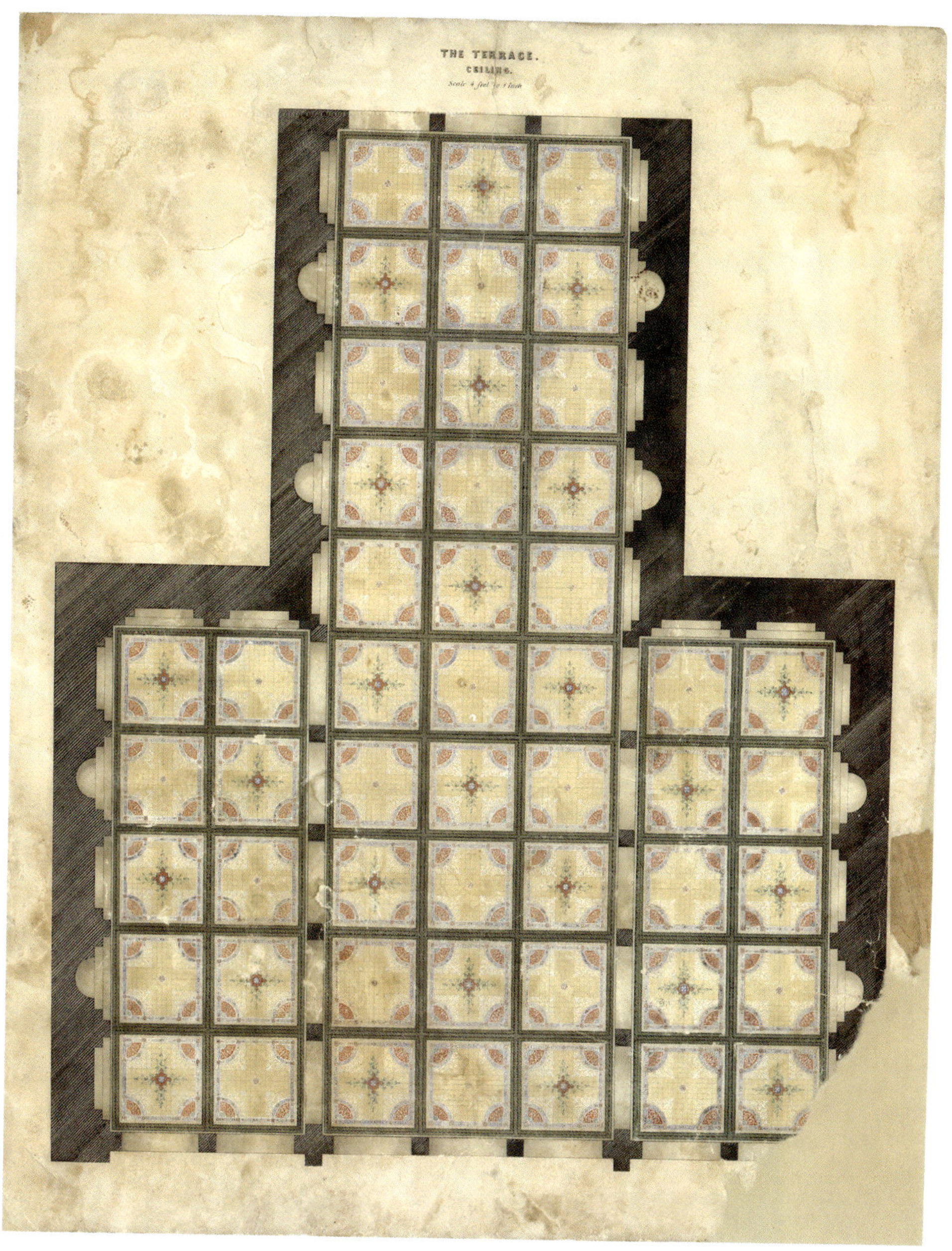

Plate 6. Designs for ceiling tiles, Bethesda Terrace arcade, ca. 1860.

Plate 7. Bethesda Terrace arcade ceiling.

Plate 8. Detail of ceiling, Bethesda Terrace arcade.

Plate 9. Design for an ornamental clock for the south end of the Mall, 1870.

Plate 10. Drinking fountain on the Bethesda Terrace esplanade, 1865.

Plate 11. Competition entry for Plymouth Church, Brooklyn, 1859.

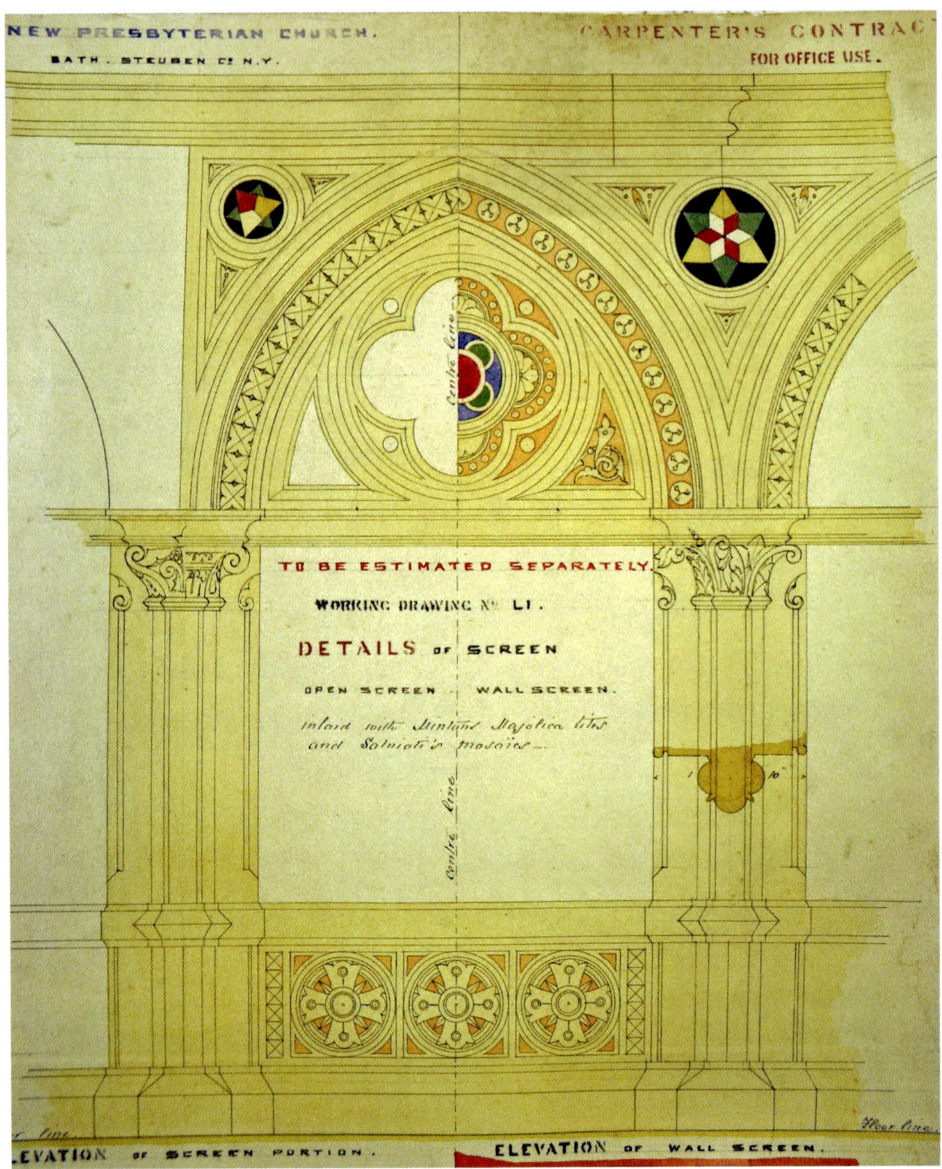

Plate 12. First Presbyterian Church, Bath, New York, details of wall, 1874.

Plate 13. Casa Dubois, Lima, Peru, detail of surviving patio tile work.

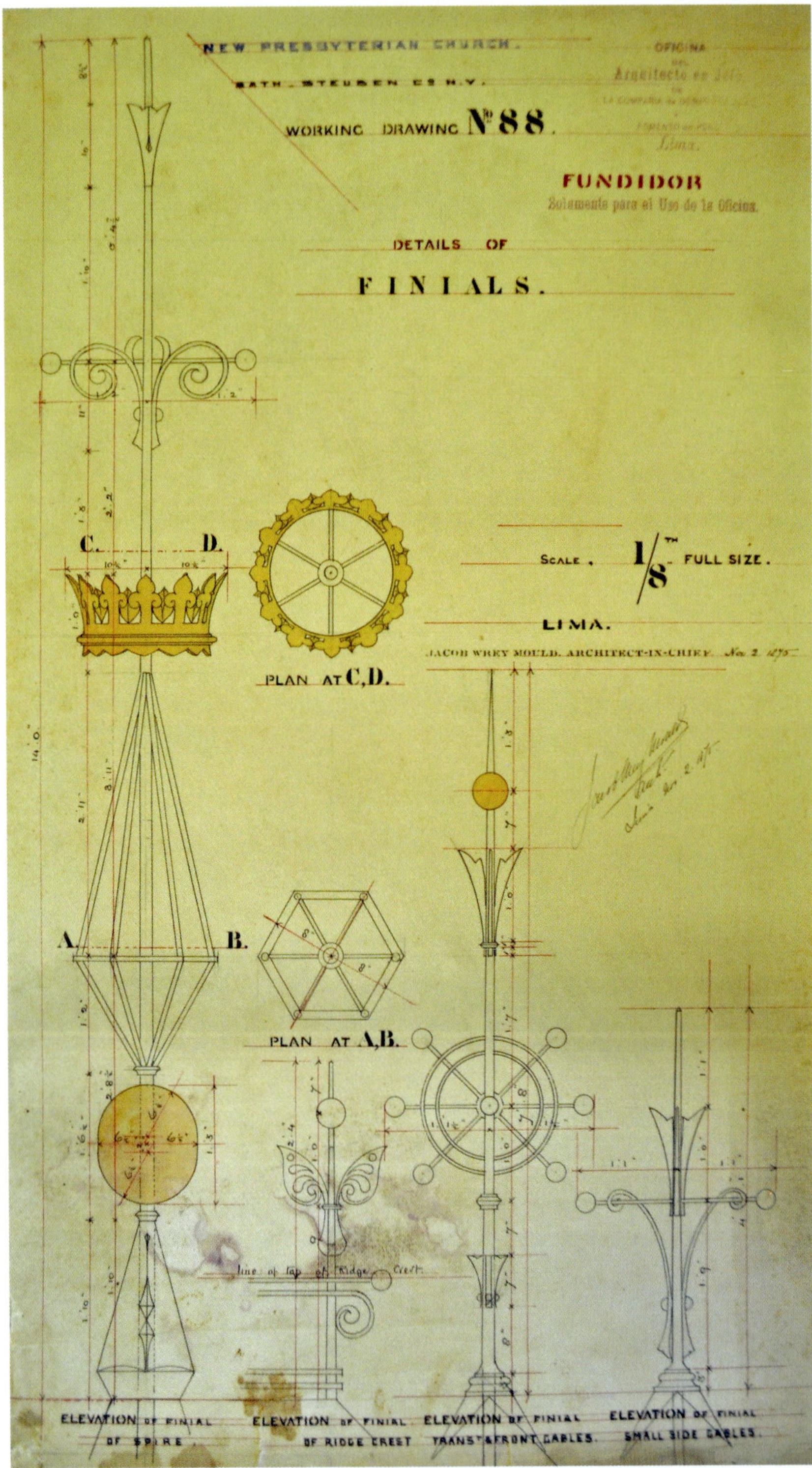

Plate 14. First Presbyterian Church, Bath, New York, drawing with details of finials, 1875.

Plate 15. First Presbyterian Church, detail of double corbels with dwarf columns supporting the roof trusses.

Plate 16. St. Mary's Episcopal Church, Lake Lucerne, New York.

Figure 49. Drinking fountain.

to become home to many species of birds. But it appears that it fell primarily to Mould, the inveterate urbanite, to design the many charming wooden birdhouses that were put up to lure hundreds of avifaunal New Yorkers to take up residence, at least part of the year, in the Ramble and elsewhere in Central Park (fig. 51). Clarence Cook made a point of illustrating one of these miniature rustic dwellings in his book on the park. It and others like it, said Cook, were erected especially for the convenience of sparrows, a breed of birds recently imported into the United States from England. Britain's nature advocate William Robinson also took special delight in Mould's sparrow house. "The sparrow, pelted from the ivy, and mercilessly dragged out of the eaves with us," wrote Robinson, "here finds himself

Figure 50. Horse drinking fountain, Cherry Hill, 1867–1871.

provided not only with a house, but with a palace. Here he may increase and multiply in peace, and by his vigorous and successful onslaught on the hordes of ugly caterpillars with which the trees in New York used to swarm, he has well rewarded the New Yorkers for their good treatment of him."[45] Cook found the then unfamiliar birds endlessly entertaining: "they are such brisk, tight-bodied, chirruping, bright-eyed chaps," he observed, "that after brief acquaintance with them, we expect to see them do everything,—fighting, love-making, eating, and drinking, with as much fuss and fury as possible." Many other park visitors young and old equally relished watching the antics of these transatlantic new arrivals. They doubtless shared Cook's view that they "look like Englishmen in miniature, for all the world!"[46]

Other breeds of birds also animated the park landscape. Some of the songful species were denizens of bulbous, delicately wrought lamp-shade-like habitations perched on carved stone pedestals (fig. 52). On the lawn near the Fifth Avenue border at Seventy-Seventh Street, a costly stone and iron dovecote was the permanent home to a large flock of doves and pigeons A billowing canopy of wire mesh prevented the residents from leaving. In addition to this spacious aviary (one of the first in the country), Mould prepared drawings for an eagle cage and several swan's nests.

Together with all of the visitor-oriented tasks, Mould presided over the

Figure 51. Bird house for sparrows in the Ramble, 1860s.

Figure 52. Design for an ornamental bird cage, 1864.

move of the Department of Public Parks offices from downtown on Nassau Street to the Arsenal within the park. The change took place in August 1871, when Mould complained that the transfer delayed the flow of work. The building, which had been originally erected in 1847 to store munitions for the state militia, had been adapted for park use mainly as a natural history museum (it had become known as the Museum Building), a function that, updated, it would continue to perform. Plans that William Martin wrote about a few years earlier in his *Growth of New York* to demolish the building and have the New York Historical Society erect in its place a "great historical library and collections, and a national museum of art, natural history, and antiquities," had been scrapped.[47] The Arsenal's new tenants undertook a good deal of remodeling work that Mould directed and Julius Munckwitz supervised. The live animal displays that had been in the basement for many years were removed and the spaces thoroughly refurbished for other purposes. Mould and other staff members occupied bright departmental offices on the main floor where Emma Stebbins's statue of Columbus, along with floral displays, greeted visitors. The upper two floors welcomed the public to view recent acquisitions of natural history "placed on a coherent and scientific shape." Exhibits included the meteorological department where, according to Mould, "the ingenious and delicate instruments in charge of, and devised by Mr. Draper, are being placed in cases more suitable for purposes of exhibition."[48] (In 1868, Daniel Draper [1841–1931] had established the New York Meteorological Observatory in Central Park.) The building, which has undergone many changes since Mould took charge of renovating it, has remained the home of Central Park's offices to the present day.

With the eviction of the animals from the basement of the Arsenal came the need to house them elsewhere. The area behind the building became the site of the city's first real zoo. In a group of structures designed by Mould in the early 1870s, a variety of animals and birds became permanent residents of the park. Parents might bring their children here to admire exotic tenants from far and wide. Historic photographs tell us that the wooden pavilions—none of which survive—were festive and fanciful in appearance. Many visitors must have found the little collection of creatures displayed in them a pleasant diversion from the pastoral walks and opportunities for socializing available to them elsewhere in the park.

The largest habitation that Mould designed for fellow creatures was the Menagerie. "The necessity to provide suitable accommodation, not only for our own stock of ruminantia, but for the numerous specimens loaned or confided to our care during the winter months, rendered the construction of a very serviceable stabling west of the Museum an absolute necessity," declared Mould. The commodious wooden structure contained enclosures for elephants, rhinos, and buffalos, together with cages for several other species. "Being a somewhat conspicuous building," wrote Mould, "the Anglo-Swiss style has been adopted in its design." But this was to be the exception, for in the design of all other zoo buildings, he would endeavor

Figure 53. Menagerie building behind the Arsenal, 1871.

to "steer clear of architectural whims and eccentricities and absurd reproductions of Egyptian and Grecian temples, that disfigure too many of the gardens in the leading cities of Europe."[49] The student of *The Alhambra* and the *Grammar of Ornament* and partisan of Ruskin did not wish to see things dressed up as what they were never able to be.

In 1867, Vaux and Olmsted laid out a full-scale modern zoo for Manhattan Square, the area adjacent to the western boundary of the park between Seventy-Seventh and Eighty-First Streets. Chiefly due to the objections of real estate interests—who feared that smells and sounds of wild animals would depress local property values—plans for this zoo were eventually abandoned. (This land became home to the American Museum of Natural History.) Neither of the original park designers wanted much of the park given over to a zoological garden, for they feared that future generations would call for the enlargement of the animal collection to the detriment of recreational parkland. During their fall from grace with the Tweed-dominated park board, however, Vaux and Olmsted helplessly watched from the sidelines as architect-in-chief Mould designed and built the Menagerie and proposed a large deer paddock on formerly open meadowland (fig. 53). Upon their reinstatement in 1872, Vaux and Olmsted had the Menagerie dismantled and the land returned to its original use and appearance. Thus, the partners turned back yet another threat to the pastoral ideal embodied in their Greensward plan.

City Hall Fountain and Fountain at Fifty-Ninth Street and Fifth Avenue

The *New York Herald* proudly touted the Bethesda Fountain as one of the two largest fountains in North America. The other one was the fountain that Mould designed in 1871 to go in front of city hall in lower Manhattan. This prominent location, as well as other parks and squares around town, had come under the jurisdiction of the Department of Public Parks, a fact that widely extended Mould's design responsibilities. Mould's exuberant creation replaced an earlier fountain installed in 1842 when the Croton Aqueduct first began bringing water into the city. "The twopenney spurts in City Hall Park are ridiculous and useless," remarked the *Herald*, but praised Mould's lavish thirty-thousand-dollar substitute as "a work of art."[50] From the corners of a square polished-granite basin, arcing sprays converged on a central feature spurting water from several spouts and crowned by an elaborate bronze finial. Semi-circular basins extended the flow from the center of each side, and gas lamps at the corners evoked a dramatic nighttime spectacle.

Mould took pains to adapt his festive design to the specific urban context in which it stood. He said that he had "aimed at producing an artistic design, rich in the effects of color, not regarding the fact that the structure faces not only the *old* City Hall but the *new* Post-office, which is to be an elaborate and massive edifice of corresponding granite" (fig. 54).[51] At the time, Alfred B. Mullett's four-story Second Empire–style post office and federal court building was under construction immediately across the street. (It was begun in 1869 and completed in 1880.) Mould chose to express companionship with Mullett's design. Moreover, directly facing city hall in the other distance, the fountain coordinated a visual link between the historic municipal institution and the enhanced postwar federal presence. Mould's fountain stayed in place until 1922 when it was removed to a small Bronx park and replaced by one designed by sculptor Frederick MacMonnies. Exile was temporary, however, and in 1999 the city reinstated Mould's restored gala water display to City Hall Park. Sadly, Mullet's "elaborate and massive edifice," a moment of Paris in New York that had informed Mould's conception, had disappeared six decades earlier.

At the time the City Hall Fountain was under construction, Mould had designed a "fountain-basin" of Malden blue stone to be erected at the Fifty-Ninth Street and Fifth Avenue entrance, the Scholars' Gate, to Central Park. According to an announcement in the local press, the commissioners may have originally contemplated placing a duplicate of the City Hall Park fountain at that prime location.[52] Instead, said Mould,

Figure 54. City Hall park fountain, 1871.

he modified his design "so as to contain less masses, and be lighter altogether in treatment."[53] In any event, in 1873, the commissioners who succeeded Sweeney's board decided to transfer Mould's yet unfinished basin to Washington Square, where it has remained to the present day.[54] The Fifth Avenue park entrance obtained its present formal character when Thomas Hastings's 1916 Pulitzer Fountain was paired with Augustus Saint-Gaudens's 1903 William Tecumseh Sherman Monument.

During his tenure as Central Park's architect-in-chief, Mould instituted several projects that did not come to fruition. Prime among these was an expanded botanical conservatory near the Fifth Avenue border at Seventy-Fourth Street (fig. 55). Mould stated that he had revised original plans by Vaux for the large greenhouse "so as to obtain greater picturesqueness of outline, more extended height inside, and a greater variety of trees and plants on exhibition." He proudly displayed his perspective drawing for it at the National Academy of Design. At the north and south ends of the central palm house, Mould appended two smaller rotundas for flora displays. (The southern one was for ferns; the northern one for camellias.) To get things just right, Mould wrote a four-page letter to Joseph Dalton Hooker, superintendent of the Royal Gardens at Kew, asking advice on a

Figure 55. Design for a conservatory in Central Park, 1871.

wide variety of subjects, including heating, drainage systems, and staircase access for visitors to reach the top of the palm trees. He also informed Hooker that New York had "oceans of money" to spend on the acquisition of cultural amenities.[55] Mould also traveled several days to Washington to consult with experts at the botanical gardens there. Nonetheless, in the end, the project languished for lack of funds. A residual element of the plan, a large water basin in front of the conservatory, today comprises the popular Conservatory Water where many people, young and old, come to sail model boats. Other big structures for which Mould prepared designs that failed to see the light of day were a Paleozoic museum, propagating house, and large casino or restaurant.

Whatever Mould designed for Vaux and Olmsted's "country park" was hardly rustic in character or appearance. His were highly sophisticated designs: complex floral and figurative reliefs, an underground room resplendent with colorful tiles and mosaics, a multicolored open-air music pavilion, quaint bird cages in the form of gossamer metal coops, curious lamps suspended on plantlike posts, hooded drinking fountains, and graceful and playful railings and balustrades. Essential to the overall carefree mood of the landscape, these seemingly inconsequential elements were calculated to sustain a mood of delight. To the evocative natural scenery and sense of "enlarged freedom" that guided Vaux and Olmsted in the grand design of the park, Mould contributed the element of whimsy.

With the defeat of the Tweed Ring administration in November 1871, Vaux and Olmsted regained control of the park. They also enjoyed the support of a new board of commissioners that included the artist Frederic Edwin Church and civic-minded businessman Henry G. Stebbins, a reform Democrat who, together with Samuel Tilden, had been instrumental in ridding the city of the Tweed Ring. In defense of Peter Sweeney's management, the *New York Times* later admitted that "the old and skilled subordinates who were really necessary to the proper management of the Park were not interfered with."[56] The new board kept Mould on the payroll but demoted him to assistant in the Department of Public Parks. Vaux, who became the department's landscape architect, apparently harbored no ill feelings toward him. Vaux and Olmsted seemed to have regarded their colleague as a wayward child who had been unable to resist taking advantage of the sweet opportunity that corrupt politicians had placed in his path. Mould's life, however, was not programmed for wealth. During his many years of service to New York's parks and public spaces, he failed to receive what he felt was just compensation for his labors.

At the Department of Public Parks, Vaux and Mould worked together on many projects. The largest of these were the Metropolitan Museum of Art and the American Museum of Natural History. These commissions under the auspices of the Department of Public Parks came to Vaux and Mould in 1869 and 1872 and would occupy them for many years.

Perhaps the first of the new collaborations was the design approved by the board at the end of July 1872 for the Merchant's Gate at the Fifty-Ninth Street and Eighth Avenue entrance to the park. Mould's designs for piers at the carriage and pedestrian gates were some of the most elaborate decorative schemes he would make (fig. 56). Mould's beautifully integrated designs covered surfaces with dense, repetitive patterns, flaring scrolls and colorful panels of polished granite. Unfortunately, budget restrictions prevented them from ever going beyond his designs on paper.

Inside the park, Mould contributed to the construction of several new bridges. In 1873, the commissioners added three bridges to the park landscape to improve the separation of pedestrian from vehicular traffic. These were the polychromatic stone Inscope Arch and the cast iron Outset Arch. The latter bore gossamer thin railings and elegant floral spandrels of Mould's creation. Looking at drawings for the slender span, which is no longer with us, archivist Cynthia Brenwall remarks that it "seemed to float between rusticated stone embankments." The Gapstow Bridge was constructed from Mould's plans to carry walkers across a narrow neck of the Pond in the southeast corner of the park (fig. 57). Made of wood to resemble metal, the bridge featured twin golden round arches formed of laminated timber held together by overstated rivets. In the manner of utilitarian Whipple bowstring truss bridges, the wide arches supported the horizontal roadway that rested at either end on stone abutments. Conceivably, Mould took to heart the writings of Viollet-le-Duc on structural expression. With the exception of the delicate iron railings that marched

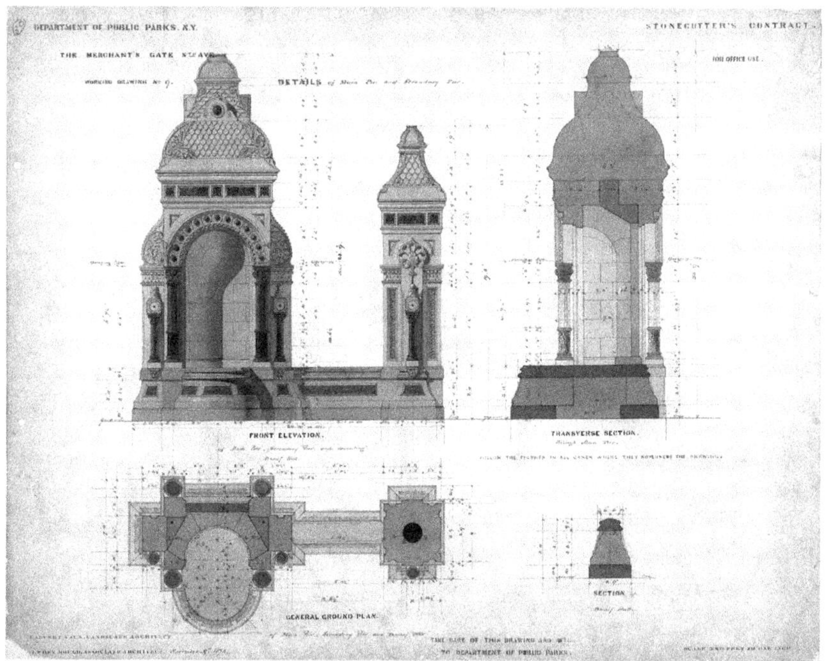

Figure 56. Design for the Merchant's Gate in Central Park, ca. 1872.

across the crossing and the cinquefoil designs that filed the central area, the curious structure bore no resemblance to picturesque bridges and viaducts in the park that Vaux had designed. As architectural historian Paula Ann Mohr has observed, "what sets it apart is the stark and frank expression of structure."[57] Yet, it, too, is gone, replaced in 1896 by the present stone bridge designed by the firm of Howard & Caudwell. A large fountain design that Mould worked on in the spring of 1874 through March of 1875 never materialized (fig. 58). It was probably the last thing he did for Central Park before he left for Lima, Peru, to join Henry Meiggs in realizing his dream to modernize that ancient city.

The year 1874 turned out to be a troubled one for Mould's employment with the Department of Public Parks. In May, the board abruptly decided to terminate his service because of the severe economic crisis that followed in the wake of the Panic of 1873. He was informed that the board might call upon him as needed in the future. Mould's dismissal ignited a fire of protest in the press, which spoke up to have him retained on the payroll. "The Mould Scandal: Pretense of Economy in the Park Department—What is the Job Hidden?" read a headline in the *World*. The *Tribune* stated

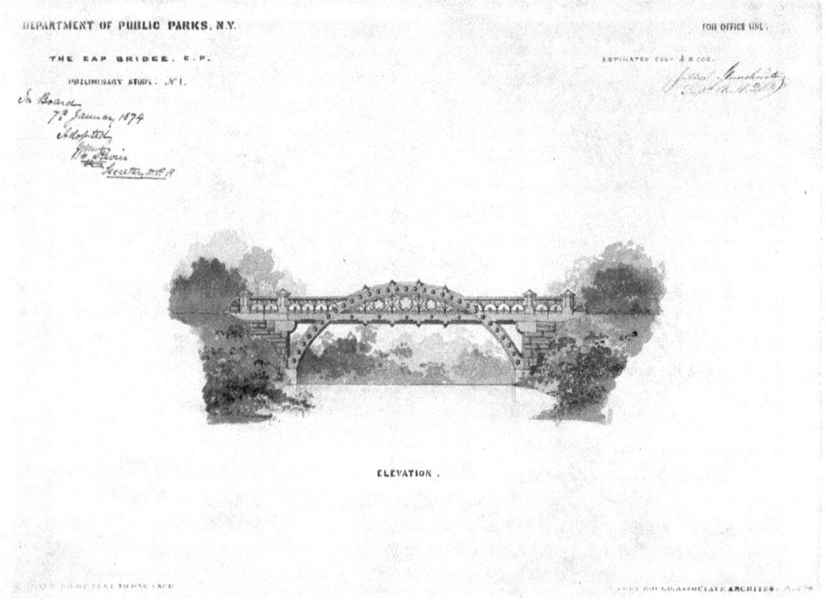

Figure 57. Design for the Gapstow Bridge, 1874.

that since Mould had begun working for the Department of Public Parks sixteen years ago he had been given little recognition and inadequate pay for his contributions to the park. "If he is thrown out in a spirit of mistaken economy he will at least have the double satisfaction of knowing that every penny of his meager pay for unthanked services has been earned by faithful work, and that he has left an enduring monument to his own taste and skill in all that portion of the architecture and ornamentation of the Park which he has been permitted to control."[58] An American correspondent to the *Builder* in England fumed: "Under ordinary circumstances, half a dozen architects would have been required to do the work which he has done alone, and which he has done in all cases with inventive genius and trained skill. The removal of a man from a post for which he is so eminently fit, and to which he has given some of the best years of his life, and where the best work of his best remaining years is still requisite is a public scandal and indecency."[59] To Mould, it must have seemed as if Owen Jones's dire prophecy had come to pass: "the Americans will wring you out like a wet rag, then drop you like a hot potato."[60]

In the end, the episode provided Mould the opportunity to have his name brought before the public and to have his accomplishments acknowledged by the wider world. It was a fortunate circumstance of history that

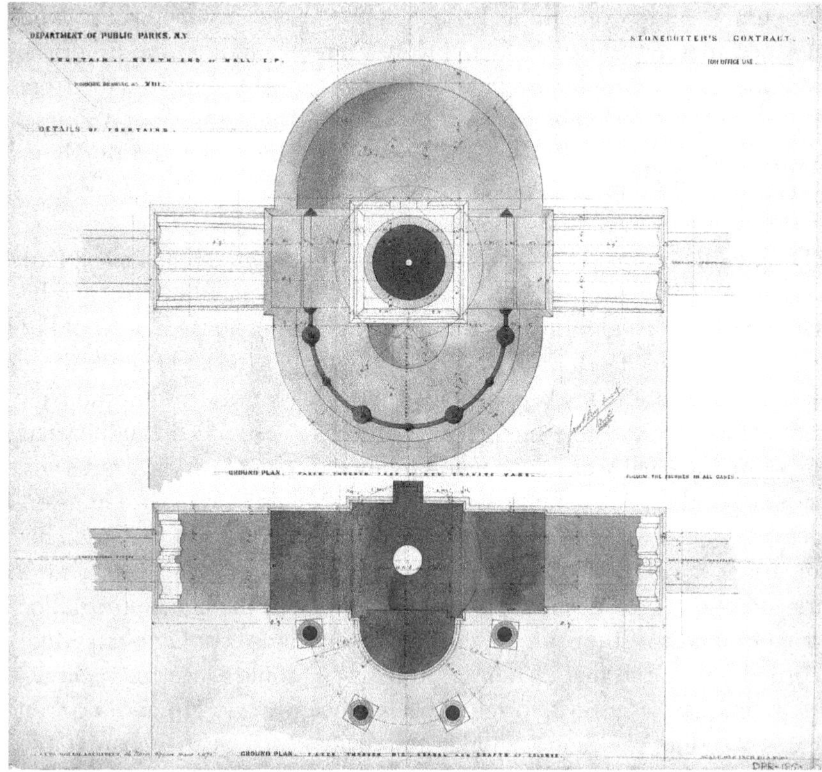

Figure 58. Design for a fountain for the south end of the Mall, ca. 1873.

Jacob Mould came to live in New York at the time when Central Park was being constructed. Here more than anywhere he was able to apply his fertile imagination to a broad variety of design topics. The fire of his creativity burned long and bright for this pioneering New World people's park. "My professional identity was absorbed and merged for so many years in the Central Park," declared Mould in later life.[61] As he worked away in the office of the Department of Public Parks, suave designs flowing onto paper, he must have thought back to his time in Jones's studio, except that now he was the master rather than the pupil. Running through his mind might well have been Owen Jones's admonition: "To put [an] ornament in the right place is not easy; to render that ornament at the same time a superadded beauty and an expression of the intention of the whole work, is still more difficult."[62] All he had learned in those happy years about High Victorian enthusiasm for the pleasurable appeal of color and ornament now was laid to work in the service of his new countrymen and their extraordinary new park. Mould's work at the Terrace, alone, was so characteristic of his renowned mentor as essentially to justify his recognition as the American Owen Jones. "Mr. Mould's best and most characteristic work is in the Central Park," wrote a knowledgeable observer to the new *American Architect and Building News* in 1876, "and is work which depends upon the detail for its effect."[63] All in all, Mould's employment in Central Park represents his most lasting contribution to American art.

Despite his complaint of being underpaid, employment in Central Park (and the generosity of his Oakley relatives) allowed Mould to indulge his fondness for the good life. He was able to purchase a house that would be his home until his death in 1886. Because his colleague and friend Alfred Jason Bloor (1828–1917) kept a chatty diary that is preserved in the New York Historical Society, we are privy to glimpses of Mould's life in the years just before the Civil War. Bloor, who was also associated with Calvert Vaux, first met Mould in the summer of 1857 when Mould shared with him several stereopticon views of architectural monuments. The two men soon became friends, with Bloor often assisting Mould on the work at both Central Park and elsewhere. Mould apparently awakened in Bloor an appreciation for opera, and together they attended performances. In October, Bloor recorded one of the first instances we have of Mould's love for yachting, which may have traced its origins to his days in Cork. He and a dozen others, including Vaux and "an old friend of Sir Walter Scott," boarded the *Diana* for a "very aggreable and gentlemanly party" that included dinner of "boned turkey Perigord pie and an abundance of champagne." (Bloor ate so well that he experienced a touch of seasickness on the way back to port.) Many other sociable gatherings, on land and sea, followed, for Mould prided himself on being a generous and engaging host. His avid attachment to boats and sailing, unusual among Mould's peers, would also manifest itself in the lives of later architects, notably Le Corbusier, Frank Gehry, Aldo Rossi, and Helmut Jahn.

In March 1859, shortly after Mould and his mother had moved into his new home at 75 East Twenty-Sixth Street, Bloor went to visit.[64] The interior, reported Bloor, is "most exquisitely finished in polychrome frescoing of his own design and superintendence." Mould welcomed his visitors at the door where the hall floor was laid in encaustic tile. "In imitation of the ancient Roman and Pompeian custom," said Boor, Mould had inscribed "the word 'Salve' in large white Roman letters on a ground of lapis lazuli." Mould had focused his greatest attention on the dining room, the future scene of many happy gatherings. "On the ceiling of the dining room," wrote

Bloor, "interspersed with the tracery and gilding are suitable texts—'Give us this day our daily bread' in old English lettering."

Mould's house would be the frequent venue for evenings of appetizing food, engaging talk, and, of course, good music. The first of these took place in April 1859 when over forty people gathered in dress clothes for an evening of Mozart. Mould played the organ accompanying some "very fine vocalists" who sang the seventh and twelfth masses. Included in the group were "a very lively French lady" who was the sister-in-law of Cyrus Field, "the Cable man," novelist and editor Caroline Kirkland, and young Henry Van Brunt, the future architect and architectural writer. On many other occasions, Mould and his mother would offer a *petit souper* and entertain guests on the organ and piano. Also heard were such stars of the day as the celebrated pianist Sebastian Bach Mills. "I never heard such playing," marveled Bloor one evening when Mills played Mendelsohn's "Wedding March" and Wagner's "Priests March" from *Tannhäuser*. "I could scarcely keep from tears," he said.

In January 1860, George Templeton Strong, had a similar experience at "one of Wrey Mould's little musical gatherings." The rooms were modest—"wee parlors are uncarpeted and unfurnished; they contain nothing but a big organ and grand piano. The chairs were evidently imported from the bedrooms and the kitchen"—but the music was memorable. There were Joseph Burke, a well-known violinist who had first made his name as a child prodigy in Ireland, pianist Sebastian Bach Mills, and Theodore Groeneveldt, a member of the New York Philharmonic orchestra, playing the violoncello. "They did full justice to a very elaborate and lovely work of Mendelsohn's (op. 56, I think)," said the hard-to-please Strong who was himself a talented musician and president of the New York Philharmonic Society. In addition, there was good singing before the evening concluded with Weber's eerie overture to "Euryanthe." "It was all unconventional and outside the common social routine," remarked Strong. Most of all, he was touched to see how "Mould's ardor in superintending was so genuine and so intense, and the people he had assembled were so keenly appreciative of the music."[65] Mould, whom Strong had earlier described as "ugly and uncouth,"[66] clearly relished the stimulus and sympathy of kindred spirits that these congenial events effected. On such evenings, Mould's home, like the park on which he toiled during the day, became an antidote to the raucous and commonplace life of the city.

If Mould's guest book had survived, one would have seen along with the signatures of Bloor and Strong, the names of Calvert Vaux and his wife,

Mary; artist Jervis McEntee and his wife, Gertrude; pianist and teacher Louise Schlarbaum; Russell Sturgis; Richard Morris Hunt and his brother, the painter William Morris Hunt; the sons of Bishop Henry John Whitehouse; Mrs. Dr. Mueller, the daughter of Italian patriot Piero Maroncelli (and a woman for whom Mould apparently nursed an infatuation—Bloor confided that he had "talked wildly to me in French [so that others should not understand] of the lady whose portrait miniature and letters he has been showing me lately"[67]); and members of the Oakley family. At times, after the music, there was work to be done. The camaraderie continued even at the drawing board. "Refreshing ourselves several times with coffee and wine we worked, talked, laughed, and now and then sighed with weariness till nearly 5 o'clock," wrote Bloor of an overnight session in May 1859 completing Mould's competition entry for Henry Ward Beecher's new church in Brooklyn.[68]

The fine times continued until 1861, when Mould's private life took a drastic turn for the worse. What would happen over the next years is not completely clear, but with the aid of Lucille Gordon's excellent archival research, one is able to piece together a plausible circumstantial story. In March 1860, Mould later testified, he had married Mary Josephine Sheridan Daly, a woman, he said, he had known during his youthful days in Cork. Perhaps she had inspired the poem he wrote in 1847: "But let me win thy dainty kiss / And laugh into these eyes / They, too, afford a heav'nly bliss / A nearer paradise."[69] One assumes from her name that she was a member of the ship building Daly family with whom the Moulds were friendly. Just how the two got together in New York is unknown, and Bloor makes no mention of her until 1861. Early in that year, he records that he found Mould and his mother "in consultation with a lawyer about a letter he has read from a certain woman in England." This was the opening salvo of the troubling return of his wife Emelie into his life.

Revelation of his former marital status would seriously damage his reputation in the eyes of his colleagues and people who had been his friends. When "some rather disreputable proceedings of his came to light," George Templeton Strong wrote in his diary, "and as I wished to avoid his house for the future, I proceeded to cut him, mildly but firmly."[70] The paramount defeat he suffered was the loss of the companionship of his mother. After March 1861, she chose no longer to live with him at the Twenty-Sixth Street house. For personal or moral reasons, she may not have wished to share the house with Mary Josephine. She moved in with her brother George Oakley on Seventeenth Street and eventually returned to England where she died in 1875. Henceforth, she communicated with her estranged son through intermediaries and by letter. Mould's conduct during this time was described as "outrageous," "miserable," a "performance," and an "affair." Nonetheless, he felt proud to appear in public with Mary Josephine. On March 30, 1861, Bloor observed Mould and his "lady" in the dress circle at Wallack's theater where he could not resist watching her "a good deal through my glass." Finally, on April 11, Bloor, who would ever more keep a social distance between himself and Mould, accompanied Mould's mother "to her outrageous son's where we talked with him and his mistress till near 10 o'clock in very plain language."

Around the same time, Mould experienced serious financial problems. Between April 1859 and October 1865, the New York County Clerk's Judgment Index lists sixteen creditors who filed complaints against him for failure to pay bills. He owed Barnet Solomon $125 for upholstery; James Reed $144 for groceries; George Curtis, an architect assistant, $114; Truman Derby $122 for clothing; and the Bank of Commerce $400 for the office he rented at Bowling Green. To haberdasher Ralph Teets, Mould owed $56 for such items as "steel mixed Cassimere coat, one pair green check Cassimere pants, one Cassimere vest, one pair of check marsales pants and one check marsales vest." Things got so bad that on May 14, 1861, Bloor reported that "Mould had been arrested on some money charge and after a confinement of two days had with difficulty procured bail." The following summer, a notice appeared in the press declaring Mould, to whom laying up coin was irrelevant, officially bankrupt.[71]

Mould's marital problems came to a head in 1866. In that year, Emelie arrived in New York from London escorted by her sister. Once she had established residency, on July 20, 1867, she became the plaintiff in a divorce proceeding against Mould in the New York Supreme Court. The charge was adultery, for since 1860, Mould had lived with Mary Josephine. Emelie apparently now believed that her husband was a man of means. In this regard, Mould's attorney had to set the record straight concerning Mould's yachting lifestyle. "The defendant is not the owner of a yacht," he said. The vessel in question belonged to his friend Thomas Kennard who occasionally permitted Mould to use the *Octavia* because Mould had superintended its decoration. Mould was indeed the owner of a house on Twenty-Sixth Street, but it was a modest domicile. The parlor floor remained unfurnished (as Strong had indicated) "for lack of means."

It appears that Mould attempted to maintain that he could not have been legally married to Emelie because she had been married to someone else before without telling him. The proof he offered was the two-year-old child her sister had introduced to him shortly after their wedding. Yet, he had no definitive way of showing that the child was legitimate. The conclusion of the process obligated Mould to pay Emilie thirty dollars per month maintenance indefinitely. Whatever the outcome in legal terms, for Mould and Mary Josephine, love gained the upper hand and endured. Henceforth, Mary Josephine would be referred to as Mrs. Jacob Mould. The 1870 census recorded them living together as husband and wife at the Twenty-Sixth Street home, which Mary Josephine inherited at Mould's death.[72] Emelie and her daughter returned to London where Emelie, who represented herself as a widow, maintained a boarding house. In 1889, she and her daughter Alice moved to British Columbia where Emelie lived until her death in 1913.[73]

Let us hope that in the midst of all his troubles, Mould took time to wander the Mall and Terrace to see how people reacted to his lovely relief carvings there and to take comfort that he was giving pleasure to others. He would have been delighted to see visitors, especially youngsters, smiling at his assortment of clever inventions: the witch, crowing cock, hooting owl, flying bat, picturesque cottage, sheaves of wheat, harvester's sturdy scythe, beckoning open Bible, beaming oil lamp, clocking hour glass, and radiant setting sun. He would have been cheered to overhear exchanges like those between Uncle Nathan and his young nieces and nephews:

> I think . . . that the rooster on the post is meant for morning, because, you know, the cock crows in the morning. . . . If the rooster stands for morning, maybe the setting sun stands for evening . . . perhaps the owl and bat stand for night . . . and the Bible, lamp, and hourglass are meant to be symbols of time, religion and—and—immortal life. . . . But what do you suppose the farmer's house, the grain, the spade, and the scythe stand for, uncle? . . . Those may be taken for symbols of agriculture or industry. In placing the grain and the cottage near the spade and scythe, the artist may have meant to say that from industry come plenty and comfort.[74]

What more would Mould have needed to demonstrate Ruskin's belief that carved decoration brought inanimate architecture to life and demonstrated evidence of love in its creation. If anybody had recognized Mould on such an excursion, they would surely have gone over to him to express their appreciation and admiration for his inspired designs. Much later, in 2018, French artist Melik Ohanian tipped his hat to Mould when, in his design for the Armenian genocide memorial in Geneva, Switzerland, he mimicked Mould's "teardrop."

5.

Building a Career

> He prepares designs, working drawings and specifications and superintends the erection of buildings in any part of the United States.
>
> —*Jacob Wrey Mould handbill advertisement, 1869*

AFTER COMPLETING ALL SOULS and before the park put solid financial ground beneath his feet, Mould reached out for other opportunities. In 1856, he submitted a design to the international competition for a cathedral the Anglican community would build in Istanbul, Turkey. The church, known as Christ Church, was to have been a memorial to British soldiers who had died in the recently concluded Crimean War, a conflict immortalized by Tennyson's poem "The Charge of the Light Brigade." The terms of the competition stipulated that the design be in the Gothic style, modified to suit the climate of Turkey. The jurors recommended the example of the Gothic of Southern Europe. Byzantine and domed entries were banned for fear of inciting confusion with Orthodox Christianity, for the church was clearly intended as a statement of imperial Britain's High Church values in the heart of the Islamic world. "That Gothic must be the main ingredient appears to us demonstrable," wrote Alexander Beresford Hope, the well-known British parliamentarian who was a staunch supporter of the Church of England, "from the fact that Gothic was the universal emanation of the mind of Christian Europe, or at least of its active portion, in the days when the polity which is now overspreading the world was cradled. It was

European—it was Christian—it was conclimatic with the chief regions of organized civil polity."[1]

Fresh from his success with the Italian-inspired design for All Souls, Mould felt encouraged to present an entry. In December 1856, before he transmitted his submission to London, Mould invited the public to view his drawings at his office on Broadway at Thirteenth Street. In this way, Mould sought to capitalize on the celebrity that his participation in such a prestigious international event would bring. The judges included Beresford Hope and Robert Willis, both of whom were associated with the influential High Church periodical, *The Ecclesiologist*. Truly, Mould must have known that it would be a long shot for him to be chosen, for some of the biggest names in modern British architecture were sure to be competitors in an event publicly supported by Queen Victoria and Prince Albert.

Mould's design, the only one submitted from America, has not survived, but from written references we know that it resembled All Souls in its banded exterior walls and cruciform ground plan. A tall bell tower stood at the end of the north transept. Mould's concept found little favor with the jurors or with critics who reviewed the entries. It must have been distressing for him to read in the *Builder* that his design was "pretentious in its claims, but wholly fails when tested by examination—the horizontal lines in the tower and spire are sufficient to quote as instances." *The Ecclesiologist*—which took the opportunity to express antipathy to Owen Jones, calling his architecture "either a tunnel or a sewer"—said of his pupil's design, "the detail is indescribable; the arrangement monstrous."[2] Despite the adverse publicity, Mould took sufficient pride in his proposal for the Memorial Church at Constantinople (he held with English Christians' preference for the ancient name of the city) to exhibit four drawings of it at the National Academy of Design in 1859. One who had seen them described them as "elaborate and delicately rendered."[3] In the end, Mould could have taken heart from having lost the competition to William Burges, one of his King's College classmates and a rising star of England's High Victorian Gothic architecture. Moreover, all seven entries from foreign architects, noted historian Mark Crinson, "received dismissive reviews."[4]

Although Mould remained a devoted Anglican all of his life, his association with Henry Bellows gave him an entree to the growing Unitarian community in New York. Over the next few years, he would design or hope to design several Unitarian churches. The first of these was for Bellow's friend Samuel Longfellow, Transcendentalist minister of the Second Unitarian Church in the Cobble Hill section of Brooklyn (fig. 59). Longfellow, a graduate of Harvard Divinity School and brother of the famous

Figure 59. Second Unitarian Church, Brooklyn, New York, 1857.

poet whose biographer he became, shared Abolitionist views with Bellows and a love for music with Mould. In the 1840s, he had published *A Book of Hymns for Public and Private Devotion*, and the year his new church opened, he introduced a popular vesper service. One wonders if he ever discussed the creation of the musical score with Mould. A religious journal of the time praised *Vespers* as "the most impressive of all orders of worship, and what is remarkable, it interests persons of the most opposite creeds and tempers, from the High Churchman to the Methodists, from the Presbyterians to the Transcendentalists."[5] The setting for the debut of this moving musical ceremony was the church that Mould designed.

Ground was broken for the Second Unitarian Church in 1857, and the building (destroyed in 1962) was dedicated in the following year. The modest, low-rise brick structure occupied a corner lot (now the site of Cobble Hill Park) and accommodated seven hundred worshippers. Mould based the plan on the nave-and-rotunda space of All Souls and many Italian medieval and renaissance churches. But unlike All Souls, the Brooklyn building was a very plain affair. The "simple Italian" exterior was covered with brown stucco relieved only by "streaks of Phila. brick round the top and bottom of the walls." Mould emphasized the main entrance on Clinton Street by a simple projecting pediment with a central stained glass oculus, a design faintly reminiscent of the façade of Leon Battista Alberti's fifteenth-century Sant'Andrea in Mantua. The overall mustering of forms, with a tall slender tower adapted from Verona's famous medieval Torre dei Lamberti at the rear, showed his developing tendency to lead the eye in an upraised movement in the architectural composition. The *Christian Register* praised Mould's "original design" and the building's "extremely neat, tasteful and harmonious" appearance. Noting that Mould had been the designer of All Souls, the editors explained that their readers should not expect to see a duplicate of that ground-breaking design. Nonetheless, "the same exquisite semicircular arch enters largely into the design, and delights the eye with its graceful sweep and chaste elegance."[6]

On March 2, 1858, Longfellow stood there before an overflowing audience to dedicate the church with a sermon entitled "The Doctrine of the Spirit." "And to-day, friends, if we would have life in our churches," declared the passionate antislavery minister who despised the Fugitive Slave Act, "if we would stay this desolating flood of materialism, the demoralizing prevalence of dishonesty and compromise, and kindle anew the dying flame of faith in human rights, we must preach, first and last, the Holy Spirit THAT IS, Living God." The choir sang "How beautiful are thy dwellings, O Lord of Hosts," and music from a large Ferris organ resounded throughout the hall.

The interior of this disremembered haven of progressive religious thought, which Longfellow referred to as the "chapel," was "chaste and simple," reported the *Brooklyn Daily Eagle*. Mould limited his choice of colors: "an open timber roof is admirably relieved by the rose tinted and molded ceiling, appearing between the heavy beams. . . . The walls are pearl gray, and the ceiling of the apse is of azure color. . . . The pews . . . are lined with crimson damask."[7] Everyone had a clear view of the apse where the pulpit was located. One of those congregants was Arethusa Hall, a New England pioneer in women's education and a founder of the Brooklyn Female Academy. She described the sanctuary as "arranged with great taste; the platform with its background of crimson drapery and its soft blue canopy, seemed to form a fitting setting for the golden hair and gentle form of its minister." The services Longfellow conducted, she remembered, "were particularly harmonious, the whole—music, prayers, scripture readings, and sermon—having the beauty and completeness of a poem. . . . I often went away from the little chapel feeling that it was . . . the very gate of heaven."[8]

The modest church received scant attention in the press, and Mould himself never talked of it or included Longfellow as one of his favored references. Yet, the influential minister expressed himself pleased with the building. "The chapel, with some things that might have been better, is very charming," he wrote, "open, social, simple and fair."[9] Unhappily for Mould, the demon in the commission, the recession that followed the Panic of 1857, had clipped his creative wings. "Owing to the financial stress of the times," wrote Longfellow's biographer, "it had become necessary to curtail the plan of the building in some important respects." One of these was a lowered roofline that "impaired the beauty of the interior." Nonetheless, Mould managed to enhance his reputation for overspending, for the final cost was "far greater than had been intended."[10] Concerning the general progress of ecclesiastical architecture, the Second Unitarian Church constituted another instance of Unitarian stylistic dissent from the Gothic Revival preferences of Episcopal, Catholic, and other mainstream denominations. Noting that a "Unitarian Chapel has been built on Clinton St., Brooklyn, by the architect of All Souls Church," the *New Path* recommended it to its readers: "In it the same general treatment is followed, and though it is a less pretentious building, it is equally worthy of careful observation."[11] The site of the church is now Cobble Hill Park; a quiet "vest pocket" park where a long time ago in a "little church around the corner" people came to hear the Fugitive Slave Act denounced, John Brown's raid acclaimed, and Black lives mattered for more than slaves.

In 1859, Mould made a bid for another Unitarian commission. In April of that year, the trustees of Plymouth Church in Brooklyn announced a competition for a new auditorium-style worship space to replace the building erected in 1850 to plans by English immigrant architect Joseph C. Wells. ("It is written upon the face of it in characters of brick and brownstone sills and lintels: 'I am the first experiment of a church of the people for the people,'" remarked one critic of Wells' plain-looking church.) The congregation had purchased twelve lots on Montague Street in fashionable Brooklyn Heights and had big plans for its new home. The competition announcement stipulated that the new building must seat six thousand, "allowing eighteen inches to a seat." One or two galleries would be required, except at the speaker's platform, where the charismatic minister, Henry Ward Beecher—"the Shakespeare of the Pulpit"—would deliver his inspiring sermons and hold mock slave auctions to raise money to buy fugitives from the South their freedom. The story of Pinky and her ring endeared him to many throughout the North. There was to be no uncertainty about the importance of Beecher and his style of ministry to the new church arrangements: "The trustees desire architects to understand that . . . , the success of the whole enterprise is staked upon the auditorium."[12]

The New York art community, however, held little store by the Brooklyn congregation's gigantic ambitions. "We supposed that no respectable architect would respond to the call," said William J. Stillman, in the *Crayon*, who styled the proposed building "an immense preaching balloon." Yet, some twenty submissions came in. Mould (who chose the moniker "Isaish, LIV.II2"), Richard Morris Hunt, and Gervase Wheeler led the roster of otherwise little-known names. When in November Stillman went to see the entries on display at the church and saw the first premium had been awarded to Charles Duggin's design, he exclaimed, "You are joking! This cannot be it." Most of the others, he declared, "trash, nonsense, bungling attempts of a carpenter, ridiculous architecture, and worse construction." But when he saw Mould's drawings, he exclaimed, "Ha, here is something!" The truth of his impression is borne out by the architect's magnificent perspective watercolor (which he proudly exhibited at the National Academy of Design in 1860) that, fortunately, survives in the Avery Fine Arts and Architecture Library at Columbia University (plate 11).[13] Describing it as the work of Mould in "all the vigor of his best vein," Stillman proclaimed it "truly a masterpiece of design, drawing and coloring." There was "his favorite campanile, his judicious molding of masses and roof lines, a truly artistic arrangement of openings, and his exquisite details strewn like sparkling gems over the whole edifice—simple, plain and withal effective."[14] Mould reinterpreted the Congregational meetinghouse in terms of the tradition of medieval rotunda churches, the vast auditorium dominating a supporting range of service rooms. And the nod to St. Mark's in Venice in the design of the bell tower, which promised to add a degree of elegance to the up-and-coming neighborhood, would not have gone unnoticed by cognoscenti of religious architecture. "The whole design, outside and in, maintains, in spite of the perplexities of the problem, the character of a church," observed Stillman, who feared that this may have prejudiced some in the nonliturgical congregation against it. Mould's colleagues at the new American Institute of Architects seconded Stillman's views. At their November 15 meeting, the members discussed the Plymouth Church competition. They condemned the first-place design as impractical and its selection as unjustified. Instead, they asserted that the designs by Mould and Hunt were "the most creditable in the exhibition."[15]

Mould had achieved an impression of monumentality rare in his architecture. Sadly, his exquisite design fell victim to his overly ambitious objectives. The trustees passed over his entry because they feared it would be too costly to build. There was no Moses Grinnell to champion his cause. In the end, no new Plymouth Church ever was erected. The outbreak of war—which some thought Beecher and his sister Harriett had helped foment—and the general economic sluggishness and uncertainty that resulted curtailed donations to the building fund. After three years, the church abandoned the bold project and sold the Montague Street property.

In 1860, Mould exhibited drawings, now lost, at the National Academy of Design for two unsuccessful bids for important commissions. In 1859, he had submitted a proposal for the recently organized Brooklyn Academy of Music concert hall. The organizers, which included his friend Edward Whitehouse, chose Eidlitz as their architect, instead. Eidlitz designed a splendid High Victorian Gothic building that seated two thousand. If one of those seats had been occupied by Mould on opening night in January 1861, he would surely have smiled to discover that the first piece on the program of the Brooklyn Philharmonic was the overture from Weber's *Der Freischütz*, the libretto which Mould had translated long ago. It was followed by arias from other operas that Mould had rendered into English. The other appointment he failed to receive was from Christ Church in Brooklyn. "[A] 'Midsummer night's dream' of Mould, more oriental pageantry, with ideas brought in from every age of gothic arabesque," remarked a reviewer in the *Architects and Mechanics Journal* who saw his now missing drawing. "The skylines, as usual, are excellent and picturesque. The crowning spirelet is extremely spiritual and elegant." The writer went on to reflect more broadly on Mould's encompassing esthetic philosophy. "Mr. Mould seeks for no authority from the archaeologists, but consults his own artistic feelings of right and wrong, and works with the unrestrained liberty which is there permitted." In the eyes of this observer of the American profession, Mould's freedom of thought "fits the age we live in."[16]

Lack of funds was no worry for Muhammad Sa'id Pasha, Ottoman viceroy of Egypt. Hailed as a modernizer of Egypt, which he ruled over with unchallenged authority, he had been responsible for building the first standard gauge rail line in his home country. In order to travel in the style which he considered his due, in 1859, Muhammad Sa'id contracted with the Thomas Wason Company, the builder of the first Pullman cars, in Springfield, Massachusetts, for a luxurious personal carriage to carry him along the new line that ran 250 miles between the Mediterranean and the Red Sea, with stops at Alexandria and Cairo (fig. 60). The viceroy envisioned no undistinguished coach but a jubilant symbol of his reign. According to the *Springfield Republican*, the ten-thousand-dollar car was in the "perfection of its mechanical features, and gorgeousness of its decoration, the finest specimen of a railway carriage ever built in the world." Intended for use primarily during ceremonial occasions—conspicuous were the national Turkish emblems of the moon and the stars—the three-part carriage featured a center open-air pavilion. "But the most conspicuous and wonder-working feature of the carriage is it decoration, outside and inside," stated the hometown paper. "Every color and shade of color is mixed and mingled until the eye is dazzled and oppressed, almost, with the vision." Wason engaged Mould to take charge of the interior appointments of the exotic mobile home, which included a large stuffed arm chair "of extra size, nearly three feet square," for the portly viceroy. Perhaps Owen Jones had recommended him for the job, for Jones had designed a carriage for the Pasha's son several years earlier. With aid of the journal's vivid description, we can place ourselves in the Pasha's seat surveying the setting of Oriental splendor that Mould had conjured:

> At the end of each saloon are two large mirrors of the size of the windows [48 × 60 inches]. The floor of each of these saloons is to be covered with a rich Turkish velvet carpet made expressly for the carriage. . . . The lower sides of the saloons under the windows are made up of inlaid work with rose wood, bird's eye maple, black walnut and tiger woods designed as to form a very rich ornament perhaps the most so of any of the decorations. The upper sides and inside roofs are finished with intricate moldings and papier-mâché ornaments, richly painted and gilded. The thresholds of the doors are in polished brass carved in the universal Arabesque style. . . . Over each saloon is an extra roof, raised above the main roof sufficiently to permit a circulation of air, and thus qualify the oppressive heat of the climate. There is hardly any variety of foreign or domestic woods,

Figure 60. State railway carriage for the Viceroy of Egypt.

> save hemlock, that does not enter more or less into the construction of this car.[17]

A reporter from the *New York Times* was among the thousands of people whom the company invited to view the car in Springfield prior to it being dismantled and sent to Egypt. Plainspoken New England farmers had the opportunity to sit in Pasha's plush chair and admire Mould's glorious decorations. The *Times* readers learned that the coach ceiling was "very showy, consisting of panels of blue and claret ground, with figures of lighter shades of the same, and of gilt, violet and drab. Narrower ribs of solid walnut, with an intricate figure in relief, extend from side to side." The dome of the open pavilion, which resembled an "oriental awing," Mould must have remembered when several years later he designed the Central Park music pavilion. The itinerant sun shelter displayed shades of violet, blue, maroon, green, white, and gold. "The effect is at once a strong contrast and a pleasing harmony of colors," noted the *Times*. The amazed writer could not help expressing chauvinistic pride in the entire work, which he praised as "a very rare and novel undertaking in a new country—supplying decorations for the old." The "most fastidious Londoner," he thought, would have found little to no fault in the extraordinary conveyance.[18]

In the spring of 1860, George Templeton Strong, one of the attendees at Mould's musical evenings, became a member of the Schoolhouse Building Committee of Trinity Church. The foremost Episcopal congregation in the city was planning to erect a new Sunday school building adjacent to its "chapel of convenience," designed in 1851 by Richard Upjohn, on Twenty-Sixth Street. Strong used his position on the committee to effect Mould's engagement as architect. "He would do our work better than any architect I know," Strong confided to his diary, "and a job from Trinity Church would be a great lift for him in his profession." The chapel was well known as the venue for weddings and funerals of New York's social elite. On April 29, Mould presented his proposed design to the building committee, which liked what they saw. Nonetheless, extravagance lurked in the details, and for even such a well-off congregation, Strong would have to work to overcome what he feared would be reluctance on the part of the vestry to agree to the price. Moreover, shortly thereafter, Richard Upjohn, the architect of the Chapel and the mother church at the head of Wall Street, got wind of the committee's doings. Feeling slighted of his perceived authority over the parish architecture, he presented, unsolicited, a plan of his own for the schoolhouse. "The design was bad," declared Strong when he saw it, "stiff, angular, and meager. Pure Yankee Gothic." The next day, Mould brought more details before the committee, which found them admirable. Soon after, despite lingering misgivings over cost, the committee gave its approval to Mould's plans. Strong said he "had the pleasure of going out to tell him that his plans were approved and adopted without a dissenting voice." According to the committee, the considerable twenty-two-thousand-dollar cost was justified because "a building sufficient for the wants of the School of Trinity Chapel and corresponding in style and dignity with the Chapel itself cannot be erected for a smaller sum."[19] Upjohn, on the other hand, in the words of Strong, was "in great wrath because we employ J. W. Mould," and began spitefully submitting outdated claims for work he had done for the congregation years before. But Mould, like Upjohn, a member of the Episcopal faith community, was in "great exultation over his retainer by Trinity Church on this schoolhouse job," which he knew would raise his profile in the city's architectural circles. "The appointment of Mr. J. Wrey Mould as Architect of the Corporation and Vestry of Trinity Church," stated the *Tribune*, "does great credit to the taste and discernment of that rich corporation, and is the highest tribute which could be paid to the merits of this distinguished architect."[20]

Trinity Chapel Schoolhouse (the present Serbian Orthodox Church of St. Sava Parish House) that Mould designed was a long narrow building, 94 by 26 feet, at the edge of the church property. Opened as a Sunday school for 300 students of both sexes, it soon became an all-boys regular school with 120 pupils occupying three floors. Originally, the Female Department occupied the first floor; male students attended classes on the second floor. The unencumbered third floor served as a chapel or general assembly room. Elsewhere in the building were a "retiring room" for teachers and a library. Water closets were located in the basement, and air refreshed all rooms through a series of flues connected to a ventilator disguised as a picturesque spire. The windows were filled with semiopaque "enamel glass, leaded up in equilateral quarries."[21] This new material dispensed with the needs for blinds and gave "an agreeable cool tone to the rooms."

For the design of the schoolhouse, Mould turned the pages of his imagination to more traditional British Gothic Revival sources. Mould described the exterior as "designed in Christian Architecture somewhat of the transition period from 12th to 13th Century, but with a certain admixture of Southern Gothic feeling in its details." For the subtlety differentiated color scheme, he specified soft red Passaic sandstone for the walls, "laid up in long thin stones averaging 8 inches in thickness and set in black mortar." He chose an olive-colored stone for the trim around the windows and elsewhere and cream-colored Caen stone for the tracery that held the tinted enamel glass in place. Bands of green and purple slate formed the roof which was surmounted with an ornamental iron ridge crest. High notes of coloration were struck at "several points in the surface" where Mould embedded encaustic tiles in the walls. He claimed that he was inspired by the new Oxford University Museum, the planning of which Ruskin had been deeply involved in. The most distinctive feature of the schoolhouse design marked the entrance to the building, which faced Upjohn's chapel across a small court (fig. 61). Students entered beneath a large stone porch that resembled a medieval Italian baldachin of the type that Arnolfo di Cambio designed in the thirteenth century over the altar of Santa Cecilia in Rome, or which surmounted the Congrande della Scala's famous fourteenth-century tomb in Verona. It was as if the architect sought to remind the pupils of the sacredness of the studies they were about to undertake (fig. 62). Here was that "certain admixture of Southern Gothic feeling in its details" that Mould told the building committee was "hitherto a want

Figure 61. Trinity Chapel Schoolhouse (present Serbian Orthodox Cathedral of Saint Sava), 1860.

in Ecclesiastical Edifices erected in this Country."[22] Finally, a picturesque bell cot and gable containing a clock high above the narrow Twenty-Fifth Street elevation proclaimed the building's educational purpose to parishioners and passersby alike.

Construction of the school began in the summer of 1860 and was completed by the end of the year. The school is the only one of Mould's New York buildings outside of Central Park to survive. During this time, however, Mould did not endear himself to his employers and to Strong. In fact, he increased his reputation as a poor money manager and businessman.

Figure 62. Trinity Chapel Schoolhouse, entrance porch.

"The committee complains of the architect and not altogether without reason," wrote Strong in September. "He is far too slow with his working plan." Moreover, "being very hard up, poor fellow, he borrows of contractors and mechanics, as an architect should not." He also borrowed two hundred dollars from Strong, promising to repay it the "day after tomorrow." It took ten years for Mould to pay him back; by that time, Strong was surprised to receive the money at all. "I fear his genius, which is unquestionable," he reflected, "carries too little ballast of practical sense." In October, the working situation had gotten worse. "Trinity School is in a bad way," lamented Strong; "heaven grant my well-intentioned efforts may not get it yet deeper into the mire." Yet, despite all the trials and tribulations, the building came out successfully. Years later, despite Strong's frustration over Mould's foot-dragging with the committee and his unacceptable marital conduct, Strong still admired him for his creative ability. In 1869, when Upjohn was presenting designs for changes to Trinity Church, Strong wrote to himself, "I wish we could avail ourselves of the Bohemian and scapegrace Wrey Mould."[23] Nonetheless, in 1871, the corporation turned again to aging Upjohn, rather than to Mould, when it built a new schoolhouse for Trinity Parish School adjacent to the Wall Street church.

The building that Mould designed for Trinity bore no resemblance to Henry Bellows's All Souls but rather partook of the High Victorian "Ruskinian Gothic" taste that was best represented by William Butterfield's All Saints Margaret Street in London. "It resembles, more than any other building we have, the efforts that have recently been made in England," wrote Peter Bonnet Wight in the pages of the *New Path*. Spherical, pointed, and segmental arches were used, and tracery patterns in the grand central window that lighted the third floor chapel and in smaller windows as well were from the fourteenth-century Decorated period of Gothic. Mould knew that up-to-date British ecclesiological churchmen had shifted their allegiance from the simple thirteenth-century Early English style that Upjohn had followed for the Trinity Chapel to the more ornamental style of the succeeding period. Mould's color contrasts in the walls were more subdued than at All Souls, with "more brilliant colors of the inserted tiles and the painted iron work" forming an agreeable contrast. Wight's main objection was one that he would make later concerning the decorative carvings in Central Park: the decorative sculpture followed Mould's drawings rather than coming directly from the minds and hands of the artisans. "Like all the carving that has been done thus far in this country, [these] are evidently copies of drawings by clever workmen, rather than thought out by the brain and wrought under the chisel of the designer." Until this practice was reformed, he admonished, "we may expect little progress to be made in the decorative part of our architecture."[24] Today, New Yorkers can see no finer expression of the High Victorian Gothic invention than Mould's schoolhouse and Frederick Withers's Jefferson Market Courthouse of 1874.

Forced to adhere to the width of a typical New York brownstone residential lot, Mould created a compact, high-shouldered building that added an uncommon note of the picturesque to his neighborhood streetscape. The building above all seemed cheerful, even mirthful, as befitted a school for youngsters. The precipitous exterior is gay with notes of color, abounds in windows, and is alive with movement. Slender lancets lengthen between two floors to culminate in banded pointed arches, and an elaborate oriel window hangs mischievously suspended from the court facade. Main lines of the design draw the eye upward to the steeply pitched roof that is composed of faceted segments and surmounted by a fancy cupola that gathers the network of internal ventilation flues. The narrow Twenty-Sixth Street elevation is made to appear even narrower by being beveled, and the central window, taller than the rest, pushes the roof into a gablet that supports a precipitously perched freestanding bell cot. The building, as P. B. Wight remarked, put to shame all the plodding school buildings that had sprung up throughout the city.[25]

The outbreak of the Civil War in April 1861 dampened the call for new construction, yet Mould found himself able to secure significant commissions beyond his employment at Central Park. Several clients asked him for designs of houses. John Allen contracted for a semi-detached dwelling for workmen on his large farm in West Meriden, Connecticut. As represented in Bicknell's *Wooden and Brick Buildings*, which published the plan and elevation, the double house appeared as one symmetrical dwelling, with a central chimney stack serving as the dominant anchoring element above a large pyramidal roof. The lives of the two families who would inhabit such a building were closely intermingled, for they shared the central stair hall and kitchen. Allen expressed satisfaction with the unconventional arrangement, telling Amos Bicknell that the building was "well adapted to the purpose for which it was built."[26]

In 1863, Mould designed a substantial brick and stone house at 653 Main

Figure 63. William Williams House, Buffalo, ca. 1863.

Street, then a fashionable address in Buffalo (fig. 63), for banker turned railroad director William Williams. People described Williams, who was involved in the creation of several rail lines and spent a term in the United States Congress, as an urbane gentleman and an astute businessman. The brick and stone dwelling, like the Trinity Chapel Schoolhouse, displayed both pointed and segmental arches and featured sculptured decoration, notably a frieze beneath the eaves and stylized floral designs on the second floor bifora window and rondel. Mould must have been pleased with the handsome window, for a few years later, he reinterpreted its design in simpler and larger form to light the vast double story hall of the Long Island mansion he designed for Thomas Clapham. There a muscular segmental arched entrance porch similar to the one on the Buffalo house advanced to welcome visitors (figs. 64 and 65).[27] Animating the façade of the Williams house by means of projecting and receding forms—tower, bay window, porch entrance—Mould expressed his passion for three-dimensionality, even in such a moderate-sized building, and anticipated his bold design of the West Presbyterian Church façade in Manhattan. The Williams house,

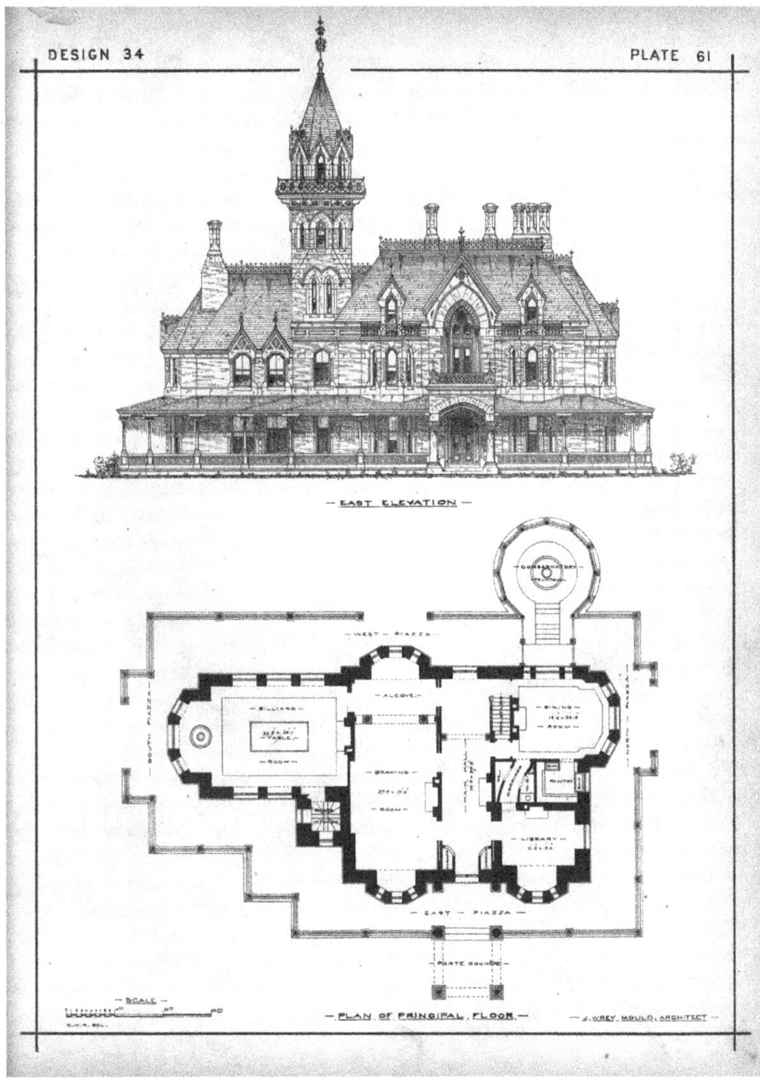

Figure 64. Thomas Clapham House, Roslyn Harbor, Long, Island, New York, 1868.

which after 1881 served the needs of clients who came from far and wide to Dr. R. V. Pierce's Invalid Hotel and Surgical Institute, introduced a forceful example of High Victorian Gothic to the city that Mould's colleagues Vaux and Olmsted would make famous after the war as the first place in America to adopt their concept of a system of parks connected by urban boulevards they called parkways.

Figure 65. Thomas Clapham House details from Bicknell's *Wooden and Brick Buildings with Details* (1875).

Another railroad personage who became one of Mould's outstanding patrons was Thomas W. Kennard (1825–1893). Kennard had an international reputation as a railroad designer before he emigrated from England to America. We do not know how Mould met the famous civil engineer, but the two men had a lot in common. Kennard, proprietor of a large Scottish iron works, had had a successful career as a builder of rail lines in

Britain—the Crumlin Viaduct spanning an immense Welsh valley was his master work, a Victorian equivalent to the Roman Pont du Gard—before he emigrated to America. In 1858, he had been recruited by William Reynolds to guide the laying of three hundred miles of track for the new Atlantic and Great Western Railroad of which he was president. The line was to link New York City with the Mississippi Valley, passing through the oil fields of Pennsylvania. Another line would connect with Cleveland on Lake Erie, then a center of oil refining. Kennard was at work by 1859 surveying the route that encompassed existing rail lines that would need to be converted to the single gauge planned for the entire line, a first in American railroading. The *Scientific American* noted, "the magnitude of the work can be appreciated when it is remembered that it required nearly one mile of railroad to be constructed daily."[28] All who knew Kennard acknowledged his genius. However, Reynolds also found him "vain and very susceptible to flattery." He was also a "show off," a self-promoter, and "reckless of expenditure."

In the fall of 1863, Kennard, who had made his home in New York, determined to install his family in a palatial house on forty acres of land he had purchased at Glen Cove, Long Island. The site, which commanded sweeping views of the water, was described as "one of the most charming spots anywhere near New York." He engaged Mould as the architect for his dream house, which involved tearing down all or part of a preexisting dwelling (fig. 66). On October 20, 1863, Kennard invited friends to see the place he had purchased and to look over the plans he had made with Mould for its improvement. Kennard, with Mould holding his arm, "spent money lavishly, as if he had been a prince."[29] With a bottomless purse at his disposal, Mould undertook to design a fabulous Swiss chalet fantasy. In September 1864, William Reynolds wrote that Kennard invited "many of the railway officials and prominent citizens of New York" out to Glen Cove to see the completed work. "The day was beautiful," wrote Reynolds: "Glencove, with its bright paint and gold and numerous banners, presented a charming sight. The grounds, flower gardens, shrubberies, fountains, statues, and lawns were in perfect condition, and altogether presented a beautiful landscape. . . . Kennard was an excellent host, and until near the hour for dinner led his guests to points of beauty and interest."[30]

So that Kennard and his guests might enjoy the scenery, Mould equipped the enormous rectangular residence with a covered terrace—Kennard preferred to call it a piazza—that embraced the entire first floor and a balconied observatory that sat atop a substantial tower. Vaux, Mould's associate at Central Park, would have appreciated the concern for scenic

Figure 66. Thomas Kennard House, Glen Cove, Long, Island, New York, 1864.

views, but would surely have been dismayed at the blatant showiness of Mould's design. Vaux had maintained that in the design of country houses "woods, fields, mountains, and rivers will be more important than the houses that are built among them." He and Olmsted made subordination of architecture to nature an article of faith at Central Park where Mould worked during the day. The exterior of Kennard's house displayed elaborately carved and gilded ornamentation that glowed brightly in the afternoon sun when it illuminated the conspicuous hilltop mansion.

"Glen Chalet," as Kennard called his fictive Alpine wonder, no longer exists, and nor do we have images of the elaborate interiors that Mould created using many different types of woods and much carved decoration. A critic writing in the *Evening Post* in 1870 singled out the Kennard interiors, along with Mould's interiors for the home of Harriet L. Packer in Brooklyn, as among the finest examples of polychrome decoration.[31] Extravagant ways eventually spelled the loss of "Glen Chalet" for Kennard, who, like Mould, was headstrong, impetuous, thriftless, and a genius at his métier. Unable to meet the expense of keeping up his grand status symbol, Kennard mortgaged the estate to his lawyer, S. L. M. Barlow, and eventually sold it to him at a steep loss. Barlow rechristened the house "Elsinore," the name by which later wealthy Gold Coast neighbors remembered it. Demolished following Barlow's tenancy, the princely site is now home to two modern ranch style dwellings. The loss is more a cautionary tale about vanity than a blow to the annals of American domestic architecture. The Kennard house was not a building that Mould could have ranked with All Souls or Trinity Chapel Schoolhouse.

Kennard was not content to live in the lap of luxury on land only, he wished to have similar splendor on rail and water. In 1863, the chief engineer acquired a personal railway car that he used to travel through the Midwest to inspect the progress of the work on the Atlantic and Great Western tracks. While thousands were dying in one of the bloodiest conflicts on record, Kennard, a British citizen, rode the rails in security in the service of primarily European investors. (Because of the war, however, he did experience difficulty at times acquiring iron and other supplies.) On board his "'elegant little dwelling house' on wheels," Kennard enjoyed the comforts of a parlor, bedroom, kitchen, and bathroom.[32] It is likely that he had turned to Mould to enhance these interiors, but we lack documentary evidence to establish his authorship. The following year, Kennard commissioned the construction of the grandiose *Octavia*, a 145-foot yacht, the first yacht powered by steam engines. (The steam-powered and sail-assisted yacht could store two hundred tons of coal and cruise for fifty days.) By all measures of the day, the ocean-going *Octavia*, which bore his beloved wife's name, was also a splendid affair. (It no longer exists.) Built in Cleveland, it sailed to New York to have engines installed by naval engineers and interior accommodations designed by Mould. For the state rooms, he created an atmosphere of opulence employing a costly variety of highly polished woods, including black walnut, rosewood, satinwood, curled maple, cherry, and holly. The ample main deck housed the dining room and a smoking room, along with a gentlemen's salon for sixteen. Below deck were living quarters for the family, together with a children's nursery. The *New York Times* asserted that the *Octavia*'s accommodations were "of a superior order and her decorations may be characterized as of regal splendor." Kennard's $150,000 expenditure included two cannons to ward off pirates.[33]

Mould became a frequent guest aboard the *Octavia*. He was not, however, one of those who accompanied Kennard and his son on the daring pleasure cruise they made in early April 1865 up the James River to Richmond, the just destroyed capital of the Confederacy.[34] At other times, Kennard apparently let Mould use his beautiful creation for himself. Perhaps, his abandoned wife, Emelie, had gotten wind of the expensive enterprise from accounts in the London papers—the *London Daily Telegraph* published a vivid description of the vessel in mid-April 1865—and thought her husband the boat's owner. This may have been what spurred her to come to America after the war to sue for alimony payments. In any event, Mould lost his opportunity to sail on the *Octavia* after 1870, by which time his free-spending friend had returned to live out his days in England.

Mould's association with Kennard extended beyond "Glen Chalet" and the *Octavia*. Mould had prepared a design dated 1862 for the Western Central Railroad terminal in Hoboken, New Jersey. Kennard was the company's engineer-in-chief (fig. 67). It appears never to have been erected. Yet, Mould took pride in the High Victorian Gothic building and gave a copy of his drawing for the two-towered façade to William R. Ware to present to the Royal Institute of British Architects when Ware visited there in 1867. The central plan terminal would have reminded many of Mould's much-admired Plymouth Church competition submission. With Middle Eastern splendor and an immense clock tower pierced by a tall lancet opening, it beckoned passengers from New York to board one of the new trains that would carry them westward to the American heartland. Nor does it appear that Mould's proposal for the Union Railroad Depot in Cleveland ever got beyond the drawing that he exhibited in 1871, together with the one for the Hoboken terminal, at the Yale School of Fine Arts.[35]

Mould was among the many invitees from New York who traveled to Cleveland to attend the gala event celebrating the opening of the Atlantic and Great Western Railway on November 18, 1863. A few days later, the *Cleveland Leader* reported that together with his position at Central Park, Mould had assumed the role of the railroad's architect. In this capacity, he had prepared plans for the company's new offices in Cleveland and may have designed the "locomotive dwelling house," an elegant rail carriage that had carried company executives from New York to Cleveland. He was even expected to spend a few months in the city while the work on the

Figure 67. Design for the eastern façade of the Western Central Railway Terminal, Hoboken, New Jersey, 1862.

Veronese Gothic–style building progressed. In addition to the corporation headquarters, the program included an exclusive private social club for railroad executives that Kennard had envisioned "on the model of the princely clubs of England." The well-appointed rooms would be grouped around a courtyard and include a domed billiard room, a well-stocked library, and drowsy reading room. When completed, the journal proclaimed, the entire building would be the "most elegant railway building in the West."[36]

Kennard had also purchased the Angier House, a well-known hotel in Cleveland built in 1854. The thorough remodeling that he financed was surely put in the hands of Mould. When the grand hotel reopened in June 1866 as the Kennard House, it featured a spectacular lobby said to have been inspired by the Alhambra. Its immense bar was among the largest and most frequented in town. For many years, the Kennard House occupied a prominent place in Cleveland's civic and social life. Several presidents and many other celebrities numbered among its guests.

"Who that has ever strolled abroad in this city does not know the church?," asked the *New York Herald* of its readers in 1893. The reference was to the West Presbyterian Church on Forty-Second Street, between Fifth Avenue and Sixth Avenue. "That accomplished architect Jacob Wrey Mould set his mind to work on the new structure and the result was a façade of such exquisite proportions that everyone who walks—not to say runs—may see that there is the work of a man of taste."[37] Many would have agreed that the church, which on paper dates from 1863 and opened in April 1865, ranked among the finest ecclesiastic buildings in New York. "The millionaire's gate to heaven," as the church was popularly known, made way in 1911 for one of the city's early skyscrapers.

Unlike Mould's earlier churches, West Presbyterian Church was not a freestanding structure (fig. 68). It was wedged between uniform rows of brownstone residences, a site that presented special challenges to the architect. One was to design an effective façade. Fortunately, Thomas S. Hastings, the minister who, in order to follow the northward migration of many of his congregants from an earlier downtown location, had acquired in 1863 a site facing the open landscape of Bryant Park (then known as Reservoir Square). From there, the sole church building was certain to command people's attention. Moreover, it was an unusually wide property. It measured seventy-eight feet along the street line. With this generous width at his disposal, Mould raised a façade of two towers, the west of which supported an elegant spire. Between these two sidewalk sentinels, Mould recessed the center of the façade behind a tall gabled porch projected forward to welcome visitors between polished granite columns. The

Figure 68. West Presbyterian Church, 1863–1865.

spirited interplay of projecting and receding horizontal and vertical units with the symmetry of the pointed arched openings resolved itself in the lofty pyramidal roof resting on a ribbon-windowed clerestory. Nor could anyone point to a particular era of Gothic architecture for its origins. "The church does not profess to have been erected according to the canons of any established style of architecture," stated Mould, adding, "the leading idea is the Italian gothic, because in its precedent, the architect has found more untrammeled freedom of detail than in any other school."[38] And true to High Victorian Gothic design principle of truth in art, the exterior faithfully related to the viewer the arrangement of the inside spaces.

Approbation for Mould's astute feat of original design was nearly universal. "The bold, fertile genius of J. Wrey Mould, the accomplished architect, has produced a façade of such rare and finely ordered proportions that every cultivated wayfarer pays it, involuntarily, the tribute of half-surprised admiration," remarked the *New-York Tribune* twenty years after its completion when Mould had been largely forgotten and H. H. Richardson dominated the American architectural scene.[39] "It is by no means a rash conclusion that the entire front elevation, with its boldly contrasted masses and beautiful iron-work and cresting, stands almost unique in its picturesque completeness," asserted the *Tribune*. The *Churchman* was equally eloquent in its admiration of Mould's remarkable accomplishment:

> The insignificance of such a church elevation is, at best, a foregone conclusion, and in most instances, the attempts of the architects to challenge and hold our consideration, are pitiful failures. But here Mr. Mould commands and holds the attention of every educated observer. There is the same bold, lavish use of color, with singular wealth of resources in proportion and perspective; and the building asserts itself immediately as an important structure. Throughout the city one will not find a simple façade with anything like the same architectural force and impressiveness.[40]

To emphasize the point, the writer could have mentioned Edward T. Potter's ungainly mid-block façade for the Church of the Heavenly Rest.

The interior plan presented Mould with the opportunity to implement an idea that had intrigued him for a while (fig. 69). Writing in the third person, he explained: "The church has been erected by the architect as the solution of a problem long entertained by him, namely: to treat an ecclesiastical building, where it is situated on a street, and in the center of a block, essentially, as a 'street front;' and by taking the major portion of the light required from the roof, to fill up the whole ground with the edifice, and not to allow a narrow alley-way on either side, which would at best give a very inadequate and meagre amount of side light." His plan focused on a seventy-four-foot square auditorium unencumbered by view-blocking supports and amply lit by a large skylight. "The height from the floor to the sky-light, formed by the intersection of the four main trusses carrying the roof, is 64 feet," he said. A later visitor marveled that "in place of columns . . . the ingenious designer resorted to four enormous round-headed arches rising from all four sides, and sustaining a vaulted skylight, or quadrangle lantern. Narrow galleries cross the three sides, and the fourth is filled with a great upper choir-space, with the organ divided on either side, and underneath a cloister-like space for the pulpit and its conveniences."[41] As there were no windows in the sidewalls, light came from above and from large pointed arched windows in the south facing façade. For nighttime illumination, gaslights glowed out of sight "being

Figure 69. West Presbyterian Church, interior.

concentrated under a series of powerful reflectors above the great skylight and also being disposed around the back of the central arch over the pulpit."[42] The pulpit occupied center stage where everyone could see its occupant; the organ console was behind it, hidden from view. Pointed arches in the wall left and right of the central arch displayed the many pipes of the large organ created for the church by Levi U. Stuart.

Mould also took pains that the decoration of the church went according to his ideas. He paid special attention to the capitals of the columns—the second examples in the city after those at All Souls to be of polished granite—at the entrance porch, which, like the bases, were formed of marble from Italy. "The foliation of the capital on the east side," said Mould, who drew the designs for the carver to execute, "is taken from *convolvulus major*, or 'morning glory,' typical of the morning." The capital on the west side represented the "night blooming ceroid." Mould also furnished the design for the *Angel of Benediction* in the tympanum over the doorway. (Perhaps he even shared his now lost drawing with Henry and Emma Stebbins when she was developing her conception of the Angel of Waters for Central Park's Bethesda Fountain.) When the church was newly finished, Mould stated that inside "a moderate amount of surface decoration is contemplated when the building will have sufficiently seasoned to allow of it." Eventually, we are told, a generous amount of polychrome and arabesque decoration, especially on the north wall, formed the backdrop to the pulpit.

Near the end of the year, the brilliant organ maker Levi Stuart finished installing the organ, which was impressive for its sound, scale, and beauty. Moreover, observed a music critic in the *New York Times*, "the instrument has been built on a novel plan necessitated by the architectural requirements of the building, being situated in the rear of the pulpit, the great organ and swell are divided by some 60 feet, the manual in the centre between the two." To celebrate the occasion of its completion, the Reverend Hastings organized a gala public concert on the evening of December 12. The program included the overture to Mendelsohn's *Midsummer Night's Dream*—"which displayed the charming antiphonal effects of the instrument"—and Bach's Fugue in G Major. But the highlight of the evening was the *andantino grazioso* from Gade's Symphony in C Major arranged for four hands and played by the celebrated organist George W. Morgan and the architect of the church, Jacob Wrey Mould. Hastings was apparently untroubled by the rumors of his guests' bigamous living arrangements. Filling the beautiful room he had created with beautiful music he loved, Mould wedded the two passions of his existence to the delight of a large "attentive and appreciative" audience.[43] It must have been among the most memorable events of his lifetime.

One would like to think that the minster's five-year-old son, Thomas, had been in attendance sitting spellbound in the exhilarating atmosphere and, perhaps, then and there, vowed to become an architect. His path to architectural fame and fortune would be very different from that of Mould, however. After study at the École des Beaux-Arts in Paris, he would return to the United States to become, with his partner John Merven Carrère, one of the leading advocates of Neo-Classicism and the City Beautiful movement.

If not to Thomas, Mould's West Presbyterian Church taught lessons that other contemporaries of his appreciated. In my opinion, H. H. Richardson found much to admire in West Presbyterian that he applied to his historic design for Trinity Church in Boston, the building that gave rise to his fame. An Episcopal church that did not follow the dictates of High Church ecclesiology, Trinity was planned for the popular pastor, Philipps Brooks, to be a preaching church. Attention was to be focused on the pulpit rather than on a liturgical chancel and altar. Like the New York church, Trinity's congregation worshiped in a majestic square space defined by four high round arches that reach sixty-four feet to a rectangular lantern or skylight. To enter Trinity, which is full of vibrant color, must provide us with the closest experience we can have of the feel of Mould's lamented building. Yet, Richardson's architecture was Beethoven to Mould's Mozart. Indeed, some contemporaries compared the New York and Boston churches. "With such a locality as Mr. Richardson found for Trinity church, Boston," wrote the *Churchman*, "Mr. Mould would have produced an edifice equally remarkable and admirable."[44] Likewise, it seems to me that Mould's friend Leopold Eidlitz had the interior of West Presbyterian Church in mind when, in 1876, he designed the vast high-arched Assembly Chamber in the New York State capitol at Albany. Given the respect that Mould's West Presbyterian enjoyed among his architect colleagues, it would not be surprising to find that its influence lay beneath many works of late nineteenth-century American architecture.

Down the street at the northeast corner of Forty-Second Street and Fifth Avenue, another, very different, church by Mould was being dedicated at the same time as West Presbyterian Church. The young Stephen Higginson Tyng Jr., the son of the highly respected rector of St. George's Episcopal Church, had recently established there a new Episcopal parish named Church of the Holy Trinity. Those who congregated there were from another class of people than the ones attending West Presbyterian, the so-called millionaire's gate to heaven. Tyng's congregation consisted primarily of the poor and dispossessed. The socially conscious Tyng, who had seen suffering humanity up close as a chaplain in the Union Army, wanted Holy Trinity to be the church of the common man. To this end, the church sponsored a broad range of social and spiritual activities. It held sewing classes and mothers' meetings, fed the poor, and hosted temperance meetings," observes architectural historian Kathryn Holliday.[45] Tyng also trained evangelists to go out into the streets of New York to recruit the fallen for Christ.

In June 1864, Tyng engaged Mould to erect a wooden church for nine hundred people that probably both patron and architect alike regarded as a temporary structure. Within nine years, the fast-growing congregation replaced it with a large brick and stone building accommodating two thousand people. Amidst national mourning for the assassination of President Lincoln, Tyng held the first service in Mould's church on Easter Sunday, April 16, 1865 (fig. 70). The building immediately attracted attention for its unusual design. "Most of the travelers who enter the grand depot in the Fourth avenue [Central Terminal occupied the block behind the church]

Figure 70. Holy Trinity Church.

notice the church which stands directly opposite, and whose architecture is very unique and peculiar," wrote a well-informed contemporary journalist. "I believe, indeed, it differs from everything of the kind in America, and my best description is, that it is not like any other edifice, sacred or profane, which I have ever seen."[46]

For this evangelical liturgical congregation, Mould rose to the occasion of working with a tight budget and designed a single-story frame building based on a Latin Cross plan. Essentially a reduction of his concept for All Souls, Holy Trinity comprised a 127-foot-long nave that broadened out into transepts at the eastern or altar end. Unlike All Souls, however, parishioners entered the church by the novel means of portals in the four angles of the transept. The ventilating spire at the juncture of the nave and transepts crowned the pleasingly varied composition of telescoping masses. But it was the steeply pitched, multifaceted roof that formed the building's leading feature. It imparted a distinctly expressive character to the seemingly modest structure. "Perhaps its most striking feature in point of construction is its low roof," noted an initially hesitant admirer, "but the erratic and original taste exhibited in it sets it entirely above criticism."[47] Articulating the poetry of the roof was becoming a signature feature of Mould's personal style. It would appear fully evolved a few years later on the Sheepfold in Central Park.

Even though he was unaccustomed to work for such a missionary client, Mould had cleverly turned the limitations of size and budget ($5,900) to good use. He may not have employed the term *cottage church* to describe the building, but others definitely noted its resemblance to domestic architecture. "Indeed for charming novelty of effect, and a cheerfulness of interior aspect, that most effectively combines the church with the *home*, we know of no ecclesiastical edifice in the city at all comparable to it," stated a reviewer of the new church in the *New York Times*. Critic Montgomery Schuyler called it a "*cottage ornée*," perhaps recognizing the evident similarity with Mould's park architecture. Moreover, Mould avoided all attempts to couch his design in any historical style, but resorted instead, noted the *Times*, to "such a combination of architectural elements as are best adapted to produce a temporary, economical and yet commodious church building." There was, notably, no attempt to follow the "carpenter Gothic" route of Richard Upjohn's board and batten church designs. Nor was there an overt sign of ecclesiological religion: no tower, bell cote, or pictorial carving. In this espousal of picturesque functionalism, Mould had "succeeded very thoroughly," asserted the *Times*."[48] The result was a snug little building that seemed appropriately expressive of shelter for a congregation that consisted largely of the dispossessed.

"The inside of the church is simple but beautiful," reported a visitor shortly before it went down, "and almost as unique in finish as the exterior."[49] Those who attended worship services here for its few years of existence found the space "sufficiently lofty" because Mould had left the roof trusses visible in the nave and transepts. Nor was there much to distract from the architecture itself. The organ and choir screen, which Mould situated behind the altar in the chancel, were "the sole decorative features of the interior," reported the *Times*. Once again, Mould treated the organ as an object of significance: "the radiating pipes of the organ being decorated and illuminated," said the *Times*, were "so disposed as to show the rich stained glass windows in the rear wall."

The success of Tyng's social ministry spelled doom for Mould's earnest bantam building. The charismatic speaker and effective spokesperson for the city's poor easily raised the funds for a larger edifice that his father's architect, Leopold Eidlitz, was hired to design. Last services in Mould's building were held in March 1873. Why Mould was passed over we will never know. Perhaps the nondenominational appearance of his wooden church had prejudiced the Episcopal hierarchy that had admonished Tyng for his ecumenical activities. Eidlitz drew up plans for an extravagant High Victorian Gothic milestone. The Gilded Age had begun. "The vibrancy of the church, so unlike the sobriety of St. George's . . . had little precedent in New York," observes Kathryn Holliday of Ediltz's splendid building: "Its only relative was Mould's All Souls Unitarian Church."

Those who wondered at the amiable cottage-like appearance of Mould's Holy Trinity were obviously unfamiliar with the small cruciform wooden church he had designed several years earlier for the First Unitarian Church

Figure 71. First Unitarian Church, Yonkers, New York.

in Yonkers, New York (fig. 71). "The lovely little wooden church," as A. J. Bloor, Mould's associate, affectionately described it, still stands at 191 North Broadway in Yonkers where it serves the needs of the Ministerio Familiar La Cosecha.

The newly formed congregation was small, fewer than three hundred, but not impecunious and favored a smart building to introduce themselves appropriately to their middle-class suburban community. The pastor was Abiel Livermore, who together with his wife, Elizabeth, co-edited the *Christian Intelligencer* newspaper. Elizabeth also took charge of the Sunday school that met in the basement lecture room. What some might call Stick Style today—Mould's contemporaries referred to it as "Swiss cottage style"—was an almost light-hearted exercise in how wood might be shaped, carved, and displayed in framework to create spirited elevations. The church beckoned passersby with a tall, multilevel tower over the crossing and welcomed visitors beneath a boldly jutting entrance porch sustained, seemingly precariously, on slender diagonal braces. Side entrances were located in the two transept angles, features that, together with the steeply gabled roof with wide eaves, Mould would develop further at the Church of the Holy Trinity. Both the openwork cross within a mandorla above the main doorway and pointed arched openings throughout imparted a vaguely Gothic appearance to the structure. The enchanting jigsaw gem occupied a small shaded churchyard that was bordered by a filigree iron fence, presumably also of Mould's design.

A contemporary account in the *New York World*, written by Manton Marble, a friend of Mould's, tells us that inside, "it is to be richly finished and furnished, and the windows are to be of stained glass of rich colors." Apparently, Elizabeth and other women of the parish had the leading hand here. "The ladies connected with the church have undertaken to raise the necessary amount to furnish the church according to their notions of the beautiful."[50] The interior decoration impressed another reporter writing in the *New York Post* as "in some degree a reflex of nature's coloring, without the crimson, orange, purple and gold, being tastefully introduced in the ornamentation of the apse, pulpit, organ loft, and windows." The writer felt no need to provide more detail than to state that Mould was the architect: "our readers will at once suppose the design and details to be all in excellent taste."[51]

Despite the ongoing war, Mould's career as a designer of expensive houses kept moving forward. "The growth of the city tends now northward along the line of Fifth Avenue," stated Mould's friend William R. Martin, a civic-minded real estate promoter and sometime Central Park commissioner. The street in its lower reaches had long been the address of distinction. Now that it was being constructed along the eastern border of Central Park it extended its reach of wealth northward. "It is the favorite route for driving to the park, and represents the life, gayety and display of the city," observed Martin. "We are now able to take pride in the park as a beautiful place to drive, or to ramble in, at a half hour's distance from our homes. This alone has given a new phase to life in New York." He probably would not have gone so far as to endorse Mould's friend Clarence Cook's proposal that the streets around the park be laid out "either in a series of terraces and crescents, or else a mixture of these with small open squares of the width of a single block, surrounded with low copings of stone, planted with grass and trees, and open at all times to the people."[52] Representing the park as it was seen by the upper crust, Martin, who Mould listed among his important references, asserted that it "will be for autumn and winter what Newport is for the midsummer." For those blessed with fortune, a dwelling along upper Fifth Avenue neighboring the people's park would permit them "to live within the midst of this beauty, to see it on spring mornings from our windows."

The first person to enjoy this view from his home was Runyon W. Martin Jr. Around 1865, Mould designed a brick-and-stone row house at 816 Fifth Avenue, just south of the Sixty-Third Street intersection, for this successful attorney (fig. 72). It was the initial dwelling erected facing the park along the avenue. From the upper windows, Martin could enjoy a panorama of the freshly minted park landscape that Mould was contributing so much of his talent to perfect. A photograph of the house from a real estate brochure of 1869 shows a Giorgio de Chirico–like image of the tall, twenty-three-by-one-hundred-foot sliver of a building standing naked and alone surrounded by eerie emptiness.[53] Like Mould's West Presbyterian Church, the Martin house aggressively asserted its independence from its future neighbors. Clarence Cook called it a "finished jewel-box." The late historian Christopher Gray caught the spirit of the house when he proclaimed it "a High Victorian Gothic sneeze of color, daring contrasts in stripes and blocks."[54]

The remarkable feature of the design was the number and size of the pointed-arch windows that filled the narrow four-story facade, reducing the solid wall surface to a minimum. Indeed, Mould took special care with the construction of the building to insure its stability. "The front wall is nearly three feet thick," reported a contemporary description, "and the projecting stones on this part all balance on the wall, i.e., each stone has more weight on the wall than on the projection." Overall, the walls contained "as many bricks as are usually placed in two houses of the same size."[55] The openings admitted abundant light into the otherwise windowless interior rooms. By the same token, the gawking fenestration capitalized on views of the park across the street. Indeed, in the same sales brochure that depicted the house, the agents published a view of the nascent park from a second floor window of Mr. Martin's house. Mould's spritely High Victorian Gothic façade was a sieve for light and a belvedere for the "new phase of life in New York."

As for the interior of the house, which long ago met the wrecker's ball, we are told that Mould enriched the rooms throughout with various hard woods and invented original designs for even the smallest moldings. Fondness for combining wood materials was a common feature of Mould's interior architecture. He must have learned to do this from his days with Owen Jones, for his English mentor had perfected this mode of decorating.

In the house Mould designed for artist Albert Bierstadt, overlooking

Figure 72. Runyon W. Martin Jr. House, New York, 1865.

the Hudson at Irvington, New York, Mould reached for higher levels of extravagance and display. Bierstadt was at the height of his fame for his large canvasses of Western scenery. "It is said that Bierstadt's brush has earned him $120,000 in the last three years," remarked a Boston newspaper in 1865.[56] He and Frederic Church were the first artists in America to earn a great deal of money from the sale of their paintings. The story goes that one day while on a sketching trip in the Hudson Valley, Bierstadt watched with fascination a hawk soaring overhead that eventually came to rest on a treetop perch high above the river. He determined then and there to choose the site for the location of a summer home. In 1866, he hired Mould, who was surely familiar with seeing Bierstadt drive through Central Park in his elegant carriage drawn by a fine team of horses, to help him erect the multistoried dwelling and studio that he called Malkasten. In the German-born artist's native tongue the name signified "paint box," but it also represented the name of an association of liberal-leaning artists founded in Düsseldorf after the revolution of 1848. Back in 1853, Calvert Vaux, Mould's Central Park colleague, had built the home and studio for Jervis McEntee, Vaux's painter brother-in-law, at Kingston. The

Figure 73. Malkasten, Irvington-on-Hudson, New York, 1866.

unassuming board and batten structure enjoyed a fine view from its hilltop site. For Bierstadt, nothing simple or finely tuned to its setting would do. His was to be a prominent mansion, an architectural statement that would command extensive views of river scenery and accommodate the large, veristic canvasses that he loved to paint and which he sold for high prices (fig. 73).

Malkasten, in the words of Mould's contemporary, the rising writer Martha Lamb, was "a large and substantial house built of rough bluestone gneiss . . . crowned with towers, surrounded with galleries, and adorned with oriel-windows."[57] What most concerned the patron and his architect was exploiting the views that the lofty property afforded. The best prospect was from the west, the direction in which the house faced. An observation tower with a typical Mould peaked dormer surmounted the four-story main elevation. From this crow's nest, one could see from Staten Island on the south to West Point on the north. The flat roof offered yet another place where one might stand, protected by a decorative iron railing, to survey the scenery. One could also commune with nature from the porch that ran around the west, south, and east sides of the ground floor and was repeated, with balcony above, on the second level. A roofless terrace continued the circuit across the north elevation. Overall, Malkasten epitomized the attraction of the "magisterial gaze" that modern art historians have identified as one of the main characteristics of Hudson River School esthetics.

The outstanding feature of the interior was the great studio that occupied the north and east corner of the house. The north side of the studio was a "transparent wall of glass" that Lamb said rendered "a magnificent landscape, a perpetual tributary" to the beauty of the space. Immense glass doors filled the eastern portion of the studio and could be opened so the artist could sketch large animals posted on the lawn that was level with the back of the house. Bierstadt combined the studio with the library to form a tall, seventy-foot-long apartment in which he displayed many of his own paintings together with bric-a-brac he had collected on his travels (fig. 74). A gallery running across one end of this room enabled him "to gain views of his own pictures and to see them as others see them, and are to see them." The artist could discreetly enter this personally reflective cosmos directly from his oriel-windowed attic bedroom. Bierstadt's lavish studio—some likened it to a salesroom for the artist's wares—"may well challenge competition in this country, perhaps in the world," proclaimed Lamb.

Mould's contribution to this vast set piece may have been less than with other clients. Surely his influence could have been felt in the contrasting exterior stonework, in the porches and tower that recall the houses he designed for Thomas Kennard and Thomas Clapham, and in certain interior decorative features, such as the frames made with "mouldings of black walnut and oak" that held Bierstadt's paintings. Lamb and others regarded the dwelling as "the outcropping of the artist-mind of Mr. Bierstadt." Yet, she had high praise for the architect who she called "an artist and architect of singular intelligence, full of the spirit of the present, informed and learned in all the glorious testimony of the past; original in his conceptions, and unprejudiced in his artistic opinions." When fire destroyed the

Figure 74. Malkasten, studio, stereoscopic image.

building in 1882, however, the *New York Times* failed to mention Mould in their coverage and stated that the one-hundred-thousand-dollar edifice "was from plans designed by the artist himself."[58] Mould himself seems to have had misgivings about the value of the project to his career, for Bierstadt's name is absent from the list of references on the handbill that he had printed in 1869.

Perhaps we should not be surprised that in 1870, when Frederic Church determined on erecting his hilltop manor house at Hudson, New York, he turned to Vaux rather than to Mould for architectural assistance. The showmanship of Malkasten surely must have put him off, as well as the bulky, box-like massiveness of the building. (It actually did suggest a gigantic paint box.) Moreover, Church, who knew Mould's work well, preferred to consult his own imagination for Middle Eastern motifs to decorate Olana, the Persian name for treasure house that he chose for his new dwelling. Like his friend Jervis McEntee's cottage, Olana expressed a more nuanced appropriation of the surrounding natural scenery for its "picture" windows than did Bierstadt's ill-fated mansion.

With the war's end, the victorious North began to think about memorializing its many soldiers who died to preserve the Union. Harvard and Yale were among the educational institutions that had sent many to the front in a variety of capacities. In June 1866, Yale asked Mould to submit a design for a memorial college chapel. The following month, Mould submitted to the building committee a design for "a cruciform church" in the "Anglo Italian Gothic" style. In a letter appended to his drawings, Mould stated that he had "endeavored to give an ecclesiastical aspect chiefly to the whole design because its *first* purpose is the worship of God—its *secondary*, the honor of Man."[59]

His building was to be divided into two sections: a memorial "pronaos" formed by the elongation of one of the transept arms and the chapel seating one thousand people (fig. 75). The pronaos was to be "entirely monumental in character, filled with memorial stained glass windows & enclosing a monumental cenotaph of highly decorative architecture, the paneled sides to be surmounted by an emblematic group of statuary—all the inscriptions inlaid in the pavement in this Pronaos & vestibule to be memorial in character & symbolical." A screen divided this area from the

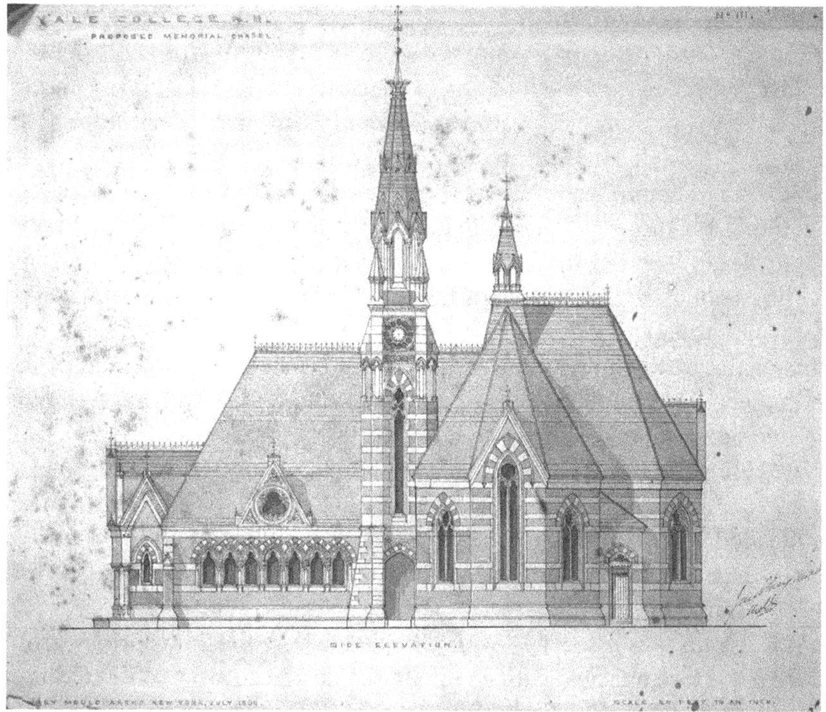

Figure 75. Design for the Yale Memorial Chapel, 1866.

chapel auditorium. The chapel itself would feature a tall open timber ceiling and seat seven hundred on the ground floor with an additional three hundred and fifty persons in galleries. The organ and choir were placed in a loft above the entrance, and sedilia, or raised seats, accommodated faculty in the chancel.

Of the drawings that Mould submitted, the one for the side elevation survives in the Yale University archives. Like Mould's Holy Trinity Church, the multifaceted roof is the most striking feature. A multistage tower resting on a ground level arch punctuates the juncture of the long low horizontal nave or pronaos unit where it meets the vertical chapel and transept. Mould reversed the usual proportions of medieval church architecture, making the chancel space taller than the nave. And once again, he devised an original design for a bell tower, an architectural element that he must have loved but which he rarely succeeded in having constructed.

Mould's description of the masonry he would use to build the memorial chapel revealed his continued devotion to architectural polychromy: "The material is to be Connecticut brown stone Rubble masonry," he said, "with trimmings of the Ohio freestone. Voussoirs of arches of North River Blue Stone & Plinth around the building of Blue Stone—Roof of Purple, red & Green Slate in ornamental patterns." Mould assured the committee that his colorful design could be erected "for the sum at your disposal."

While the committee was still debating the merits of Mould's plans, together with those of other architects who had been invited to submit ideas, Mould, apparently desperate for cash, wrote to ask for part of his promised compensation. Perhaps his anxiety was in reaction to the arrival of Emelie in New York. "Will it be possible by any means to forward me 100$ of the forthcoming $200 in the course of the next 2 or 3 days," he petitioned. "I presume the appropriation has been made whatever course the decision may take." The two hundred dollars was due him no matter what the outcome of the building committee's deliberations. "If 100 can by hook or crook be sent to me it will greatly oblige & accommodate me," he pleaded.[60] Whether or not the committee forwarded him his requested partial fee is not known; however, they ultimately declined to hire him for the job, giving the palm instead to Frederick Clarke Withers.

While Vaux was associated with Olmsted and Withers on various projects, he was also engaged with Mould in the design of two grand buildings associated with Central Park: the Metropolitan Museum of Art and the American Museum of Natural History. Vaux assumed the role of lead architect in both endeavors, with Mould serving as his close associate.

When the Metropolitan Museum was first opened on March 30, 1880, the *New York Times* published an authoritative article recounting for its readers the more than two-decades-long evolution of the institution. The hero of the piece was the former city comptroller (and Olmsted nemesis) Andrew Haswell Green. This avid New Yorker, who wanted to see the city take its place among the cultural capitals of the world, first conceived the idea to create a large public art gallery to be located within Central Park. It was at the time when the park, to which he became devoted, was just getting under way. After many years promoting his notion, Green succeeded in May 1869 in having the state legislature authorize the creation of an art museum in the park and to appropriate money for its construction. By this time the site for the museum and a plan for it had already been developed by Vaux and Mould as architects employed by the Department of Public Parks.

The following year, when the new Tweed city charter took effect and transferred authority over the park from the state to the city, a group of private New Yorkers incorporated themselves as the trustees of the Metropolitan Museum of Art. It would be the primary goal of the trustees to amass a collection and to manage the institution. They also soon came to an agreement forged by Green to have the city construct the museum building. "The Trustees of the Museum, very possibly, might have wished to have had a public competition for the plan of the building," stated the author of the *Times* article, "but the department having fixed on a certain general scheme looking to the future, and having for a great many years before matured their plans, . . . were forced to decline the offer of a competition."

The building that Vaux had planned consisted of a series of galleries surrounding six courts or quadrangles. These units could be built individually over a number of years as funds became available. The trustees insisted, however, that he add a hall for the display of statuary and other objects that might reach as high as fifty feet. The program was said to involve no significant architectural display. "The only portions presenting a finished appearance," observed the *Times* of the new two-story building, "are the fronts that face the courts of the future quadrilateral. These are of granite and brick, in plain, massive style."[61]

From Mould's point of view, the *Times* author's account of the museum's early history generally coincided with his memories of those years. He especially appreciated the acknowledgement of Green, but he felt that his own role had been slighted. To correct the impression, he sent a letter to the editor insisting on his part in the creation of this grand building. He did not dispute Vaux's lead in the development of the design nor his generosity in treating him as an equal. (This had taken place at the time when Mould had his troubles with Emelie.) Nonetheless, he left the impression that his participation, as indispensable as it might have been, was confined to offering valuable suggestions and preparing all the drawings:

> I worked at the drawings in the top room of the Bank of Commerce building in Nassau Street over the then Park Commissioners' office, and many were the quiet hours passed there with Mr. Andrew H. Green, Mr. Vaux, and myself in the discussion and elaboration of the plan—in fact Mr. Green used to come up stairs every half hour he could spare and take interest in the results of my drawing board. . . . I am too proud with my intimate connection with the scheme to allow the fact to pass unnoticed, that not only was the original plan of the complete museum conceived in 1868, but the matured plans,

> elevations and sections made in 1870, accepted by the department, officially signed, and all photographed (there are numerous copies in circulation) were each and severally signed "Calvert Vaux and J. Wrey Mould, Architects," and up to the date of my leaving for Peru [spring 1874] all the plans, details, and working drawings, with the exception of some interior changes, were prepared by my own hands, at my residence, 123 East Twenty-sixth street, in the evening hours, after my daily duties at the Park office were concluded. There Mr. Vaux came to consult with me, and with him Mr. George K. Radford, an engineer of high scientific attainments, to whom we entrusted the constructive portions of the iron-work of the building . . . my professional identity was for many years absorbed and merged in the Central Park that I cannot allow any non-recognition of the above truths to pass current even for a single day. The pecuniary commission on that building as well as on the Museum of Natural History was shared equally with me by Mr. Vaux, who made the last remittances thereof to me in Lima, Peru.[62]

Despite the "plain, massive style" of the building, there was a call for Mould's skills as an ornamentalist. A beautiful drawing signed by Mould in January 1870 for galleries of painting and sculpture exists in the archives of the Department of Public Parks. It envisions future exteriors that were to be lavishly composed of rusticated pink granite piers, banded Florentine arches, and carved figurative rondels (fig. 76). Moreover, the man who was "hell on color" surely gave his advice on the paint scheme for the new galleries: "Colors have been judiciously toned, and with proper reserve," observed the *Times* author, "attention is purposely directed toward the objects exhibited, and not to the building itself." Supports and columns throughout were painted a deep maroon and the floors were laid with tessellated stone. The large double-story hall that the trustees had requested displayed the Cesnola collection of reputed ancient Cypriot statuary. This impressive room was covered by glass skylights supported by semicircular exposed iron arches. Unfurling vines decorated the spandrels and small circles sprinted across the surfaces of the arcs. The frank use of exposed metal suggested a close reading of the theories and practices of Viollet-le-Duc. The rich ornamental treatment of the arches implied Mould's deft hand. Moreover, Mould's reference to George Radford and his later incorporation of similar wide arches in one of his own commissions suggests that this element of design of the statuary hall, now used for the display of medieval armor, may have been due primarily to Mould.

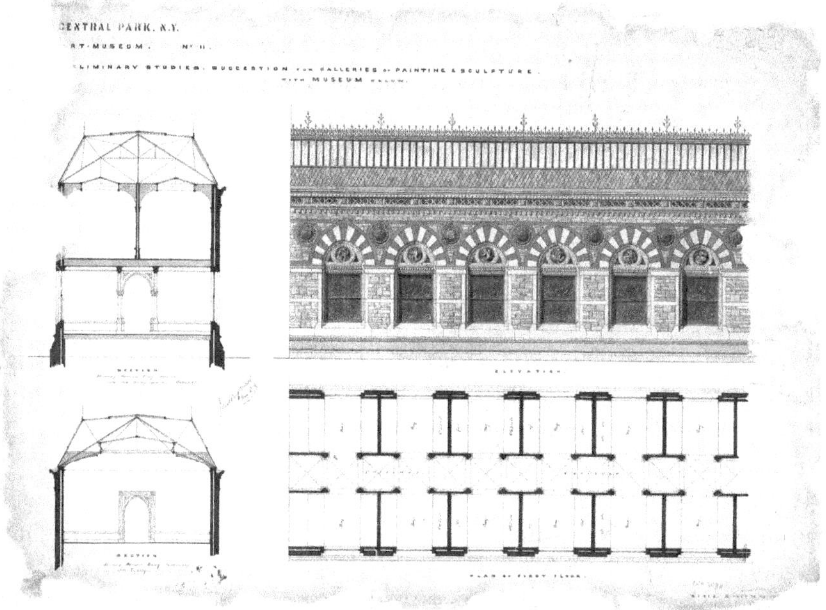

Figure 76. Preliminary study for the Metropolitan Museum of Art, 1870.

Not long before Mould's dismissal from the Department of Public Parks in May 1874, he had the good fortune of being asked by the congregation of the First Presbyterian Church in the small upstate town of Bath, New York, to design a new church for them. The pleasant Cohocton River town in the heart of a prosperous agricultural region enjoyed a comfortable existence as the county seat of Steuben County. The congregation had been contemplating building a new church for several years. Finally, in March, they had raised enough money to establish a building committee with John Davenport as chair. As a member of the leading family of Bath, Davenport and his brother Ira had been the major donors to the new church building fund. Apparently, John, who was president of the board of trustees, had contacted Mould on behalf of the six hundred parishioners. Mould, who must have been eager for work after losing his job with the Department of Public Parks, speedily prepared plans for the replacement of an earlier building that since 1825 had graced the south side of lovely Pulteney Park, the little square that defined the center of Bath.

In August 1874, the local newspaper revealed what the new church would be like. The reporter, who must have had access to Mould's narrative description of his plans, depicted the church substantially as we see it today. For the walls, Mould chose a local stone laid up in rusticated courses enlivened with black and white marble for voussoirs in numerous arched openings. The handsome facade would feature two-eighteen-foot-square towers to either side of a columned vestibule behind which rises the end wall of the nave pierced by a large rose window. (Having a tall tower in the plan must have been a requirement, for the former church was proud to boast the tallest bell tower in the county.)

Inside, the "audience room" measured a comfortable ninety feet long by forty-eight feet wide. Paired lancet windows, Mould said, were "adapted to give an abundance of light as well as a warm, cheerful look to this space, which he proposed to span with the daring device of sweeping round arches resting on stone corbels. Mould's plan would emphasize the pulpit-end of the hall by expanding its dimensions to fifty-two feet wide, raising diagonal ribs into the ceiling, and introducing a grouping of a single large window flanked by two smaller ones. By these means, he attempted to give "the effect of a transept." Externally, this pseudo-transept appeared as a pyramidal roof culminating in a ventilation turret.

One can imagine that older members of the congregation who could remember the former Carpenter Gothic church must have been bewildered to read that the style of their new house of worship embraced "Venetian Gothic, partaking of a somewhat Oriental character, and combining some of the leading features of both the Byzantine and Saracenic architecture."[63] Its exotic flair surely raised the eyebrows of the congregants of nearby St. Thomas Episcopal Church, designed in 1871 by Mould's New York colleague and fellow British immigrant Henry C. Dudley. He had emulated fourteenth-century English parish churches, the architectural model favored by most Anglican and Episcopal clients. The contrast between the designs of the neighboring buildings serves to underscore Montgomery Schuyler's contention that, in spite of Ruskin's widespread influence on architectural theory and taste and the championing by such practitioners as George Edmund Street, Italian Gothic "found little favor with Anglican Gothic Revivalists as a 'churchly' style, either in England or in this country."[64] As the chief protagonist for this style, Mould received, observed Schuyler, commissions for his work mainly from non-Episcopal clergy.

Over the next two years, Mould would send one hundred drawings and plans to Bath for the local builder, Edward Clark, who began to erect the church in August 1874. Many of these plans exist today in the archives of the church, the largest repository we have of such documents for any Mould building outside of Central Park. Working from his home on Twenty-Sixth Street and an office on Union Square, Mould completed and forwarded in the summer of 1874 and early part of 1875 many drawings. These included those showing the dramatic upward progression of roofs (before the towers received their upper stories; fig. 77), the framing of the

Figure 77. First Presbyterian Church, Bath, New York, drawing for front elevation, 1874.

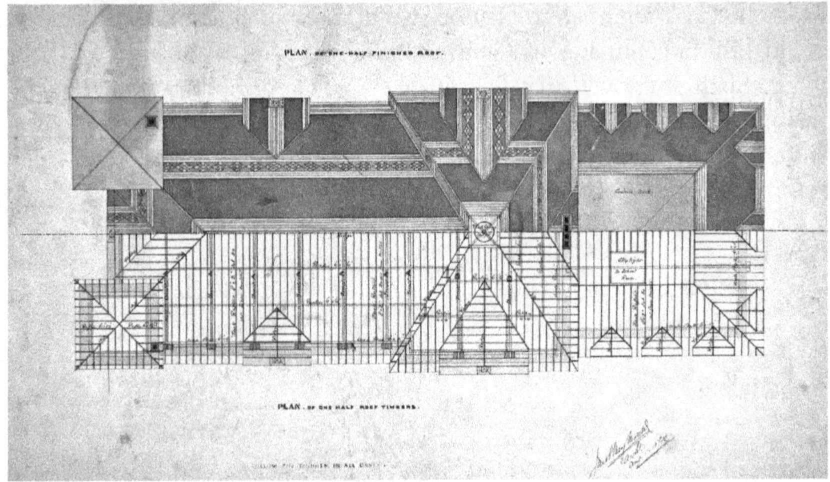

Figure 78. First Presbyterian Church, details for roof, 1874.

roof rafters and their exterior slate covering (fig. 78), the construction of the impressive wooden trusses that span the auditorium, the of mosaic-filled blind arches on the sanctuary wall (plate 12), and the capitals of the porch columns. In October, the Reverend James M. Platt, pastor of the church, laid the cornerstone. After that, Clark took two more years to complete the body of the church. As costs mounted, John and Ira Davenport supplied the bulk of the needed funds.

6.

Greater Expectations

What do you think of that? It came in consequence of all the fuss made last May by the New York papers which were seen by Mr. Henry Meiggs . . . he sent for me.
—Jacob Wrey Mould to John Davenport, February 23, 1875

AFTER THE COMMISSIONERS DISCHARGED Mould from his position with the Department of Public Parks in May 1874, they continued to keep him on the payroll for several months. In the aftermath of the Panic of 1873, he faced a bleak market for his services, and he must have fretted over how he would support himself and Mary Josephine. Jobs for architects were scarce. The severe depression had left the national economy in flux, and building projects in New York went on hold.

On February 23, 1875, Mould told John Davenport in Bath that he had been unable to write recently about the church because his time had been taken up with an extraordinary new venture. "When you turn the page you'll understand," Mould wrote, instructing Davenport: "Now, prepare yourself . . . Brace your nerves And Turn over." On the next page he scrolled: "I am appointed Architect and Engineer in chief to the Board of Public Works of the city of Lima, Peru, at a salary of 10,000$ in gold and all fees paid down of 5,000 gold besides, 1st class passage for my wife and I all expenses paid—500$ gold to lay out and salary starting a week from Sunday. I sail March 13th!" Mould went on to explain that "it came in consequence of all the fuss made last May by the New York papers which were seen by Mr. Henry Meiggs, the great Peruvian . . . & he has sent for me—'rather a horse of another color' from Mr. Andrew H. Green is it not?"[1]

Henry Meiggs was a complex, fascinating individual. To a visionary entrepreneur he wedded political operative, generous philanthropist, lover of music, and extravagant *bon vivant*—a bred-in-the-bone Gilded Age mogul. In the 1870s, he was the most powerful figure in Peru. His biographer, Watt Stewart, called him the "Yankee Pizarro."[2] Born in Catskill, New York, in 1811, he grew up to manage the family's successful lumber business. Eager for a larger stage to exercise his talents, he moved to New York City in the 1830s. There he continued in the lumber business in partnership with his brother-in-law. Meiggs soon achieved considerable financial success and developed a taste for high living.

Ever restless for greater challenges, Meiggs set his sights on California during the gold rush years. San Francisco, until then a small village, was poised to grow quickly into a major city. He foresaw a highly profitable market for cut lumber. A vast amount of timber grew in California, but finished lumber was almost unavailable. In 1849, he sailed to San Francisco with a shipload of construction-ready wood. A large profit from the sale of the cargo provided him with capital to launch the California Lumber Company. Exploiting the sequoia and other forests brought Meiggs yet greater wealth. With a filled wallet, he became active in many areas of public life, giving magnanimously to charities and the performing arts and assuming a leadership role in civic affairs as a powerful member of the city council.

Seizing the opportunity to buy cheap land in North Beach, with its potential for a ship anchorage, Meiggs plunged into city development. He used his position on the council to get several streets built from the business center of town to connect to the port area. He anticipated that property values would increase quickly and borrowed heavily to augment his investment. Circumstances, however, failed to bear out his optimism. A decline in real estate values occurred following the Panic of 1853. The next year, Meiggs declared bankruptcy. When it became impossible for him to raise cash from investors, Meiggs turned to illegal practices. Taking advantage of his access to the city's pre-signed books of blank promissory notes, he proceeded to fill in his name and the amounts needed. Since, as an alderman, he had used these forms of payment legitimately in the past, no one questioned these documents. Nobody suspected that this generous and delightful man, often called "Honest Harry," was a financial sham. When business failed to revive, he was so heavily in debt that it became impossible for him to repay his obligations. Late in September 1854, Meiggs made the decision to flee California and his creditors. Taking ship with his wife and three children and his brother John, he sailed for Chile. Meiggs's default caused many businesses to temporarily suspend operations, and angry mobs of creditors searched the streets for "Honest Harry."

In Chile, Meiggs's fortunes made an astonishing rebound. In April 1859, the *New York Times* reported:

> Henry Meiggs, the famous forger, whose performances made a great stir in San Francisco four years ago, is now the most successful financier in Chile. He is reported to be worth already some two million dollars. . . . He lives with his family, in very good style, in a French Hotel at Santiago. . . . He has obtained a contract from the Government for constructing the first section of a railroad from Santiago to Talca about two hundred and twenty miles, and it is almost certain that Meiggs will have the contract for building the entire line.[3]

Meiggs's remarkable success was due both to his audacity and to his genuine concern for people. Don Enrique, as he was now called, understood the local customs and respected them, and his generous nature gained him the trust of the huge work force he had assembled. The men repaid him by willingly undertaking dangerous tasks and fulfilling them on deadline.

Meanwhile, Meiggs had developed an interest in building a railroad from the coast of Peru across the Andes to Arequipa, Peru's second largest city. He had made a proposal as early as 1863, but nothing came of it. With a revolutionary change in government in Peru in 1867, however, the scene was set to welcome Meiggs. The new president, Jose Balta, believed the nation's growth could be achieved through foreign financed public investments. In 1869, the Balta government canceled its contracts with local capitalists for guano fertilizer, Peru's most important export commodity, and signed an exclusive financial arrangement with the Dreyfus bank of France. In return for its monopoly on the European guano trade, Dreyfus agreed to assume the servicing of Peru's foreign debt and to advance substantial new loans. Balta began to spend abundantly on public works. His most ambitious project was the construction of railroads between the nation's coastal ports and inland precious metal mines. He turned to Henry Meiggs to build these pioneering railways. Boasting that he could build a railway anywhere a llama could tread, Meiggs proposed building six Peruvian lines. Soon, he was at work on tracks that linked Callao, the port of Lima, with the Andean mining town of La Oroya (aka Oroya), a line sometimes called the "railway in the clouds."

As Meiggs became indispensable to the Peruvian government, he also assumed a major role in Lima, where he came to live, and which he genuinely hoped to transform into a modern metropolis. He dreamed of turning Lima from a hodge-podge of dusty hovels into a capital as splendid as any in the Old World. Already, just before Mould had arrived, Meiggs had leveled the walls that had hemmed in the city since the seventeenth century. In their place, he projected a tree-lined boulevard. It was in the area west of central Lima that he foresaw the city would grow, joining the historic capital—Pizarro's City of Kings—to Callao, the port on the Pacific some seven miles away. It was near here that Meiggs lived in splendor on a country estate called Villegas. From his elaborate villa, which was often the scene of lavish entertainments, Meiggs enjoyed a panoramic view of the harbor at Callao at one extreme and the Andes at the other. Meiggs, whose reputation for myriad adulterous liaisons was probably exaggerated, was a product of his age, a man of great vitality who made no little plans but created schemes that stirred men's souls. Mould, who was drawn to men like this throughout his life, believed that he was to have a major role in implementing Meiggs's ambitious plans for Lima's new buildings, parks, and boulevards. Probably with full knowledge of the high-powered character of his sponsor, Mould, at age fifty, set out to Lima eager for new possibilities. It was into an environment of wealth, privilege, and sharp dealings that in April 1875, Mould entered, armed with an initial contract to work for two years with Meiggs's Office of Public Works.

Mould could have read about his new home in the pages of Alexander von Humboldt's *Cosmos*, which the great geographer published in installments from 1845 to 1862, based on his voyages in South America from 1799 to 1804, as well as in Charles Darwin's *Voyage of the Beagle* (1839). In 1873, just two years before Mould moved to Lima, James Orton, professor of natural history at Vassar College who many regarded as a another von Humboldt, made his second journey through South America. While he regarded most towns of northern Peru as nothing more than "vast pig-sties containing human habitations," he found Lima outstripped his expectations and "justified the sobriquet of 'Little Paris.'"[4] "Lima is beautiful from the sea," wrote Orton, as he approached by steamer, the way Mould and Mary Josephine would arrive two years later. "Its stately domes and spires rise out of the plain only seven miles from the ocean . . . and just behind the city the glorious Andes ascend abruptly to the sky, while in the foreground are busy Callao and gay Chorrillos."[5] The population of 160,00 was made up of people from all over the world. "Probably no other city in the world, not even Constantinople, can present such a variety of physiognomy and complexion," observed Orton. "Limenians of the upper class are educated, refined, courteous," and English was nearly as prevalent as Spanish. "The ladies," reported Orton, "no longer shrouded, now promenade with open faces; the *manto*, or veil, is worn simply as a head-dress."

The heart of the city that honored its founder, the brutal conquistador Francesco Pizarro, and its liberator from colonial rule, Simón Bolivar, was the Grand Plaza. This five-hundred-foot-square open space was overlooked on the east by the great Baroque cathedral, the towers of which, Orton stated, were built of "wicker-work" (a building technique known locally as *quincha*) so they could sway during earthquakes, which were frequent. On the north side of the square stood the large Government Palace. The other two sides were shaded by arcades that were filled with shops. "At evening, the crowd of every rank and fashion loitering in the illuminated arcades, the band playing on the cathedral steps, and the fine turn-outs, equal to those of Central Park, dashing around the Plaza, make up a very attractive scene," reported Orton. Also worthy of a visit, said Orton, was the unusually long bridge that spanned the Rimac River that ran through the city. The 530-foot span had survived over two hundred and fifty years of earthquakes.

As for domestic architecture, most of the city's dwellings were made of adobe, had flat roofs, and were divided into rooms by walls of plastered cane. The steady mild and dry climate dispensed with the need for hearths and chimneys; "the sun is the fire-place of Peru," said Orton. (When Orton's friend Charles Darwin spent six wintertime weeks in Lima in the 1830s, he found otherwise; Darwin despaired of the thick drizzle the locals dismissed as "Peruvian dew.")

Shortly after arriving in Lima, Mould wrote to John Davenport on stationery of the office of the architect-in-chief of Meiggs's Compania De Obras Publicas y Fomento Del Peru, describing his trip from New York. Approaching the city from the sea, Mould was "totally unprepared" for the sight of the Peruvian mainland. "The coast is totally destitute of verdure on the mountains," he told Davenport, "without a tree or blade of grass—& the appearance is desolate & awful in the extreme."[6] After a journey of twenty-four days—eight days on the Atlantic, eight days crossing Panama, and eight days on the Pacific—the Moulds disembarked at Lima at 7:30 PM on April 12. Two days later, Meiggs took them with his family on a ride on the spectacular Oroya rail line. A description of the route published at the time calls it "among the most daring achievements of modern engineering." One can easily imagine on the journey Meiggs employing words similar to these of a biographer to explain the extraordinary railroad that connected the port at Callao on the Pacific with the headwaters of Atlantic navigation at Oroya:

> The height ascended by this road is within 136 feet of that of the summit of Mont Blanc. The road bends upon itself with sharp angles as it ascends the mountains and pierces the obstructing peaks with thirty-two tunnels, which often come together so closely that they seem continuous to the traveler. Great gorges had to be traversed and torrent streams spanned by bridges that seem to hang in midair. In several places the mountain-sides were so precipitous that the workmen could only reach the point at which a tunnel started by being let down with ropes from the edge of the cliff and held there until they had cut for themselves a foot-hold in the rock. . . . One of the bridges over a chasm 2000 feet deep, leads to a tunnel at either end. The difficulties of the work were increased by the necessity of transporting all the implements, materials, and workmen to these almost inaccessible heights.[7]

Where they stayed that night, at two in the morning, an earthquake rudely jolted them awake. "It is not a pleasant sensation, I assure you," Mould declared. (Lima itself was known to experience over forty shocks every year.) Nor did he enjoy later in the week being taken to a bullfight. He and Mary Josephine set up house in a large, rented second floor flat or "alto." Socially, the Moulds were quickly accepted into local society, which included many expatriates from the United States and Europe. Soon after their arrival, the Moulds began to receive invitations. "We have been twice to drink and hear the band at Chorrillos—the watering place where all the fashionables are," he told Olmsted.[8] One of the people they met was, Heinrich Witt, a well-liked German businessperson who was a fixture in the Peruvian financial world. He would become a patron of Mould's.

From letters Mould wrote to Davenport and Olmsted, we can piece together his general impressions of the city.[9] He found himself in a place where few people had heard of Owen Jones, read Ruskin, or followed the *New Path*. "I seem to have come to the Antipodes!" he exclaimed to Olmsted. "Everything is so utterly and totally unlike all I have been accustomed to all my life—these narrow streets, these two-story houses, these projecting balconies, . . . the whole backed by that mighty Cordilleras with their harmonious outlines, wonderful effects of aerial perspective, & utter bareness & desolation—without a blade of grass or a tree on their slopes—together with the incredible climate—completely bewilders me."[10]

As to local architecture, almost all of Lima's buildings were made from "horrible yellow adobe," said Mould, and in a style unsuited to his taste.[11] "The innumerable churches, with their everlasting ding-dong, &

impossible architectural details," he said, "[displayed] every vice intensified of the worst period of the Renaissance." A single afternoon touring architecture in Lima, suggested Mould, would "bring down the gray hairs of John Ruskin in sorrow to the grave."[12] Both he and Mary Josephine lamented the oppressive sway the church held over the general population, which was poor and uneducated. "Woe be to the US if ever she gets into the clutches of the Priesthood," Mould, the Anglican, declared to his Presbyterian client John Davenport. "My wife who is a Catholic is horrified and disgusted by what she sees here—Keep to your Bible and free public schools and freedom of thought and speech everywhere or god help you!" Moreover, Mary Josephine missed her walks in Central Park. "If you go beyond the city limits you are swollen with dust and devoured by sand flies—besides ladies are cooped up, and if they go into the streets [they are] muffled up in Mantillas like wives at a funeral." [13]

On the other hand, Mould generally took delight in the climate. Steady trade winds brought fresh, cool air every day into town, keeping the temperature at around seventy degrees. A lover of fresh air—he constantly had a window open at his New York office—Mould found the trade wind "deliciously cool." The weather was also agreeably predictable, something unknown to him in London or New York. The trade wind, he said, "sets in steadily as a clock from the SW every afternoon & together with the 'Humboldt current' from the Straits of Magellan forms the wonderfully temperate & enjoyable climate of Peru. Go into the sun, & that luminary immediately infuses you with one unforgettable fact. *13.3′ from the Equator*—go into the shade, & you are cool at once."[14] In the summer month of February, fresh fruits were abundant and flowers bloomed profusely, but every night was cool enough to require a blanket. He and Mary Josephine, however, would find the winter months of June and July less enticing. "We are shivering here," he wrote to Davenport, "a fireplace in Lima does not exist," Echoing Darwin, Mould complained "it is a cold Scotch mist for 4 months."[15]

Mould held a low opinion of how successive Spanish governments, royal and republican, had managed, or, in his opinion, mismanaged the country's fabulous resources. "No doubt Peru in the hands of the Anglo-Saxon race, could be the richest country on Earth," he told John Davenport, "as it is, it is the poorest—what a climate, every day in the year a working day, no frost, no rain, the oak & cocoa . . . side by side. Sugar & wheat, maize & clover, gold, silver, coffee, iron & coal in abundance & across the Cordillera, the richest & finest hinter land in the world!! O, that Henry VII had not been so mean, but given Columbus the means, & this would now be a

Southern U.S."[16] Mould told Meiggs, Peru was "a most delightful country to work in, but a poor one to play in."[17]

His new employer saw to it that his new architect was comfortably installed in his working quarters, which he rented from Heinrich Witt. At 92–94 Calle de Zarate, Mould's spacious private office opened onto a patio that was filled with tropical plants. He had "every convenience even luxury placed at my disposal in the office," said Mould; "such rolls of paper, piles of colors and brushes—lashings of pencils, instruments and materials all in 1st class English style." Moreover, Meiggs had already paid him one thousand dollars and reimbursed all of his travel expenses. "Rather a contrast to the two penny halfpenny way in which the D.P.P. is being managed," Mould told Olmsted.[18] He also proudly informed Olmsted that in Peru, professional men like himself enjoyed a high degree of respect.

Despite the enviable position Mould found himself in, after years in London and New York, he clearly held reservations about living in provincial Lima. To Olmsted and Davenport, he forthrightly admitted his longing for New York. He told Olmsted that, "As far as I can see . . . when I achieve a moderate independence, I shall return to New York and would rather have 5000$ there than 20,000$ here and whenever she chooses to give me a decent reliable proposal and proper appreciation, I am ready to return to her service."[19]

Misgivings aside, Mould believed that the Lima he had come to was a most promising place for an architect. For real estate developer William R. Martin's benefit, especially, he wrote: "When I see the enterprises contemplated here in this city of 160,000—the joinder of Lima & Callao & 7 miles of city to be built, I blush for the stagnation & political state of coma into which poor New York has drifted."[20] Mould had a two-year contract with Meiggs, starting March 10, 1875. Contingent on Peru soon recovering its credit after a disastrous financial crisis, Mould saw "work in preparation for [himself] which no 2 years or 10 years or 12 years can complete." Projects that occupied Mould's attention in Lima included a large dwelling for Edward Dubois, a mausoleum in the main cemetery for Heinrich Witt, and a masonic lodge in Callao. In addition, he talked of building large workshops for Meiggs's company; of constructing "a structure of 'adobe' being a 'Callejon' or residences for some 40 working men and their families, with a foreman's house at the end"; of being asked to design a theater; and of preparing plans "to lay out a new part of the city on towards Callao . . . projected ultimately to join Lima & Callao." To Olmsted he confided the possibility of building a public park. "There is nothing I can't grow," he told Olmsted, "Palms, Bananas, Coconut . . . they have them in profusion—then for water effects I have the Rimac," the river that flows from the Andes through Lima to Callao.[21] The stage was set for this improbable turn in Mould's affairs to begin.

One of the initial buildings that Mould designed in Lima was the new quarters for Peru's oldest Masonic organization, the Cruz Astral lodge in Callao (fig. 79). Meiggs supported the erection of the new Scottish Rite temple that rested on foundation stones imported from Scotland. The historic temple still stands at Pedro Ruiz Gallo 240. An article in the *South Pacific Times*, a newspaper published by the expatriate British community of Lima and later translated into Spanish by another local publication, noted that the temple was the first building erected by Meiggs's Compania de la Obrus Publicas. The *South Pacific Times* writer stressed its importance as the first example of its style of architecture in Peru; it was, he pointed out, the sort of building one might find in London or New York. Located across the street from the Municipal Theater that had opened in 1860, Mould's revelatory design, which he supervised during construction until it was completed in December 1877, must have attracted much attention from the cultural *cognizante* of the day.

Although somewhat altered and garishly painted, the small Masonic temple still reveals the major elements of Mould's design. The two-story symmetrical facade features a wide central entrance with small office rooms to either side. Mould added drama to the façade with a balcony, a traditional element of Lima's architecture, on the second floor fronting a deeply recessed bay with two windows. Ornament is modest by High Victorian standards, and consists of an iron entrance gate, incised designs in the flat lintels over the windows and arrowroot plants rising from the ground on either side of the central entrance. The *South Pacific Times* critic singled out for special mention the planarity of the design, which, in a region that had little rainfall, prevented the accumulation of dust on the façade's decorative components.[22] Until a few years ago, the members of Cruz Astral lodge continued to meet in the second floor skylighted assembly room that was the heart of the building.

Mould's first private client in Peru other than Meiggs was Edward C. Dubois. Originally from Poughkeepsie, New York, Dubois pursued a successful international career as a railroad engineer. He played a major role in the design of lines in Mexico, Panama, and Columbia before becoming associated with Meiggs in his Chilean enterprises. There, Dubois earned Meiggs's enduring trust, and when Meiggs came to Peru, Dubois came with him. (It was said that together with American-educated superintendents, almost everything Meiggs used on his railroads came from the

Figure 79. Cruz Astral Masonic Lodge, Callao, 1877.

United States, including Troy cars, New Jersey locomotives, and Ames shovels.)

Dubois participated in Don Enrique's audacious railroad building projects and invested heavily in Peruvian silver mines. In 1873, he married Manuela Emilia González de Orbegoso, the European-educated daughter of a former president of Peru and the sister of the wife of Auguste Dreyfus, the French financier who, with his brothers, established the Dreyfus Frères bank in Peru. In 1869, Auguste had signed the so-called Dreyfus Contract that gave the Parisian bank the monopoly on the sale of guano fertilizer. Eventually, Dubois himself became the agent for the Dreyfus bank in Lima. Fortune smiled many times on Edward Dubois. Mould himself reported that the year of his arrival in Peru the Dubois family had "just found a silver vein worth $1000 a ton, and the vein is growing richer as they dig deeper. A great tunnel is to be built to drain the celebrated 'Cerros de Pessos' mine, 1000 feet in length, according to a plan now being prepared, proposed by Trevithick in 1795, who estimated the value, from what was visible of the mine, at about $130,000,000."[23] Money would be no object when Edward Dubois came to build his mansion. What a splendid concurrence of circumstances for Mould that he was there in Lima available to be architect to another fabulously wealthy client. To Olmsted he boasted: "I have already got settled to work in earnest. My first job is to be a . . . house, 200 feet × 60 feet (3 stories) for a Poughkeepsian (a Sr Dubois) who has married into a wealthy Peruvian family. They are extremely *rich* & will *go* it."[24]

The enormous Casa Dubois (aka Casa de Piedra) is unlike any dwelling that Mould had yet designed (fig. 80). It stands much diminished in the heart of Lima on the Jiron de la Union at the corner of Jiron Maquegua. The once proud and distinguished edifice is partially empty, its subtle maquillage is covered by garish paint, and it suffers sundry crass indignities at the hands of contemporary commerce. Moreover, it is shorn of its original mansard roof—as if the city had taken offence against such an insult to its level skyline (fig. 81). Nonetheless, one can still appreciate the building's exceptional beauty, and the architect's plans have survived to give us a better account of its original appearance than does the actual building.

Despite their wealth, the Dubois family felt comfortable living in a building that along with gracious domestic life provided space for commerce. The ground floor consists of a series of segmental arched spaces intended to house shops. Two stout polished granite columns frame the entrance that leads to the interior court or patio. The taller second story

Figure 80. Casa Dubois, Lima, 1875.

accommodated the family's private living quarters. Faced with brick laid in panels, this *piano nobile* consists of a series of large windows framed by Florentine banded arches that impart a festive gaiety to the building. (One wonders if Mould told Dubois that these arches were up-to-date cousins to those that he had left behind on the plan that he and Vaux had developed for the as yet unbuilt Metropolitan Museum of Art or if he mentioned that the thin iron balustrades under the windows imitated the railing he had designed for the Graywacke Arch in Central Park.) The major feature of the 210-foot-long façade is the sumptuously detailed iron balcony (fig. 82). A masterwork of filigree ornament, the triple arch design suggests the triumphal arch motif that often drew attention to the entrance of Peruvian Baroque churches. The elaborate construction, which highlights the main salon, may be a later addition, for it does not appear on Mould's elevation drawing. Nonetheless, it bears all the elements of his style, and surely is from his hand.

Mould maintained that the Casa Dubois was the first true masonry building in Lima. Instead of adobe, the walls consisted of red Philadelphia face brick and "artificial Frear stone," a precast concrete building material. When asked how he obtained the materials for such a revolutionary construction, he replied that he got them "where the Dutch got the first

Figure 81. Casa Dubois, ca. 1915.

houses in New York. We imported the house piecemeal. The brick and cement for the stone came from New York. The Granite is the red granite from Scotland. It was the cheapest and surer way to import rather than attempt to quarry."[25] Mould must also have sent his designs for the ironwork of the main balcony and the windows to the United States for manufacture, as he did for another commission in Lima.[26]

In a short time—and perhaps at the insistence of his client's wife, who came from a distinguished Peruvian family—Mould had taken a sweeping architectural history lesson and succeeded in understanding the chief elements of traditional large houses in Lima. "I have added to my stock

Figure 82. Casa Dubois, iron balcony.

of experience some of the strange architectural conceits and vagaries to be found in Lima 'of the Kings,'" he later admitted.[27] In his design for the Casa Dubois, the interior patio, ground floor shops, and second floor private rooms, all conformed to longtime local usage. But the most remarkable feature of the building was out of sight. For the fabrication of the walls, Mould reinterpreted the earthquake-resistant method of construction used by the Incas and adopted by the Spanish colonial builders. Known as quincha, this vernacular way of building employed wood and mud—wattle and daub—that endowed the walls with a certain flexibility allowing them to move during a tremor. Mould's drawings reveal the wooden framing and cross-bracing system (that resembled a balloon frame construction) that he used (fig. 83).

Visitors to the Dubois first entered the building into the spacious patio

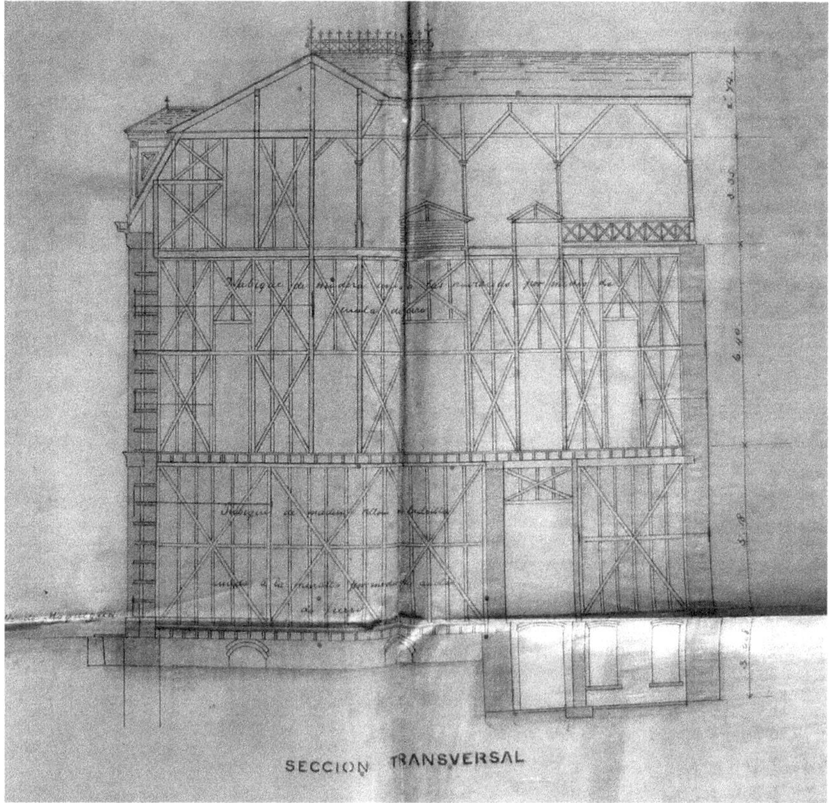

Figure 83. Casa Dubois, Mould's drawing for the side elevation, transversal section.

or courtyard (fig. 84). Mould made this refuge from the work-a-day world opulent with banded arches and colorful tiles (plate 13). Large landing windows and a skylight bathed the scene in gentle light and widely spaced, vertiginous columns on the second level imparted a sense of loftiness to the grand floor above. If Mould's old mentor, Lewis Vulliamy, had been able to visit this magnificent patio, he would have been pleased to see how much his youthful assistant remembered of the famous stairway in London's Dorchester House. Like that impressive foyer that Robert Holford proudly mounted and descended, Mould's Casa Dubois patio drew natural light from above and was encompassed by a spacious gallery supported on coupled columns. When Mould once again saw Vaux and Frederic Church, he could have told them that, in Lima, he had outdone even their gorgeous staircase at Olana, the artist's Hudson Valley mansion.

Mould's imposing stairway once conveyed visitors in proper splendor to

Figure 84. Casa Dubois, interior patio, ca. 1915.

the second level of the house where the Dubois received them in luxuriously decorated quarters. These included a large central living room, dining room, library, and billiard room. Sadly, most of the original decoration of the rooms has disappeared, for after the 1930s, the building changed hands and uses a number of times. We have, however, an evocative description of their former beauty by Etoile Castillo, a painter and writer on art well known in early twentieth-century Peru. In 1915, Castillo visited the house, which was still in private hands, and furnished the journal *Variedades* with an account of the experience. "Transported through the entrance gate," remembered Castillo, "the first impression we received, when we were in the patio, bears a similarity to the one that we feel in our colonial cloisters, something of cold, sad asceticism; but soon the sensation of the rich, fine, worldly and aristocratic prevails before the wide grand stairs encrusted with enamels, the massive, opulent railing, the wide, sonorous galleries, the slender iron columns which, support the sumptuous coffered ceiling, the immense crown of the frieze through which the splendid light of heaven spills. . . . This house does not seem to be made of stone but of crystals.[28] Some areas of the "encrusted enamels" remain, an enduring testament to Mould's passage in Lima.

Armed with knowledge of Lima's past, Mould substituted for the ubiquitous late Baroque style he disliked forms and details drawn from his vocabulary of High Victorian Gothic design. The five-hundred-thousand-dollar mansion was, Mould said, "not ornamented with every inartistic abomination and sham known to South American builders."[29] In essence, with the Casa Dubois, he repeated what he had done with All Souls in New York: brought a new language of architectural design to his adopted city. "It is the only house in Lima that I know of that is worth speaking of as a piece of architecture," Mould proudly proclaimed.[30]

Unlike All Souls Church in New York, the magnificent Casa Dubois—which he would never see completed, for he left it unfinished at the time of his departure from Lima in the summer of 1879—failed to spark a significant change in local architectural attitudes. Yet, modern affection for this local monument remains ardent. Mould would be pleased to read the praise afforded his remarkable building by authors of a modern architectural guidebook: "Although nowadays many of the original materials have been painted over and the merits of the house have been diminished, it still remains an exceptional work due to the consistency and quality of its architecture and execution."[31]

One of those who surely admired it was the German expatriate businessman, Heinrich Witt. Witt had lived in Lima since the 1820s and kept a detailed diary of his many and varied doings. On September 4, 1876, he wrote that "at 8 o'clock Mr. Mould, the architect in the Compania de Obras Publicas y Fomento del Peru, walked out with me to the pantheon [in the Cementerio Presbítero Maestro], where we met Enrique [presumably Henry Meiggs], Ricardo, and the administrator of the cemetery. Jointly we chose a spot six varas long [approximately seventeen feet], and

Figure 85. Mausoleum of Heinrich Witt, 1876–1878.

six broad, where I intended to have a chapel constructed, containing inside an altar, and two sarcophagi, into one of which the coffin containing the mortal remains of my dear wife was to be deposited." On December 19, Mould, Meiggs, and three assistants went to the cemetery to measure the plot and begin laying the mausoleum foundations.

After numerous delays—including Peruvian financial troubles and a prolonged wait for the arrival of the bronze doors from the United States—Mould completed the tomb at site 391 in the fall of 1878 (fig. 85). The Florentine arch with which Mould dignified the entrance was characteristic of his architecture but would have been new to the eyes of his client and others who visited the vast city of the dead. It seems likely that he derived the design for the compact freestanding structure from the impressive stone dormers that he and Vaux had included in their

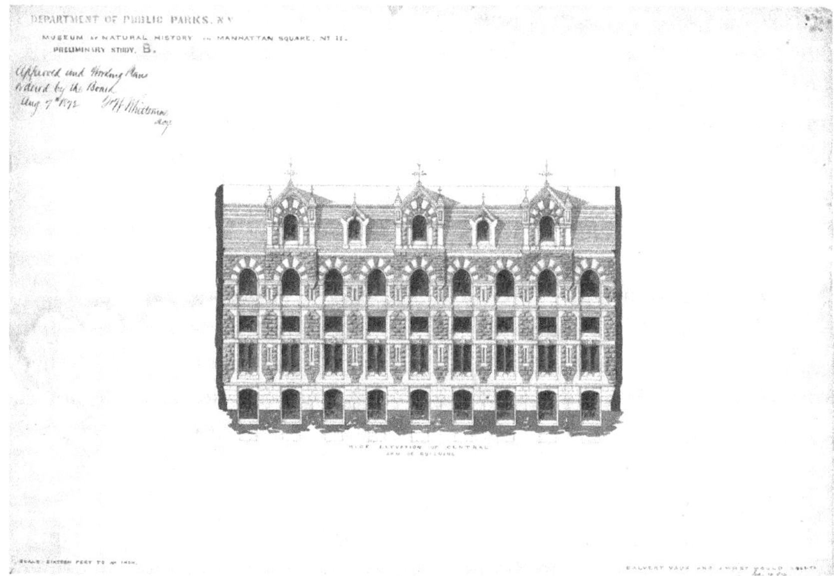

Figure 86. Calvert Vaux and Jacob Wrey Mould: Museum of Natural History, elevation drawing for central section, 1872.

1872 design for the central portion of the American Museum of Natural History in New York (fig. 86). Mould's 1865 proposal for a gatekeeper's house in Central Park may also have been in his mind when he took up the challenge of designing this unique example in his career of a mortuary building. On October 1, 1878, Witt supervised the transfer of his wife's remains from the niche where they had been kept since her death in May 1876. "It was a melancholy duty which we had to perform," he wrote, "but nevertheless I was glad that we had decided upon building this chapel with its two sarcophagi."[32] In November 1892, bearers conveyed Witt's own coffin through the Italian Gothic chapel doorway to join that of his beloved Enriqueta in eternal rest.

Mould spent a considerable amount of time in Lima concluding his commission for the First Presbyterian Church back in Upstate New York. He soon found that postal service between Bath and "this out of the way place"

was slow, expensive, and unreliable.[33] A series of letters, mostly to John Davenport, reveal the difficulties he had in transmitting drawings and receiving information on the progress of the work. At times, he had thought items he had sent had gotten lost because he had had no word of their reception. It could take a month for his correspondence to reach Bath and sometimes longer for Davenport's to reach him. He would usually forward items through Bryce Grace & Co. of Callao, unless he knew someone personally who was going to the United States who would carry material for mailing there. To save money on mailing costs, Mould told Davenport that he would make all his drawings on lightweight tracing paper rather than on the usual more durable cloth. He instructed his client that once he had gotten the paper documents to "please have some good flour paste made & paste it carefully on muslin—tack the muslin out *taut* after wetting—then paste on your tracing & leave a day—keep in a dry place—follow same rule with all details I shall send from Peru."[34]

The correspondence also provides a glimpse of Mould's working methods and how he dealt with clients. The month after his arrival in Lima, he promised to send Davenport details for the eave cornices, iron finials, plaster cornices, and the pulpit as soon as he could get the drawings made. Once he received word back from Davenport that he approved of the designs, Mould promised to "prepare all the drawings together [with] details & all, & send in a bunch." In any event, he was delayed in finishing the preliminary drawings because, he later wrote, he had only obtained "a drawing board in my private office" in early June. By October, 1875, Mould was readying further details, including designs for door hinges, plaster cornices, and finials (plate 14). With these, he enclosed written instructions for the woodwork, celling, and walls. He also told Davenport that he had made the first study for the taller façade tower (which he would refer to simply as "the tower"), but as yet he had "not satisfied myself upon" its design.

His letter also addressed the matters of lighting and stained glass. For the former, he included a sketch showing how he wished the stone corbels that supported the roof trusses to have tiny gas jets for nighttime illumination. Gas lamps would also be suspended from the corbels, he said. Mould had already written to his friend Vance of Mitchell, Vance & Co. in New York, telling him to send Davenport photographs of suitable fixtures. The firm, he said, had the only "factory ones for a gothic church." Moreover, Mould proposed "to suspend from under the center of the intersection [of the] nave & Transept" one of Mitchell, Vance's Corona Lights—hanging level with the lights on the corbel brackets. For the stained glass windows, Mould told his client to deal with Henry E. Sharp in New York and to order the glass from England. Mould was of the firm opinion that no good stained glass could be secured in America. He recommended that Davenport be in touch with Frederick Withers for the address of the London firm that had made windows for Withers's St. Luke's Episcopal Church in Beacon, New York.[35]

In January 1876, with no news from Bath for over two months, Mould fired off an anxious letter to Davenport telling him, "I am getting alarmed—everything save the Front Screen & Pulpit has gone up to you—all the particulars of the Stained Glass windows—& I have not had a word from you . . . I hope nothing is wrong."[36] A month later, he sent a list of nine drawings he had forwarded for various details because he still had not heard if they had been received. In April, he requested "a clear, systematic list of all the dgs [drawings] received with numbers, to compare with my book here." With much relief, he wrote in May to Davenport, "I only received yours the other day—& until then knew whether or not all the plans I had sent reached you—or miscarried!! Especially the last lot in December 1875." He also informed him because of the press of other business, "the study for the Spire must wait till June 21st & then you must approve it & let me know before I get out wkg dgs."[37]

It was not until July 21, 1876, that Mould sent the last drawings for the body of the church and promised to forward shortly the design for the tower. Now, he said, it was time to go into "a little Arithmetic," to calculate his three-and-three-quarter-percent commission.[38] The tower design, however, still waited to be concluded. On September 20, after Davenport approved his scheme, Mould wrote that he was progressing with his study for the spire that he felt "looks to promise well." He assured his client that "you will be able to make a . . . start on Tower in 1877 & receive all Plans before Ice heals up." By then, he had submitted over one hundred drawings to Bath which led him to reiterate his request for payment, being careful to stipulate his commission would not include "the balance of Tower & Spire in anyway."

On the evening of February 22, 1877, "a large congregation assembled to look upon the handsomest church rooms to be found in this part of the state," reported a local newspaper of the ceremony marking the opening of the church for worship (fig. 87). "It is large, airy and roomy, without pillars or obstructions, making it one of the very best arranged rooms for oratorical effect," observed the writer (fig. 88). Moreover, the journalist asserted that when "the towers are complete, hardly a church in Western New York will be found to surpass the new church in real architectural beauty and design." Sensing the Orientalism in the look of the

Figure 87. First Presbyterian Church, 1874–1878.

Figure 88. First Presbyterian Church, interior.

new building, a correspondent for the *Steuben Courier* evoked *The Book of One Thousand and One Nights*. He cast Mould as a magical genius. "Aladdin in his supposed day and generation could scarce excel" the present building, he asserted. Nor could the writer help but reflect upon how different Mould's creation was from its predecessor. "This day," remarked the *Courier* reviewer, "the beholder stood within the grand building which has sprung up from the seed of its respectable ancestor—the old white church. What a wondrous change! . . . Yesterday the ancient style building, prim and puritanical! Today, the magnificent structure embellished by all the touches of tasteful art."[39]

Presumably, Davenport met the architect's deadline for payment for his services on October 15. Mould's total stipend was $1,613.50. And there would be more work to be done in the future. Earlier in the year, Mould had admonished Davenport, "Do not *think* or *dream* of interior decoration for 4 or 5 years to come, when I may be back in the U.S. to attend to it."[40] Despite all the difficulties Mould experienced working long distance, he succeeded in making Bath's First Presbyterian Church one of his finest works.

The First Presbyterian Church bears witness to predecessors in Mould's career. To a significant degree, the West Presbyterian Church survives in the façade of the Upstate building. The two flanking towers, one tall the other short, the recessed nave wall behind a projecting porch, the pyramid-roofed monitor crowning the small tower, and the mounting roofline dominating the façade all recall the aspects of the earlier urban sister. Moreover, the large wheel window that Mould took such pride in when he introduced it on the front of All Souls here reappears to fill the entire façade gable. Its circulating tempo animates the façade's balance of horizontal and vertical lines. The tall northeast tower also pays homage to the larger tower of the West Presbyterian Church, but the open arched base and nearly independent position identify the steeple as the corporal offspring of Mould's All Souls campanile that was destined to exist only on paper.[41]

For the inside of the Bath church, Mould reinterpreted the Reverend Hastings's church. A long, high nave space inflates into a transept-like area at the sanctuary end. In place of the intersecting arches that defined the West Presbyterian church interior, here great exposed curved trusses made of wood arch majestically over the congregation. Visitors to the Metropolitan Museum of Art statuary hall that opened a few years after the church would recognize the similarity. Some people who knew both buildings would possibly have sensed the influence of Eugene Viollet-le-Duc's daring proposal that appeared in his book *Entretiens sur d'architecture* of 1863–1872) for masonry and iron vaulting. Mould's wooden arches, which consist of separate pieces held together by iron rivets, provide support to the heavy timber framed roof (hidden behind the paneled ceiling) and distribute the weight from the apex of their curve down onto the walls where double corbels support them (plate 15). Mould surely derived these curious double stone corbels commanding dwarf columns from the illustration in Viollet-le-Duc's book, where they also appear.

We do not know just when Mould received the bad news that his mother had died in early December 1875 in Chislehurst, but it must have been a serious blow to him. Whatever had caused her to return to England, she had been a potent influence on Mould's life, and he surely would have acknowledged it. Compounding the tragedy was the death of his aunt Louisa the month before his mother's passing. Mould could not have forgotten how she had so generously sustained him financially during his first months in New York. Regrettably, Mould would never see the modest grave that the two sisters shared in St. Nicholas Cemetery in Chislehurst. Now that Owen Jones, who had shown him the way to his life's journey in art, had died in April 1874, Mould faced the future devoid of those who had been his important supporters. His sense of aloneness must have been especially acute, living in far-off Lima so distant from good friends and his mother's kindly family in New York.

Although returning to the United States was not on Mould's mind in a serious way in 1875, it would become more and more a reality two years later. In the spring of 1877, Henry Meiggs became grievously ill and on September 29, 1877, he died prematurely. All of Peru mourned his untimely death. Banks and businesses closed, and many thousands of people of all classes attended his funeral on October 3. Heinrich Witt reflected that "there is no doubt that Mr. Henry Meiggs had been a wonderfully enterprising, energetic, and very charitable man, but whether his integrity had been without blemish, was a question I would not decide."[42] After the services at the venerable Baroque church of Le Merced in Lima, Meiggs's body was conveyed to a mortuary vault built by Mould on the grounds of Meiggs's villa at Villegas. Mould's last interview with Don Enrique had been on August 15, at which time he discussed plans for an elaborate mausoleum that Mould apparently had committed to paper before Meiggs's death but which was never built.

Meiggs also had confided to Mould other ambitious plans. "Before his death, Meiggs had secured the cooperation of Mr. Mould in a series of architectural changes, which would have transformed Lima from a collection of adobe structures into a modern city, fit to be the capital of a progressive State, noted the *New York Times*."[43] When asked by a reporter from the *World* what plans Meiggs had laid out for Lima had he lived longer, Mould responded effusively:

> He had contemplated the building of a street to connect Lima and Callao (seven miles long) and on either side it was to be lined with suburban villa residences. It would have been under the plans he had approved for its construction, the most beautiful drive in the world. In views it would have been unsurpassed, for the Cordilleras would have been seen on one side and the Pacific Ocean on the other. The buildings were to be palatial in style, and midway between the two cities, on the slope, was to be a park about two-thirds the size of Central Park. With the fecund soil of that country, this road and the

> park of San Lorenzo would have been worth a journey across the Pacific to see, in all their beauty. They could not have been matched on the surface of the globe, for there is no other Peru; and there is no other Henry Meiggs.

As to the progress that had been made on fulfilling his dream, Mould explained:

> I had prepared plans and general drawings and was working out the plans in bulk. It was to be the private property of Meiggs, and was intended by him as a speculation. He would have certainly carried it out, and it would have been to him a paying investment, even after the millions it would have required had been expended. But when he died his projects, his aims and his ambitions came to as sudden an end as he himself, and not one of his successors has energy or capacity enough to carry these vast plans.[44]

Thus, Mould was denied the opportunity to have his Lima take its place in urban history alongside Haussmann's Paris, Le Corbusier's Chandigarh, Louis Kahn's Dacca, Walter Burley Griffin's Canberra, and Richard Neutra's Brasília.

Misapprehension over his future status in Lima steadily increased in Mould's mind in the months following Meiggs's burial. Eventually, on July 17, 1879, when the steamship *Colon* arrived in New York, Mould was on board. (Mary Josephine had stayed in Lima for the time being.) Unlike Olmsted, who twenty years earlier had returned to New York with bright prospects in view after the failed gold mine venture in California, Mould faced an uncertain future in the United States. "Mr. J. Wrey Mould, whose name was a familiar one in the City some years ago as that of an architect of much originality and culture," had returned, announced the *New York Times*. He would be staying in Brooklyn for some weeks, the journal stated, presumably, because renters still occupied the house on Twenty-Sixth Street.[45] He talked freely to the press about the situation he had left in Peru, which was on the verge of war with Chile. Most of all, he aired his grievance over the way his benefactor, Henry Meiggs, had been treated by Balta's successor, Manuel Pardo, and the campaign, as Mould saw it, to disparage his memory and the enormous contribution he had made to the advancement of Peru in general and Lima in particular.

One of Mould's first visits after this return must have been to All Souls Church, which, in his absence, had undergone remodeling of the interior by Henry Hobson Richardson and his partner, Charles Gambrill. The nature of the alterations, which took place in 1875, and whether Richardson consulted Mould are unknown. It seems, however, that the work, which cost only $1,300, involved relocating the great organ from the north wall to over the west entrance, where it appears in historic photographs. At the time, Richardson, who had moved his office to Brookline, Massachusetts, in 1874, was also at work on his foremost ecclesiastical commission, Trinity Episcopal Church in Boston, the design and decoration of which surely owed a debt to the example of All Souls. Indeed, it was a tragedy of history that Mould's extraordinary masterpiece no longer exists so that we might experience its reality together with its Boston progeny, the two most influential examples of ecclesiastical architecture of their time.

Over the summer of 1879, Mould debated whether or not to return to Lima. In August, to escape the heat of the city, he spent time at the Wayside Inn in Lake Luzerne, New York. The village, with which Mould was familiar from earlier days, overlooked the Adirondack lake that borrowed its name from the renowned Alpine location. "Everything about the place reminds you of Swiss scenery," wrote the *New York Times* in 1875, "even the boats lying idle in the lake awaiting your orders have a foreign look, and the guests, themselves, greet you with a continental grace, corresponding to that given to Americans when abroad, and the place may be called 'the Switzerland of America.'"[46] Two rivers, the Hudson and Sacandaga, come together nearby, and the Little Falls add more interest to the naturally picturesque setting.

The popular inn was run by Benjamin C. Butler, whose name Mould included on his 1869 handbill as a reference. That year, Butler had opened his commodious hotel, together with several rental cottages. Perhaps Mould had participated in the design of both, although no documentation has surfaced to substantiate an attribution. (Fire destroyed the inn in 1938, but several of the wood frame cottages, which were of the sort that Mould designed for Dr. Henry Owen and which appeared as Design 20 in Bicknell's *Wooden and Brick Buildings* [1875], remain.)

In 1879, during his time of anxiety over his future course of action, Mould must have found comfort in being in the Adirondacks, a nurturing natural place where he had often summered, both at Lake Luzerne and with the Oakley family at their Lake George cottage. As he continued to think things over, he undoubtedly reflected on his life's chronicle of inconstant fortune. To Olmsted he wrote that prospects "as to whether I go or stay in the U.S. are dubious."[47]

The success of Butler's Wayside Inn and its several cottages had been the engine driving the influx to Lake Luzerne of Downstate families. They came there, stated Butler, "to find converse with nature's charms amid rural simplicity and among rural people, who know but little of town life, except that it is brought to their notice by summer visitors." Until recently, a modest chapel had served the requirements of the locals. Henceforth, said Butler, "to meet the larger, more varied and cultivated taste for the city visitor, as well as the increasing number, requires a larger temple."[48] In 1868, Mould had furnished plans for a new St. Mary's Episcopal Church, for which he was paid $120. For an additional thirty dollars, he had appended a design for the rectory.

Among the summer people was Henry Evelyn Pierrepont, the "father" of Green-Wood Cemetery in Brooklyn. He had recently taken to vacationing at Lake Luzerne, where he owned property. A member of the New York Ecclesiological Society, he put up much of the money for the new Episcopal church and donated the land on which it stands. The site is an especially pleasant one, for as Benjamin Butler noted, "it commands a fine view of lake and mountain scenery in all directions."[49] At first, it seems the congregation might have hired Richard Mitchell Upjohn to plan the new church. Pierrepont lived in a splendid house designed for him by Richard Upjohn, Richard Mitchell's father, with whom he had also worked at Green-Wood. But, in the end, perhaps through the influence of Benjamin Butler, who also donated significantly to the project, the job went to Mould. In August 1874, Butler, the longtime warden of St. Mary's, officiated at the laying of the cornerstone. Workmen completed the church for two hundred and fifty people, except for the tower, the following June. At that time, Mould had been in Lima. His latter-day stay at the Wayside Inn provided him with the first opportunity to see his handwork accomplished.

The unassuming church so at ease in its tranquil surroundings is in its way evocative of Swiss vernacular churches, as popular descriptions maintain (plate 16). There were no fancy Florentine arches, colorful inset tiles, or richly carved reliefs. Instead, Mould showed his sympathy for the emerging Arts & Crafts esthetic. Composed of a motley assortment of stone quarried nearby, the walls hum a soft tune of color. Banded slate roof tiles added a now-missing note of multicolored contrast. Dispensing with a proper chancel, Mould instead honored the altar by sheltering it beneath a high pyramidal roof, a sort of dome ascending to a small turret, a musician's gesture of counterpoint to the dominant tower.[50] The leading feature of the church is the tall, broach-spired bell tower, here reduced to its elemental forms of base, carillon, and spire. While Mould was in Lake Luzerne in August 1880, he had the opportunity to give final instructions for finishing it; the building committee voted to proceed with its completion in the following month.

Inside the church, Mould largely ignored the Gothic Revival practices to which many of his contemporaries, including the Upjohns, adhered. A series of round-arched trusses marches down the nave, spanning the all-embracing space. Similar arches appeared again roofing the grand exhibition hall in Vaux and Mould's plan for the Metropolitan Museum of Art, sheltering worshipers in Mould's First Presbyterian Church in Bath, and carrying pedestrians across the Gapstow bridge in Central Park. Mould gave expression to the sanctuary with a large stained glass window in the end wall and by expanding the roof overhead into the peaked, tent-like ceiling.

Mould may have come back to Lake Luzerne for the dedication of the completed church on July 23, 1885. The services were conducted by Bishop Doane of Albany, another person who lent his name to the list of references on Mould's 1869 handbill. Sadly, Benjamin Butler had died three years earlier. Together with the First Unitarian Church in Yonkers and the First Presbyterian Church in Bath—which is St. Mary's architectural progeny—the Lake Luzerne church is one of three houses of worship by Mould that survive. Looking at the church with the eyes of our own time, one seconds writer Sally Svenson's assessment: "The complexity of the low-slung mass, with its assortment of hipped roofs, gables, and breaks was characteristic of Mould's approach. His ecclesiastical architecture expressed an intricate three-dimensionality and introduced sharp-contrasts in form."[51]

In November, Mould was back in New York staying at the Astor House. He had again been in contact with Olmsted, who had painted a dark picture of the state of the architectural profession in New York in recent years. What Olmsted had told him, said Mould, chimed in "with the Jeremiad chanted both by Vaux & Radford as to their doings during my absence." The dire history they had related made him take heart that he had made the right decision by leaving town when he did. "Luckily, by going to Peru," he wrote, "bad as it was—I did more than I could have had I stayed in New York, out of the Park, and such professional stagnation as has occurred." Looking ahead, he declared that it will "not be my own fault, if I don't get into the stream again. I shall take good care to let the Public know I *am* back. The Tropics have *not* enervated me I can assure you."[52] Over the next months, Mould was both negotiating to get his old job back with the Department of Public Parks and seeking to reestablish himself in the American architectural profession.

To that end, in the spring of 1880, he and Mary Josephine moved to Detroit, Michigan, where Mould became associated with another British-born architect, Gordon W. Lloyd. Lloyd had arrived in Detroit in 1858. Over the years, he had amassed a successful practice there that brought him commissions throughout the Mid-West and as far east as Buffalo. He was especially in demand for ecclesiastical architecture. For many parishes, he had construed model Gothic Revival churches. While Mould was with him, the Westminster Presbyterian Church in Detroit commissioned the office to design their new house of worship (fig. 89). It was unlike anything in Lloyd's prior repertoire. "Mr. Mould came to this city three months ago and in that brief period as an evidence of his genius, I may point to his beautiful and original designs for the Westminster Church on Woodward Avenue," wrote "FLANEUR" in a letter to the *Detroit Free Press* in September 1880. The writer, who was obviously cognizant of the local architectural scene, noted that Mould had come to Detroit "simply with a view to form a copartnership with Mr. Gordon Lloyd."

Mould's hand is clearly visible in the Westminster Church design which

Figure 89. Mould and Gordon Lloyd, Westminster Presbyterian Church, Detroit, Michigan, 1880–1884.

centers on a domed auditorium that is the dominant feature of the compact architectural composition. Revisiting his competition entry for the Plymouth Church, Mould took full advantage of the building's corner site along Detroit's foremost thoroughfare. Two large Florentine Arch windows—giant versions of those on the Casa DuBois—provided abundant light from two directions to the grand worship space and brightened the sober red brick exterior. A barrel-vault canopy sheltered the corner entrance that reached out to welcome visitors from both streets. Mould's Detroit legacy ended in 1918 when the building fell victim to progress and was demolished to make way for C. Howard Crane's Orchestra Hall.

The partnership with Lloyd was short lived. As FLANEUR noted, Mould's three-month period of probation had barely expired when he received word that he was appointed architect-in-chief for Morningside Park in New York City at a salary of $250 per month. "The department has providentially stepped in between me & serious financial difficulty," he confided to Olmsted.[53] On October 4, Mould informed Olmsted: "I am writing at my old desk and in my old room (and of yours) thank God!!"[54] The last phase of Mould's career had begun, and he was back in New York where he felt most at home, and where he had made his major contributions to the progress of America's built environment. "The more enduring monuments of his skill, taste and versatility, to be found in Central Park, New York City, are matters of national repute and familiar to most of your readers," FLANEUR told the *Detroit Free Press*. "Detroit has thus lost one of the ablest architects of America."[55]

Morningside Park in Upper Manhattan had been originally proposed by Andrew Green in 1867 because he saw that the topography of the high escarpment would have made extending the typical grid of city streets a very difficult and expensive task. "From 110th street north to Manhattan Valley, the ridge of rocks almost verdureless, mainly between 9th and 10th avenues, breaks so abruptly towards the east as to render the streets that have been laid over it in rigid conformity with the plan of the city, very expensive to work, and when worked so steep as to be very inconvenient for use," reported Green in 1867.[56] By 1873, the land—"where the steep cliff catches the rays of the rising sun," acclaims architectural historian

Andrew Dolkart[57]—had come under the jurisdiction of the Department of Public Parks, which engaged Olmsted and Vaux to create a park plan. In October, they submitted their ideas, a major feature of which was a promenade along the street adjoining the high ground on the western border. Strollers on Morningside Avenue, as this thoroughfare is known today, would enjoy fine views as far distant as Long Island Sound. A large retaining wall would be necessary to sustain this "terrace road mall" along which Olmsted and Vaux hoped to create numerous viewing balconies as well as provide several entrances to the park with stairways descending to the lower landscape. Other park elements were to be a lagoon with tropical plants, a wild area resembling the Ramble in Central Park, and an exhibition hall. Although the city adopted Olmsted and Vaux's plan, it was slow to implement it, and for nearly fourteen years, little progress was made on its construction.

Eventually, in June 1880, the state legislature authorized the Department of Public Works together with the Department of Public Parks to construct the high western roadway and necessary retaining wall. This action prompted the park department to hire Mould in September. It is likely that Olmsted, who had been consulted concerning the new work, had suggested Mould for the design of the park's improvements. Otherwise, Olmsted relied for such architectural assistance on Thomas Wisedell, another British émigré architect who was second only to Mould in devising beautiful landscape features. (Wisedell's designs for the walls around the grounds of the US Capitol, which Olmsted planned in 1874, attest to his genius.) In October, Mould wrote to Olmsted, "I do not desire to consult you in any official sense, but as I do not vitiate the integrity of your original plan, & the modifications I propose do not militate against the former design I wished to have your advice on the few points in which I deviate." Above all, Mould wished that he and Olmsted "should be in perfect harmony and accord" over what was to be done. By the following April, he had prepared preliminary studies for all the streets bordering the park, and by September 1881, he had his ideas firmly in place. "Now, the actual conditions of the most important avenue bounding Morningside Park, that to the west and known as Morningside avenue, present at a glance a departure from the stereotyped and commonplace method in which our streets are ordinarily treated and by which New York with all its wealth ranks architecturally below many cities one-tenth its size," Mould said. He proposed a remarkable series of features to make the most of the unusual urban topography:

Morningside avenue rises on a hill from One Hundred and Tenth street to One Hundred and Sixteenth street to a height of sixty one feet by a series of irregular grades, which irregularity suggests a treatment such as may be found in London, Paris, Florence, and even in such provincial towns in England, as Clifton-on-Avon, Bath, Fleetwood-on-Wyre, etc., namely, that of constructing the sidewalk leading to the crown of the hill by a series of terraced esplanades, reached by flights of easy steps, no flights having more than six steps. Morningside avenue thus treated will afford a delightful resort for pedestrians and loungers, commanding as it does a view toward Mount Morris Park, the East River, and Hell Gate. The view already is a superb one and can be much improved by judicious tree-culling. The attraction will entice, I believe, fully half of the visitors to the Park to stroll up the hill for the sake of the view.

To enhance the charm of this promenade I propose that ten feet of the thirty feet sidewalk on the other side of the avenue, rising with the grade of the street, be laid out as a grass border, within handsome granite curbs, to be planted with hardy shrubs. The border is to be interrupted at different streets by pedestals carrying the street lamps, and at the centre of each block I want a polished granite vase supplied with flowers from the Park. Along the terrace walk on the Park side of the avenue I propose a series of semi-octagonal bays as places of rest and conversation. There are seven of these shown on the plan, each twenty-five feet wide and similar in effect to those on the "Balcony" or "Pulpit" bridge in the Central Park. Morningside avenue seen in perspective from its foot at One Hundred and Tenth street will be disagreeably undulatory in effect, presenting an ugly and unsatisfactory line. The terracing will obviate this and take off the harsh contour of the roadway.

I have omitted the introduction of shade trees on the avenue because, in the first place, anything attaining height would seriously detract from the property on the west side of the avenue by shutting off the view I have mentioned; and, secondly, the grade of the avenue has been regulated by rough stone filling, in some places ten feet deep, in which no tree will take root.

The other streets bounding the Park I design with the ordinary sidewalk curb and gutter, bordered with trees. The architectural treatment of the parapet or boundary wall must form one homogeneous design with the terraced and octagonal bays. I have prepared

> plans and details for the mall, and have also worked out the most important and most expensive of the entrances to the Park—that at Morningside avenue at One Hundred and Sixteenth street where the flights of stone steps descend from the avenue into the park, a distance of forty-two feet. The parapet wall will consist of a low dwarf wall coped with granite, one foot ten inches in height, surmounted by an open cast and wrought iron railing, the total height from the ground to the top of the railing being three feet eight inches. The wall is broken at intervals of thirty feet by low granite posts.
>
> The chief entrance to the Park was planned in 1873 upon a magnificent scale. The approach of the elevated railroad will subject this plan to alterations. The estimated cost to completing the wall streets and sidewalk surrounding the Park is $244,000. The cost for the fourteen entrances to the Park and of the octagonal alcoves along Morningside avenue will be about $225,000.[58]

In this, the heyday of the Richardsonian Romanesque, Mould recommended rusticated gneiss laid up in random ashlar courses for the retaining wall and balcony parapets. The age of polychromy was over. Presumably, Olmsted lent his assent to Mould's farsighted concept for fulfilling his and Vaux's original creation. The department gave its approval to Mould's brilliant design and directed him to proceed with making detailed working drawings.

Unfortunately, the course of Mould's association with the Morningside Park project proved transient. In December 1882, when he had completed drawings for the park, he was once again terminated. The reason the department gave for its action was financial. It lacked funds to keep him on the payroll during the nonconstruction months. Nonetheless, in January 1883, Julius Munckwitz, a longtime colleague with whom Mould enjoyed bantering in German, took up the task of preparing working drawings and specifications. From February to July, Mould was reengaged, but only as Munckwitz's assistant at $5 per day. After that, he would not see service with the Department for another two years. Angered by what he regarded as shabby treatment, Mould sued the city for $500 in lost wages that he believed were due to him. Unhappily for him, the judge failed to agree.[59]

"Those detestable parties in Union Square," Mould wrote in a letter to Olmsted recounting his grievance, "'bounced' me in July 1883. I was not, unfortunately, independent enough to 'bounce' myself, as both you and Vaux did." He further confessed, "I am, comparatively speaking, doing *nothing*." At the same, time, he gingerly offered his services to Olmsted who had lost the assistance of Thomas Wisedell because of his untimely death. "Of course knowing Wisedell's professional relationship with you," Mould ventured, "I have felt delicate ever since my return from Peru, in approaching you on the subject, but now that Death has removed him, can we not 'cooperate again'? Of my powers & qualifications I need say nothing to *you*, except that 10 years' experience have vivified & strengthened what the 'World' said in 1874. . . . In fact, my creative ability is now stronger than ever, & my energy undiminished. I am as the Spanish say 'a la disposición de yo.'"[60] For whatever reasons, Olmsted failed to take him up on his proposal.

According to Jay Shockley in the New York City Landmarks Preservation Commission report on Morningside Park, by the time of Mould's death in June 1886, "the only completed feature of the park was the main portion of the western retaining wall, with its overlook bays and stairways south of 116th Street" (fig. 90).[61] The following year, the city called back Olmsted and Vaux to revise their original plan for the park and proceeded to fund its construction. The two men generally respected Mould's splendid designs. His contribution still gives pleasure to contemporary park users. Mould's conception was in its way as remarkable as Le Rampe and Piazzale Michelangelo that Giuseppi Poggi built in 1869 in Florence, the Rue Foyatier that opened in 1867 climbing to the Montmartre butte in Paris, and the other places Mould alluded to in his statement. Morningside Avenue—with its balconies, ramps, and stairs that Mould had designed—deserves to be better known among the favored productions of Belle Epoch urbanism (fig. 91).

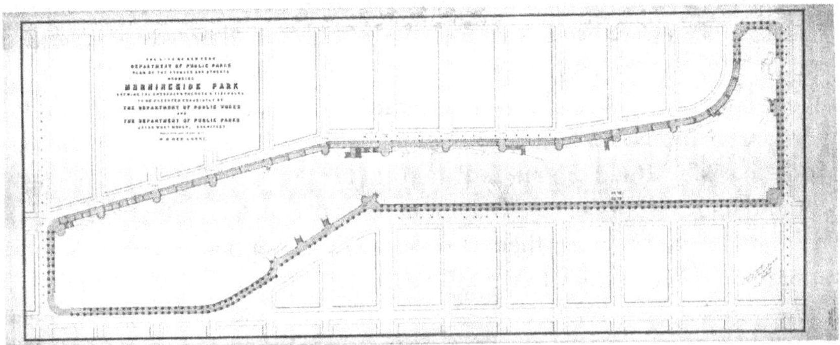

Figure 90. Design for walls around Morningside Park, 1881.

Figure 91. Morningside Park walls and ramps, ca. 1889.

"The appointment of Mr. J. Wrey Mould to his old position of Architect to the Park Department is an excellent one for the parks and the public," stated the *Record and Guide* when Mould returned to work at the Department of Public Parks in July 1885. The popular real estate journal took the opportunity to reflect a bit on history, reminding its readers that "Mr. Olmsted, Mr. Vaux and Mr. Mould are the three men to whom we mainly owe the Central Park." Regarding Mould in particular, the journal recalled: "When we think what the level of public and private architecture was in New York when the Park was begun it is awful to consider what we might have had if an architect on that level had been employed to do the park work. In fact no better work of its kind has been done since in New York than Mr. Mould did in the Park from twenty to twenty-five years ago." Although the editors agreed that there was not much architectural work to be done in the park just then, they saw Mould's appointment as "a guarantee that what there is to do will be well done, and that what is already done will not be spoiled."[62] By August 1885, Mould had prepared plans for an addition to the park. The charming red brick Lawn Tennis Club and Ladies Cottage, however, failed to go beyond the beautiful drawings he made for two slightly different versions of the home-like building. It was his final bid to contribute to the landscape that had benefited so much from his fertile imagination.

Once he was back in the United States, Mould renewed his association with the Davenports in Bath. In June 1883, he had the opportunity to visit the Upstate town to create plans for the remodeling of the Davenport offices and to see his completed First Presbyterian Church and perhaps fulfil his promise made in Lima to John Davenport to give him firsthand advice on matters of decoration. In March 1885, Mould visited Bath to remodel the interior of Riverside, the Davenport family forty-eight-room, Federal-style dwelling overlooking the Cohocton River. Although nothing survives of what Mould did beyond a few black-and-white photographs, we are told that the house was "a spacious and beautiful one." Mould had created a suitable setting for the elegant parties the family enjoyed giving and for a sizeable collection of "articles of *vertu*, rare paintings, engravings, and statuary." We know from a contemporary description that the Davenport library contained "thousands of handsomely bound volumes, comprising not only the standard authors but many books of great value, including many shelves of works by American writers."[63]

Mould also furnished designs for the carriage barn located behind the walled rose garden just inside the entrance to the grounds of the Davenports' country seat (fig. 92). For the last time, the architect indulged his taste for sturdy textured wooden exteriors that had distinguished such

Figure 92. Carriage House, Davenport estate, Bath, New York, 1883–1885.

earlier buildings as the First Unitarian Church in Yonkers and Holy Trinity Church on Fifth Avenue. The walls of the Davenport carriage house are divided into panels, each section consisting of clapboard base, board-and-batten center, and teardrop frieze. Chamfered edges, faceted bosses, carved brackets, and exposed eave rafters embellish the happy structure. The handsome wooden barn, which looks like it might have strayed from Central Park, is the sole remnant of Mould's many contributions to the Davenports' home and business properties.

More unusual was the addition Mould designed in 1883 to the Davenport gatehouse, which had been erected around 1850 by local mason James Plaisted (fig. 93). For the new wing he built, Mould adopted Plaisted's vernacular cobblestone building method particular to Central and Western New York. Mould may also have replaced the original roof and installed a bracketed hood over the entrance. A massive brick-and-stone chimney towered above the unusual octagonal room that Mould's addition contained and that apparently served as an office for the estate. It is a pity that this

Figure 93. Gate House to Davenport estate, Bath, New York, 1883.

rare example of a High Victorian architect respecting a venerable craft tradition (it originated with English immigrants who began settling in the region in 1820s) was lost in 1970 to a highway project.

The last important work by Jacob Wrey Mould came unexpectedly in July 1885. On the morning of July 23, President Ulysses S. Grant, hero for the Union cause in the Civil War, died in office. His widow expressed the desire to have his body interred in New York because the people there had been so supportive of her husband through his many years of service to the nation. The city scrambled to nominate a suitable site to erect a tomb for America's most celebrated soldier. On July 28, the first clod of soil was removed from an eminence overlooking the Hudson River at the end of Riverside Drive. The little knoll was beloved as the first spot in the vicinity to announce the arrival of spring and the last to welcome winter.

The task of quickly designing the tomb to hold temporarily the president's remains fell to Mould, the architect of the Department of Public Parks (fig. 94). The brick-and-stone edifice he planned in twenty minutes was finished in record time at noon on August 7. The reason Mould could adapt to the circumstances with such dispatch, he said, was that he had fashioned the Grant tomb after the one he had built for the remains of Henry Meiggs on his estate at Villegas. The only difference was that the Grant tomb would be made of brick, which had not been available in Peru. Although quickly built—workmen toiled day and night under the close supervision of the park commissioners—the tomb was not shoddily built. The construction measured seventeen feet long by thirteen feet wide and rested on a granite foundation that supported three-foot-thick walls of brick. The front and sides were composed of alternating courses of red face brick and black brick set in black mortar. Grant's indestructible steel-encased coffin stood alone inside the single barrel-vault space, several steps below the surface of the surrounding ground. On August 8, 1885, the tomb was ready, merely sixteen days after the president's death. Many thousands of mourners came over the next twelve years to pay their respects and view the hero's sarcophagus through a metal gate.

The vault would be temporary while ideas flowed forth from many quarters for a lasting shrine to the venerated war hero. Olmsted and Vaux offered their opinions on where the permanent monument should be and

Figure 94. Temporary tomb for Ulysses S. Grant, Riverside Park, New York City, 1885.

how it should honor the debt of gratitude the Union owed to Grant. Vaux insisted that the matter be put in the hands of a committee of artists, who would then conduct a competition limited to other artists they would ask to submit proposals. Mould seconded the notion of a solicited event. "Open competition never produced a great work of art or a great building, and it never will," Mould told a reporter from the *New York Herald*. He went on a length elaborating on the subject:

> My own idea is that say ten artists and architects should be paid $1000 each for their designs and there the rest be left to competition. The great designers will not waste their time upon the chance that their designs will be accepted. Less important men will be glad to compete without pay. The great Wellington monument was designed by paid competition. On the other hand, the Albert Memorial, in London, was given to Scott without competition, and it is, in my opinion, the most radical specimen of Beaconsfieldian architecture, a mass of gimcrakery and gingerbread. We want the Grant memorial to be something grand, simple and pure. It ought to be of the most severely classical character. My own idea is to build a great Pantheon having a series of granite columns with bronze capitals on the sides and great stairs leading up to it from all sides. It ought to have a splendid dome, and in the centre of its interior, I would have a sarcophagus such as that in which Napoleon's remains rest.

Beyond that, he preceded to propose a truly extraordinary notion: "In this sarcophagus I would place the bodies of Grant and his noble foe, Robert E. Lee." When asked by the astonished reporter if he did not think that the interment of Grant and Lee together "would jar upon the feelings of many people," Mould replied:

> No, sir; sleeping side by side in a great national mausoleum they would be the most noble symbol of a reunited country, with no North, no South, no East, no West. The last message that General Grant gave to the public was the letter dictated in the presence of Dr. Douglass in which he said, as it were with his dying breath, that he was thankful to have lived long enough to see the people united again and to know that his late foes had forgiven him. That is the idea such a memorial would express. No sight could be more touching or thrilling; no lesson could be more profound than that of the two great soldiers side by side in death. It would do more than anything else to wipe out the bitterness of the past.

To the impression of an out-of-touch eccentric he must have given many *Herald* readers, he added the portrayal of curmudgeon. When asked by the reporter if artists ought to consult the people for the idea of a design for the Grant memorial, he responded:

> I think that the American people are the most inartistic people in the world. They must be severely led in artistic matters. Look at the Metropolitan Opera House. It was built in imitation of La Scala, and there it is! If $2,000,000 was spent on the building it ought to have been endowed with $2,000,000 more. The miserable trash called soldiers' monuments which contractors—I will not call them stonecutters—have dumped all over the country ought to be a warning to us. This Grant memorial should be not only be a colossal work, but it should be the best artistic expression of the nation's regard for the great General that America can produce.[64]

There would be no competition. The Grant Monument Association chose James Hemenway Duncan to design the present Neo-Classical tomb that opened to the public on April 27, 1897. For a while after that, Mould's "very simple, yet substantial" tomb could be seen "in the shadow of the granite monument, unguarded and unsung." The proximity of the old and new tombs prompted one thoughtful observer at the time to reflect that "the one impresses even the most careless observer with idea of temporal power, wealth and grandeur; the other—the old tomb—in its simplicity is an emblem of sorrow which seemed to center the natural sadness that hovers about the memory of a hero and to concentrate those memories to one little poetic spot."[65] To many who may have come to the spot, people like Olmsted, who had actively participated in the war, Mould's unpretentious burial ground mausoleum and its resident must have evoked more the ghosts of a terrible past than the glory of victory that Duncan's tomb proclaimed.

On June 14, 1886, Jacob Wrey Mould died in his home at 123 East Twenty-Sixth Street. While America eulogized Richardson, who had died the month before, Mould's passing was noted only briefly, and mainly by members of the architectural profession. The editors of the *American Architect and Building News* took the opportunity to reflect on the immigrant architects who had come to this country "not in these days, but years ago, when, from a foreigner's standpoint there was little to attract, or to promise a successful career in his chosen calling." Mould, in particular, was to be esteemed for "the spirit of enterprise that had led him to immigrate to this country in 1852 had endured throughout his life." That spirit had prompted him years later "to join one of the most adventurous Americans, Henry Meiggs, in his railroad undertakings in Peru." Mould would be chiefly remembered for his superb contributions to Central Park. "There was so much to do," stated the obituary, "and so many possibilities of doing the wrong thing that we cannot be too grateful that the work fell into hands no less skilled than his."[66] Others expressed admiration for his architecture. The keen observer of the New York cultural scene, George Templeton Strong, called him a clever architect and "universal genius"; architectural critic Russell Sturgis agreed, referring to him as "that strange genius"; and Clarence Cook said that Mould seemed to him "a more original artist than Richardson, or than anyone of those among our architects in whose reputation the quality of originality plays the greater part."[67]

A modest funeral took place at Mould's home at 2 PM on June 15 conducted by the Reverend G. H. Houghton of the Church of the Transfiguration. Among those present were architects Henry Dudley and Frederick Diaper. The New York music profession was represented by the composer Robert Stoepel. At the time of his death, Mould had left unfinished a translation of the libretto to Wagner's *Tannhäuser*. Theodore Thomas, the celebrated interpreter of Wagner, had commissioned Mould to provide the English version for an autumn performance by the American Opera Company. Others from the musical world lamented Mould's passing. On his coffin rested a splendid bouquet of lilies sent by Zélie de Lussan, a rising star in the international world of opera. Interment took place without pallbearers in the Oakley family plot in Brooklyn's Green-Wood Cemetery where a simple granite headstone marks Mould's grave (fig. 95).

His rightful memorial lies elsewhere. Central Park, affirmed a

Figure 95. Jacob Wrey Mould tombstone, Green-Wood Cemetery, Brooklyn, New York.

contemporary, "will be a lasting and an honorable monument to Mr. Mould."[68] This grandson of a notorious slave trader, who was probably unaware that he had distant relatives in Africa, had influenced the course of American architecture, made the enjoyment of grand opera accessible to many, and contributed significantly to the life-enhancing environment of the New World's foremost and ever beloved urban park.

J. WREY MOULD,

ARCHITECT,

(PUPIL OF OWEN JONES, ESQ., OF LONDON.)

ARCHITECT TO THE BOARD OF COMMISSIONERS OF THE CENTRAL PARK.

ARCHITECT OF THE WEST PRESBYTERIAN CHURCH, ALL SOUL'S CHURCH, TRINITY CHAPEL SCHOOL, CHURCH OF THE HOLY TRINITY, ETC., ETC., ETC.

Begs to give notice that he prepares DESIGNS, WORKING DRAWINGS, AND SPECIFICATIONS, and superintends the erection of buildings in any part of the United States, on the following scale of terms, exclusive of traveling expenses:

Preliminary Studies, .	1 per cent.
Plans and Elevations, .	1½ per cent.
Working Drawings, .	1¼ per cent.
General Superintendence,	1¼ per cent.
	5 per cent., (the usual commission of Architects.)

For works costing less than $5,000, or for Monumental and Decorative work, Designs for Furniture, &c., a special rate in excess of the above. Drawings, as instruments of service, remain the property of the Architect.

Art Design.

J. WREY MOULD also begs to announce that he prepares Designs and Working Drawings for the several subsidiary branches of Art herein mentioned. DECORATION IN COLORS for the Interiors of Churches, Public Buildings, or Dwellings. STAINED GLASS, for the further enrichment of ditto. ART PUBLICATIONS: Title Pages, Vignettes, and Ornamental Borders and Covers for all forms of Illustrated and Illuminated Works, designed and drawn, either on the wood block or in lithography. BANK NOTES drawn in outline or in vignette. BOOK BINDERY: Enriched and Embossed Covers designed. CERAMIC WARE: Designs prepared for all works in Pottery or Porcelain. BRONZES, SILVER and ORNAMENTAL GLASSWARE, ORGAN CASES, TEXTILE FABRICS, and PAPER HANGINGS: The patterns drawn on the block, so as to repeat; and all other Designs provided for subjects in any way co-relative with Ornamental Art.

REFERENCES.

(By express permission.)

The Right Reverend the Bishop of Illinois, D. D.
The Right Reverend Bishop Doane, D. D.

The Rev. Stephen H. Tyng, D. D.
The Rev. Stephen H. Tyng, Jr.
The Rev. Henry W. Bellows, D. D.
The Rev. Samuel Osgood, D. D.
The Rev. Henry Ward Beecher.
The Rev. John H. Hopkins, M. A.
The Rev. Thomas S. Hastings.

Henry G. Stebbins, esq.
Moses H. Grinnell, esq.
Andrew H. Green, esq.
Manton Marble, esq.
U. A. Murdock, esq.
T. W. Kennard, esq.
Runyon W. Martin, Jr., esq.
William R. Martin, esq.
Wm. M. Prichard, esq.
Benj. C. Butler, esq.
George L. Lorillard, esq.
John Allen, esq.

OFFICE AND RESIDENCE, 123 (late 75) EAST TWENTY SIXTH ST., NEW YORK.

MDCCCLXIX.

End Piece: Mould's handbill advertising his services, 1869.

ACKNOWLEDGMENTS

I first must thank my dear friend Lucille Gordon for all the many good times we shared talking about Mould and the progress of her research into his varied life and work. I owe to her daughter Jamie Gordon the delivery of two large boxes of her mother's research notes that formed the foundation for this book. I am equally grateful to her sister, Ellen Gordon, for encouragement to complete her mother's quest and for many helpful suggestions that improved the manuscript. The contributions of the late Dennis Francis to our understanding of Mould's life and work were of enormous value also.

Many people who generously offered suggestions for research and interpretation include: Carol A. Hrvol Flores, associate professor emeritus, College of Architecture and Planning, Ball State University, and author of the definitive book on Owen Jones, for much valuable advice and information regarding Mould's relationship with Jones and his circle; Sara Cedar Miller, historian and photographer, Central Park Conservancy, for generous aid with many aspects of the book, especially Mould's association with Central Park, and for overall moral support; Cynthia Brenwall, conservator, New York City Municipal Archives, for much valued help with the large repository of Mould drawings at the archives and whose splendid volume *The Central Park: Original Designs for New York's Greatest Treasure* is a visual and studious resource to which I returned many times and which I recommend to readers seeking to appreciate extent of Mould's contribution to the great park; Rosanna Kuon Arce, Conservadora y Restauradora de Pintura de Caballete, Investigadora del Centro de Investigación y Conservación del Patrimonio–UTEC, for taking many photographs of Mould's work in Lima; Martin Wachadlo, independent architectural historian, who kindly took many photographs and a dear friend with whom I enjoyed talking about Mould's varied contributions to American architecture; Amy Picard, rare book librarian, Buffalo and Erie County Public Library, and her assistant, Nicole Konziela, who facilitated scanning of images from that institution's remarkable collection of nineteenth-century architectural books and periodicals; Cynthia Van Ness, librarian of the Buffalo History Museum for pointing me to images of the long vanished Williams House; John Bewley, archivist emeritus, Music Library, University at Buffalo, for much helpful advice and many references concerning the role of music in Mould's career; Michele Bewley for helping me navigate the mysteries of genealogical research into Mould's ancestry; Michael Marissen, Daniel Underhill Emeritus Professor of Music, Swarthmore College, for reviewing the sections dealing with Mould's musical life; Mosette Broderick, director, Urban Design and Architecture Studies, Department of Art History and Urban Design and Architecture Studies, New York University, for many helpful suggestions concerning Mould and the New York of his day; and Charles Beveridge, editor of the Frederick Law Olmsted Papers, for help with Mould's correspondence with Olmsted.

I am indebted to the following individuals for valuable assistance concerning specific Mould projects:; Irene Ayad; Quentin Beran; Luis Martin Bogdanovich, manager of PROLIMA; Helen Brink, historian of First Presbyterian Church, Bath, New York; Enrique Daniel Rodríguez Castillo; David Dulanski; Samantha Hightower, Office of Metropolitan History, New York City; Kirk House, director, Steuben County Historical Society; Juan Jose Pacheco Ibarra, Universidad Nacional Mayor de San Marcos, Lima, Peru; Paula Mohr; Pam Morin, Lake Lucerne, New York, town historian; Paul Pasquarello; William Rhoads, Professor of Art History Emeritus, SUNY New Paltz; Stephen Smith; Agosto Tamayo-San Roman; Ty M. Reese; Jane Westenfeld, research and instruction librarian, Pelletier Library, Allegheny College; and Voysest Zöllner.

NOTES

Introduction

1. Carol A. Hrvol Flores, *Owen Jones: Design, Ornament, Architecture, and Theory in an Age in Transition* (New York: Rizzoli, 2006), 238.

2. Mark Crinson, *Empire Building: Orientalism and Victorian Architecture* (London: Routledge, 1996), 34.

3. Flores, *Owens Jones*, 242.

4. Montgomery Schuyler, "A Great American Architect: Leopold Eidlitz," *Architectural Record* 24, no. 3 (September 1908): 178.

5. "Street-Musings on Architecture," *Crayon* 6 (February 1859): 60.

6. Clarence Cook, "Obituary—Jacob Wrey Mould," *Studio*, n.s., 2 (July 1886): 15.

7. Jeffrey W. Cody, *Exporting American Architecture, 1870–2000* (London: Routledge, 2003), 4.

8. *The Diary of George Templeton Strong*, ed. Allan Nevins and M. H. Thomas (New York: Macmillan, 1952), 2:233.

9. Montgomery Schuyler, "Concerning Queen Anne," reprinted in *American Architecture* (New York: Harper & Brothers , 1892), 41. The polychrome phenomenon may be said to have attained its zenith in 1901 at Buffalo's Pan American Exposition, the celebrated "Rainbow City." There, all of the Spanish Baroque style pavilions bore tints determined by an elaborate color scheme that purported to trace the history of civilization.

10. Schuyler, "Great American Architect," 178.

11. Montgomery Schuyler, "Italian Gothic in New York," *Architectural Record* 26, no. 1 (July 1909): 46.

12. "Correspondence. Building in Philadelphia," *American Architect and Building News* 1 (October 14, 1876): 335.

13. Peter B. Wight, "Reminiscences of the Building of the Academy," *New York Times*, November 22, 1900.

14. In the early 1870s, the church hired Richardson to do some remodeling of the interior of All Souls. He may have been responsible for moving the organ from the north side to a gallery over the main entrance.

15. Sarah Bradford Landau, *Edward T. and William A Potter, American Victorian Architects* (New York: Garland Publishing, 1979), 99.

16. [Montgomery Schuyler,] "Jacob Wrey Mould," *Record and* Guide 37, no. 952 (June 19, 1886): 797.

17. The essay appeared in *Concerning Architecture: Essays on Architectural Writers and Writing Presented to Sir Nikolaus Pevsner*, ed. John Summerson (London: Allen Lane, 1968).

18. J. W. Mould, "An Account of Mozart's 'Il Don Giovanni,'" in translated score of *Don Juan or the Libertine Punished (Don Giovanni)* (London: Boosey, 1850), x.

19. For Mould's membership, see Nevins and Thomas, *Diary of George Templeton Strong*, 4:540.

20. Charles Jencks, "Architecture Becomes Music," *Architectural Review*, May 6, 2013, accessed July 2021, https://www.architectural-review.com/essays/architecture-becomes-music.

21. Schuyler, "Jacob Wrey Mould," 797.

22. Jervis McEntee, diary entry, June 21, 1886. Archives of American Art, Smithsonian Institution, Washington, DC.

23. "With the Respects of the Artist V. Prévost," preserved in the George Eastman Museum in Rochester, NY.

24. It is possible that Mould shared a friendship with Victor Prévost. Prévost had come to New York from France around the same time that Mould had arrived from England. Like Mould, he had had a background in lithography. During his time in New York, Prévost advanced the cause of photography, being the first to use paper negatives rather than glass plates to hold images. (Prévost took his Central Park images using glass plates.)

25. Daniel J. Sharfstein, *The Invisible Line* (Princeton, NJ: Princeton University Press, 2011), 3.

26. Allyson Hobbs, *A Chosen Exile: A History of Racial Passing in American Life* (Cambridge, MA: Harvard University Press, 2014), 54.

27. Robert Fikes, *The Passing of Passing: A Peculiarly American Racial Tradition Approaches Irrelevance*, BlackPast.org, December 30, 2017, accessed October 15, 2022, https://www.blackpast.org/african-american-history/passing-passing-peculiarly-american-racial-tradition-approaches-irrelevance/.

1. Family Territory: England, Africa, Ireland, America

1. Beth Kaplow, *African Merchants of the 19th Century Gold Coast* (Ph.D. dissertation, Columbia University, 1971), 28–29.

2. St. William St. Clair, *The Door of No Return: The History of the Cape Coast Castle and the Atlantic Slave Trade* (New York: Blue Bridge, 2007), 167.

3. Vincent Caretta and Ty M. Reese, eds., *The Life and Letters of Philip Quaque: The First African Anglican Missionary* (Athens, GA: University of Georgia Press, 2010), 15.

4. Quoted in Caretta and Reese, 15.

5. Rachel A. A. Engmann, "Unearthing Mixed Raceness at Christianborg Castle," in "Constructing Race and Architecture, 1400–1800, Part 2," *Journal of the Society of Architectural Historians* 80, no. 4 (December 2021): 385–415, accessed January 2022, https://doi.org/10.1525/jsah.2021.80.4.385.

6. *Gentleman's Magazine*, XCIII (1823), 271.

7. Thomas Pennant, *Of London* (London: Robert Paulding, 1790), 54.

8. "Ameublement," *Luxus und der Moden* 16 (February, 1801): 123.

9. Benjamin Oakley, *Letters on Miscellaneous and Domestic Subjects* (London: self-pub., 1823), 23.

10. Helen Goodman, "Women Illustrators of the Golden Age of American Illustration," *Woman's Art Journal* 8, no.1 (Spring–Summer, 1987): 13. Of her grandfather's association with the National Academy of Design, Violet said that he "was deeply interested in its success." Violet Oakley to Mrs. M. A. Nicholas, January 1, 1909. In the collection of the National Academy of Design archives.

11. Quoted in Bailey Van Hook, *Violet Oakley: An Artist's Life* (Wilmington, DE: University of Delaware Press, 2016), 7.

2. Youthful Years in London: Architecture and Music}

1. Mould's tombstone in the Oakley plot in Brooklyn's Green-Wood Cemetery states that he was born in Chislehurst. The Oakley family lived in Chislehurst, so it is possible that Mary Ann could have been staying with her relatives there at the time of the birth of her son.

2. Review of "Evening," *Fine Arts Journal Weekly* 17 (Nov. 7, 1847): 147.

3. J. Wrey Mould, "Editor's Preface," *Der Freischütz* (London: Boosey & Co., 1849).

4. Mould, "Editor's Preface."

5. Mould's application to the Council of King's College, Junior Department, dated August 9, 1838, is signed by Rothery and preserved in the King's College Archives where further information about Mould's time at King's College is available.

6. Roth Quoted in Leland Roth, eds., *America Builds Sources and Documents in American Architecture and Planning* (New York: Harper & Row, 1987), 225.

7. Frank Miles, *King's College School: The First 150 Years* (London: Graeme Cranch, 1979), 18.

8. Oliver Brackett, et al., *An Introductory Review of English Painting, Architecture, Sculpture, Ceramics, Glass, Metalwork, Furniture, Textiles and Other Arts during the Reign of George III* (London: B. T. Batsford, 1929), 20.

9. Census of 1841.

10. William A. Coles, ed., *Architecture and Society: Selected Essays of Henry van Brunt* (Cambridge, MA: Harvard University Press, 1969), 165.

11. Nicholas Adams, "Buildings from Book, Books from Buildings," in *Building Buffalo: Buildings from Books, Books from Buildings*, exhibition catalog (Buffalo: Buffalo & Erie County Public Library, 2017), 31.

12. Andrea Marie Johnson, *Incongruous Conceptions: Owen Jones's Plans, Elevations, Sections and Details of the Alhambra and British Views of Spain* (PhD dissertation, University of South Florida, 2016), 32.

13. Carol A. Hrvol Flores, *Owen Jones: Design, Ornament, Architecture, and Theory in an Age of Transition* (New York: Rizzoli, 2006), 23.

14. Joanna Merwood-Salisbury, "The 'New Birth of Freedom,' The Gothic Revival and the Aesthetics of Abolitionism," in Irene Cheng, et al., eds., *Race and Modern Architecture: A Critical History from the Enlightenment to the Present* (Pittsburgh: University of Pittsburgh Press, 2020), 127.

15. "Owen Jones," *New York Times*, May 4, 1874.

16. "Exhibition of Decorative Works at the St. James's Bazaar," *Illustrated London News*, April 27, 1844, 266.

17. Mould, "Editor's Preface," *Der Freischütz*.

18. "The Standard Lyric Drama," advertisement, *Athenaeum*, July 10, 1847, 752.

19. The illustration for the cover of a song published in 1849 by Boosey, "The Fairy Polka" by Marschan, is attributed to Mould.

20. *Spectator*, December 16, 1848, 1214.

21. Quoted in Bob Kosovsky, "Jacob Wrey Mould: Architect of Central Park and Lyricist," New York Public Library, January 18, 2011, accessed July 23, 2022, https://www.nypl.org/blog/2011/01/18/jacob-wrey-mould-architect-central-park-and-lyricist.

22. Emanuele Senici, *Landscape and Gender in Italian Opera* (New York: Cambridge University Press, 2005), 87.

23. Clarence C. Cook, *A Description of the New York Central Park* (New York: Scribner's, 1869), 50.

24. Vulliamy Papers, RIBA Archives, VUL/1/3, box 1. Clarence Cook and Mould's other contemporaries stated that Mould designed the grand staircase at Dorchester House during a protracted absence due to illness of Vulliamy from the office. Mould may have made the ambiguous claim that he had planned a staircase in Dorchester House that Cook inflated to refer to the grand staircase itself. It is highly unlikely that Vulliamy would have left to an assistant the design of so important an element.

25. Entry of Marriage between Jacob Wrey Mould and Emelie Annie Davies, August 16, 1851. General Register Office, London, England.

26. Undated letter from Jacob Mould to Emelie Davies in New York County Clerk's Office Division of Old Records, Supreme Court reference number GA-323 M-3.

27. Divorce decree and referee's reports, Emilie [*sic*] A. Mould (plaintiff) and Jacob W. Mould (defendant), July 20, 1867, New York County Clerk's Office Division of Old Records, Supreme Court reference number GA-323 M-3.

28. Divorce decree and referee's reports.

29. Lucille Gordon (see preface) diligently searched for Ambrose Henry Davies, said by Emelie to have been a professor of botany employed at Kew Gardens, and could find nothing in contemporary records regarding birth, marriage, death, or professional or educational affiliations.

30. Gordon's research. This was a generous sum at a time.

31. Gordon's research.

32. Gordon's research.

33. "Treatment of Architects in America," *Builder*, July 18, 1874, 611.

3. Fresh Prospects in New York

1. "Exhibition of the Architectural Association," *Morning Post* (London), August 10, 1850.

2. *New York Times*, July 14, 1856.

3. *New York Times*, October 22, 1852.

4. *New York Times*, November 11, 1852.

5. Benjamin Oakley, *Letters on Miscellaneous and Domestic Subjects* (London: self-pub., 1823), 267.

6. Letter from Jacob Wrey Mould to John Davenport, August 7, 1874, Davenport Papers, Cornell University.

7. George Carstenen and Georg Gildermeister, *The New York Crystal Palace: Illustrated Description of the Building* (New York, 1854), 21.

8. Horace Greeley, *Art and industry as represented in the exhibition at the Crystal Palace, New York—1853–4; showing the progress and state of the various useful and esthetic pursuits.* (New York, 1853), 258.

9. "Chromatic Decoration of the New York Crystal Palace," *Builder* 11, no. 565 (December 24, 1853): 783.

10. "Opening of the Exhibition," *New York Times*, July 15, 1853.

11. "Treatment of Architects in America," *Builder* 32, no. 1640 (July 18, 1874): 611.

12. Samuel Kerfoot, *Bishop Whitehouse and the Diocese of Illinois* (Chicago: Thompson & Day, 1860), 6.

13. Mould to Whitehouse, January 24, 1853, Henry John Whitehouse Papers, Archives and Historical Collections, Diocese of Chicago. Quoted in Daniel Bluestone, *Constructing Chicago* (New Haven: Yale University Press, 1991), 91.

14. Mould to Whitehouse.

15. Whitehouse to Mould, March 4, 1853. Henry John Whitehouse Papers, Archives and Historical Collections, Diocese of Chicago. Quoted in Bluestone, *Constructing Chicago*, 91.

16. "Rev. Dr. Bellows Church," *New York Times*, October 12, 1874.

17. "Rev. Dr. Bellows Church."

18. David Van Zanten, "Jacob Wrey Mould: Echoes of Owen Jones and the High Victorian Styles in New York, 1853–1865," *Journal of the Society of Architectural Historians* 28, no. 1 (March 1969): 44.

19. Victor Fidel, *The Quest for Religious & Community Identity: The Story Behind the Architecture and Evolution of All Souls Church, New York City* (New York: Lapine Press, 2010), 26.

20. Walter Kring, *Henry Whitney Bellows* (New York: Skinner House, 1979), 125.

21. Kring, 293.

22. Bellows, *Fortieth Anniversary Sermons*, quoted in Kring, 126.

23. H. W. Bellows, *The Moral Significance of the Crystal Palace* (New York: G. P. Putnam & Co., 1853), 14.

24. Letter from Mould to C. E. Butler, February 11, 1856, Henry Whitney Bellows Papers, Massachusetts Historical Society.

25. Bellows to Cyrus Bartol, April 18, 1853, quoted in Kring, *Henry Whitney Bellows*, 128.

26. Quoted in Clarence Cook, "Obituary—Jacob Wrey Mould," *Studio* 2 (July 1886): 15.

27. Bellows to Eliza Bellows, June 27, 1855, Bellows Papers, Massachusetts Historical Society. Quoted in Kring, *Henry Whitney Bellows*, 149.

28. Van Zanten, "Jacob Wrey Mould," 41.

29. Henry W. Bellows, *The First Congregational Church in the City of New York. Addressed to his Parishioners: January Fifth and Twelfth, 1879, on occasion of the Fortieth Anniversary of his Settlement*. (New York: Church of All Souls, 1899), 22.

30. Quoted in Helen W. Henderson, *A Loiterer in New York* (New York: D. H. Doran, 1927), 232.

31. "Pulpit Sketches," *New-York Tribune*, March 30, 1884.

32. "New Churches in New York," *Builder* 11, no. 563 (November 18, 1853): 705.

33. "New Churches in New York."

34. "Pulpit Sketches."

35. A description of the church while under construction stated that "four intersecting iron trusses, which span the central square, will support an octagonal lantern of brick" ("New Churches in New York," 705). If this were true, it would mark one of the earliest uses of iron trusses in a church interior, predating Victor Baltard's Saint Augustin in Paris by several years.

36. "Art," *Churchman* 54, no. 19 (July 24, 1886): 94.

37. The congregation was officially known as the First Congregational Church in the City of New York. The trustees approved Bellows's suggestion to name the new church building All Souls Unitarian Church. The former church building on Broadway at Crosby had gone by the name Church of the Divine Unity.

38. [Richard Morris Hunt,] "All Souls Church," *Crayon* 5, no. 1 (Jan., 1858): 21. Mintwood, "A Sheep Among Shepherds," New York World, December 11, 1870.

39. Hunt, "All Souls Church."

40. Mintwood, "A Sheep Among Shepherds."

41. At some point, it appears that the organ was moved from the north transept to above the main entrance at the western end of the nave. This may have been part of the remodeling of the church undertaken by H. H. Richardson in 1875.

42. Cook, "Obituary—Jacob Wrey Mould."

43. Cook.

44. "Pulpit Sketches."

45. Clara Beames writing in 1869, quoted in Peter Cameron, "A Contemporary Sketch of Richard M. Ferris and Levi U. Stuart," *Tracker* 12, no. 2 (Winter 1968): 13. After Ferris's death in 1858, Levi U. Stuart continued the business under the name Ferris and Stuart and later simply by his own name.

46. Some of Mould's contemporaries saw a relation between New York's All Souls and the Basilica of St. Boniface, dedicated in 1850 in Munich. See "All Souls Church," *Frank Leslie's Illustrated Newspaper*, January 5, 1856.

47. Thomas L. Donaldson, "Memoir of Louis de Zanth," *Papers read at the Royal Institute of British Architects, Session 1857–58* (London: printed by the Institute, 1858), 17.

48. "Pulpit Sketches."

49. High Howard, *Architects of an American Landscape: Henry Hobson Richardson, Frederick Law Olmsted, and the Reimaging of America's Public and Private Spaces* (New York: Atlantic Monthly Press, 2022), 151.

50. Minutes of the board of trustees, July 8, 1853, 113, New York Historical Society.

51. Van Zanten, "Jacob Wrey Mould," 47.

52. James O'Gorman, *The Architecture of Frank Furness*, exhibition catalog (Philadelphia: Philadelphia Museum of Art, 1973), 27.

53. December 27, 1855. Quoted in Kring, *Henry Whitney Bellows*, 162.

54. Henderson, *Loiterer in New York*, 233.

55. "Pulpit Sketches."

56. [Peter B. Wight,] "What Has been Done and What Can Be Done," *New Path* 1 (October 1863): 70.

57. Nicholas Dean to Henry Whitney Bellows, January 12, 1854, New York Historical Society.

58. "New-York Church Architecture," *Putnam's Monthly* 2 (September 1853): 237.

59. "The New Unitarian Church of Dr. Bellows," *Journal of Commerce*, December 27, 1855.

60. "Art," *Churchman*, no. 54 (July 24, 1886): 94.

61. General Convention Central Committee, *A book of plans for churches and parsonages: published under the direction of the Central Committee, General Congregational Convention, October 1852; comprising designs by Upjohn, Downing, Renwick* . . . New York: Daniel Burgess, 1853).

62. Clarence Cook, "Letters on Art—V," *Independent*, September 14, 1854, 1.

63. "The New Unitarian Church of Dr. Bellows."

64. Hunt, "The Church of All Souls," 20–22.

65. Kathryn Holliday, *Leopold Eidlitz: Architecture and Idealism in the Gilded Age* (New York: W. W. Norton, 2008), 70.

66. Jacob Wrey Mould, "Letters to the Editor," *New-York Tribune*, January 22, 1880.

67. "The Millionaires Gate to Heaven," *New York Herald*, December 3, 1893.

68. "The Church of the Pilgrims in Brooklyn," *Evening Post*, June 15, 1870.

69. "Art," 94.

70. Peter B. Wight, "Reminiscences of Russell Sturgis," *Architectural Record* 26, no. 1 (1909): 123.

71. Mould to Butler.

72. Mould to Butler.

73. Quoted in Leland Roth, ed., *America Builds Sources and Documents in American Architecture and Planning* (New York: Harper & Row, 1987), 225.

74. Hunt, "The Church of All Souls," 22.

75. Minutes of the February 23, 1857, meeting of the American Institute of Architects, Archives of the AIA, Washington, DC. Active with the AIA group at first—he attended dinner meetings and, in 1859, lectured on "Monumental Architecture"—Mould let his AIA membership lapse after 1861.

76. For Vaux's attempt to establish professional standards and fees, see Francis Kowsky, *Country Park and City: The Life and Architecture of Calvert Vaux* (New York: Oxford University Press, 1998), 87.

77. No title. *American Architect and Building News* 38 (1892): 50.

78. Report of the forty-first annual convention of the American Institute of Architects, *Carpentry and Building* 30 (1908): 7–11.

79. Henderson, *Loiterer in New York*, 232.

80. "The Fire at All Souls," *Brooklyn Daily Eagle*, August 23, 1931.

4. Embellishing Central Park

1. Cynthia Brenwall, *The Central Park: Original Designs for New York's Greatest Treasure* (New York: Abrams, 2019), 28.

2. Quoted in Carol A. Hrvol Flores, *Owen Jones: Design, Ornament, Architecture, and Theory in an Age in Transition* (New York: Rizzoli, 2006), 91.

3. Samuel Parsons and W. R. O'Donovan, "The Art of Landscape Gardening in Central Park," *Outlook*, no. 84 (September 1906): 230.

4. George W. Curtis, "Editor's Easy Chair," *Harper's New Monthly Magazine* 19 (1859): 841.

5. Moses Grinnell, another early park commissioner, could also have supported hiring Mould.

6. [William James Stillman], "Street-Musings on Architecture,' *Crayon* 6 (February 1859): 59. For Stillman's views on art and architecture, see Stephen L. Dyson, *The Last Amateur: The Life of William J. Stillman* (Albany: SUNY Press, 2014).

7. "An Architect's Appeal for Justice," *New-York Tribune*, November 20, 1875.

8. [Whitelaw Reid,] "An Architect's Appeal for Justice," *New-York Tribune*, November 20, 1875.

9. Thomas J. Campenella, *Republic of Shade: New England and the American Elm* (New Haven, CT: Yale University Press, 2003), ix.

10. Annie Nathan Meyers, *My Park Book* (New York, 1898), 66–67.

11. Mould's 1868 design for the pedestal for Ward's soldier commemorating New York's Seventh Regiment was passed over in favor of one devised by Richard Morris Hunt.

12. "Music in Central Park," *New York Herald*, July 11, 1859.

13. See Hazel Conway, "The Royal Horticultural Society Bandstand Mystery: Or, What Happened to the First Cast-Iron Bandstands?" *Garden History* 29, no. 2 (Winter, 2001): 214–216.

14. Fredrick Beecher Perkins, *The Central Park* (New York: Carleton, 1864), 36–37.

15. Olmsted and Vaux, "A Review of Recent Changes, and Changes Which Have Been Projected in the Plans of the Central Park," in *Forty Years of Landscape Architecture Being the Professional Papers of Frederick Law Olmsted, Senior*, ed. F. L. Olmsted Jr. and Theodora Kimball, reprinted as *Frederick Law Olmsted, Landscape Architect, 1822–1903* (New York: Benjamin Blom, 1970), 2:252–253.

16. Vaux to Clarence Cook, June 6, 1865, Frederick Law Olmsted Papers, Library of Congress, Washington, DC.

17. Henry Bellows, "New York and Its Parks," *Atlantic Monthly* 7 (April 1861): 426–427.

18. Owen Jones, *Grammar of Ornament* (London: Day and Son, 1856), 4.

19. He also showed two drawings for mosaic work on the Terrace. See Smithsonian American Art Museum Pre-1877 Art Exhibition Catalogue Index, accessed September 24, 2022, https://americanart.si.edu/research/art-exhibition-catalogue-index.

20. Owen Jones, *The Alhambra Court in the Crystal Palace* (London: Bradbury & Evans, 1854), 37.

21. *Brooklyn Union*, July 12, 1867, 1.

22. Ruskin from *Stones of Venice*, quoted in Peter Quennell, *John Ruskin: The Portrait of a* Prophet (New York: Viking Press, 1949), 67.

23. *Third General Report of the Board of Commissioners of the Department of Public Parks* (New York: William C. Bryant, 1875), 8.

24. Elizabeth Barlow Rogers, *Saving Central Park* (New York: Knopf, 2018), 75.

25. Kathryn Ferry, "Colour and Geometry: The Tile Designs of Owen Jones," *Journal of the Tiles and Architectural Ceramics Society* 11 (2005): 4.

26. Francis Forrester, *Little Peachblossom; or, Rambles in Central Park* (New York: Nelson & Phillips, 1873), 39.

27. Clarence C. Cook, *A Description of the New York Central Park* (New York: F. J. Huntington and Co., 1869), 52–53, reprinted by New York University Press in 2017 with an introduction by Maureen Meister. The 1986 restoration of the Terrace and the Arcade ceiling provided the opportunity for modern conservators to assess Mould's system. See Jean Parker Murphy and Kate Burns Ottavino, "The Rehabilitation of Bethesda Terrace: The Terrace Bridge and Landscape, Central Park, New York," *Bulletin of the Association for Preservation Technology* 18, no. 3 (1986): 24–39.

28. Clarence Cook, "Obituary—Jacob Wrey Mould," *Studio: Journal of the Fine Arts*, n.s. 2 (July1886): 14.

29. Some of the "conventional" ornament here resembles certain designs in Lewis Vulliamy, *Examples of Ornamental Sculpture in Architecture. Drawn from the Originals of Bronze Marble and Terra Cotta in Greece, Asia Minor, and Italy* (London: Priestly and Weale, 1818–1821).

30. [Peter B. Wight,] "What Has Been Done and What Can Be Done," *New Path* (October 1863): 74.

31. Vaux to Clarence Cook, June 6, 1865, in the Frederick Law Olmsted Papers, Library of Congress, Manuscript Division.

32. Vaux to Cook, June 6, 1865.

33. "Mr. Mould's Record in the Central Park," *New-York Tribune*, May 30, 1874.

34. Jacob Wrey Mould, "Report of the Architect-in-Chief," in *First Annual Report of the Board of Commissioners of the Department of Public Parks for the Year 1871* (New York: printed by the department, 1872), 421.

35. Mould seems to have capitalized on his Central Park reputation to obtain the commission in 1872 to design a large bridge in Oakwood Cemetery in Troy, New York. The beautiful iron span resting on stone abutments resembled Vaux's Bow Bridge. Gone now, it once conveyed carriages over Round Lake in a rural cemetery landscape not unlike that of the park. (See "Beautiful Oakwood," *Troy Times Supplement, November 8, 1890.*) The commission may have come to Mould through his friendship with George B. Warren (1828–1905), the one-time mayor of Troy, whom Mould described as "a most charming fellow, highly cultivated [who] has one of the finest collections of English watercolors in the country" (Mould to Olmsted, June 28, 1872, Frederick law Olmsted Papers, Library of Congress). One is tempted to believe that Mould may also have lent his advice to Warren as he assembled an impressive collection of Oriental porcelains, now housed in the Frick Museum in Pittsburgh. Another work by Mould in Oakwood Cemetery is the 1873 Dudley Family Monument.

36. Quotes from Mould, "Report of the Architect-in-Chief," 399–401.

37. CITIZEN, "A Forsaken Garden," *New York Times*, December 10, 1877, 10.

38. CITIZEN.

39. Mould, "Report of the Architect-in-Chief," 391.

40. Mould, 408.

41. [Henry Bellows,] "Cities and Parks," *Atlantic Monthly* 7 (April 1861): 424.

42. [William Robinson,] "Public Gardens: The Central Park at New York," *Garden* 1 (May 4, 1872): 524.

43. Cook, *Description of Central Park*, 83.

44. Cook, 416.

45. Robinson, "Public Gardens," 545.

46. Cook, *Central Park*, 142.

47. [William Martin,] *The Growth of New York* (New York: G. W. Wood, 1865), 32.

48. Martin, 409.

49. Martin, 397.

50. "Rus in Urbe," *New York Herald*, December 9, 1872.

51. Mould, *First Annual Report*, 414.

52. "Metropolitan Parks," *New-York Tribune*, July 21, 1871.

53. Mould, *First Annual Report*, 414.

54. *Third General Report of the Board of Commissioners of the Department of Public Parks for the Period of Twenty Months from May 1st, 1872, to December 31st, 1873* (New York: William C. Bryant, 1875), 56.

55. Letter from Jacob Wrey Mould to Sir Joseph Dalton Hooker, June 11, 1870. Directors' Correspondence, Library and Archives at Royal Botanic Gardens, Kew.

56. "The Ruins of Our Parks," *New York Times*, August 12, 1877.

57. Paula Mohr, "'Artificial Constructions' and Object Lessons in a Sacred Landscape: The Art and Architecture of Central Park" (PhD dissertation, University of Virginia, 2007), 198.

58. *New-York Tribune*, May 29, 1874.

59. "Treatment of Architects in America," *Builder* (July 18, 1874): 611.

60. "Treatment of Architects in America."

61. Jacob Wrey Mould, "Mr. Mould and the Museum of Art," *New York Times*, May 1, 1980.

62. Jones, *Grammar of Ornament*, 2.

63. "Correspondence: Building in Philadelphia," *American Architect and Building News* 1 (October 14, 1876): 335.

64. In later years, the city changed the number to 123 East Twenty-Sixth Street.

65. Diary of George Templeton Strong, January 5, 1860, New York Historical Society.

66. Allan Nevins and M. H. Thomas, eds., *The Diary of George Templeton Strong* (New York: Macmillan, 1952), 2:381.

67. Diary of Alfred Janson Bloor, February 27, 1860. New York Historical Society.

68. Diary of Alfred Janson Bloor, May 31, 1859. New York Historical Society.

69. J. W. Mould, "A Maiden Sought the Dewey Grove," *Courier* (London), March 27, 1847.

70. Strong, March 28, 1870, quoted in Nevins and Thomas, *Diary of George Templeton Strong*, 4:280.

71. "In Bankruptcy," *Commercial Advertiser*, August 4, 1868.

72. Mary Josephine's age remains a mystery. The 1870 census form lists her age as twenty-four (Mould's was listed as forty-five). Yet, during the divorce proceedings, Mould said that he had met Mary Josephine Sheridan in Ireland about the year 1843, which would have been three years before her supposed birth. Either the census taker was mistaken or she lied about her age. She sold the house at 123 East Twenty-Sixth Street in 1897. See "Real Estate Market News: Recorded transfers," *New York Herald*, September 14, 1897.

73. When Emelie died in 1913, her granddaughter indicated on her death certificate that her father's name as Davis; her mother's maiden name was "not-known."

74. Francis Forrester, *Little Peachblossom or Rambles in Central Park* (New York: Nelson & Phillips, 1873), 40–41.

5. Building a Career

1. Mark Crinson, *Empire Building: Orientalism and Victorian Architecture* (London: Routledge, 1996), 140.

2. "Constantinople Memorial Church Competition," *Builder* 15, no. 735 (March 21, 1857) and "Competition for the Memorial Church at Constantinople," *Ecclesiologist* 18 (February 1857), 113.

3. An Art Amateur, "The Monumental Christian Temple at Constantinople," *Evening Post*, December 3, 1856.

4. Crinson, *Empire Building*, 143.

5. "Longfellow's Vespers," *New York Times*, December 15, 1861.

6. "New York Correspondence," *Christian Register* (Boston), March 6, 1858.

7. *Brooklyn Daily Eagle*, March 3, 1858.

8. Quoted in Olive Hoogenboom, *The First Unitarian Church of Brooklyn: One Hundred Fifty Years; A History* (New York: printed by the church, 1987), 48.

9. Joseph May, ed., *Samuel Longfellow: Memoir and Letters* (Boston, MA: Houghton, Mifflin & Company, 1894), 196.

10. May, 196–197.

11. [Peter B. Wight,] "What Has Been Done and What Can Be Done," *New Path* 1, no. 6 (October 1863): 71.

12. Noyes L. Thompson, *The History of Plymouth Church* (New York: G. W. Carleton, 1873), 103.

13. The drawing is preserved in the Lamb Collection at Avery Library where it is mislabeled "Pilgrims Church in Brooklyn." The confusion may have arisen from the fact that the Church of the Pilgrims (that occupied a church designed in 1844 by Richard Upjohn) merged with Plymouth Church in 1934.

14. [William J. Stillman,] "Sketchings," *Crayon* 6 (December 1859): 374.

15. "Architecture," *Crayon* 6 (December 1859), 373.

16. "Architects' Drawings in the National Academy of Design," *Architects and Mechanics Journal* 2, no. 6 (June 9, 1860): 81.

17. "Correspondence of the Springfield (Mass) Republican: American Cars in the East," *Commercial Advertiser* (New York), January 6, 1860. The article credits William Child, an employee of the company, with "the design and execution of the ornamental painting." The author, however, believes that Mould must have had a strong influence on the design of the entire carriage.

18. "Scientific Notes," *New York Times*, January 11, 1860.

19. Minutes of the Vestry, Trinity Church, June 4, 1860.

20. "Trinity Church School," *New-York Tribune*, June 11, 1860.

21. "Trinity Church School."

22. Minutes of the Vestry, Trinity Church, June 4, 1860.

23. These quotes are from the Strong diary in the New York Historical Society for the following dates in 1860: April 19, April 29, May 2, May 3, May 11, May 30, June 4, September 6, October 6, and February 4, 1869.

24. Wight, "What has Been Done," 70.

25. According to his friend and colleague Alfred Bloor, Mould was working on the design for another schoolhouse on Staten Island.

26. Amos J. Bicknell, *Wooden and Brick Buildings with Details* (New York: A. J. Bicknell, 1875), vol. 1, design 7.

27. Bicknell, *Wooden and Brick Building with Details*, design 34.

28. "A Grand Continental Railroad," *Scientific American* 8, no. 10 (March 7, 1863): 153.

29. "A Princely Home in the Suburbs of New York—How Railroad Princes Live," *Horticulturist* 28, no. 327 (1873): 268.

30. William Reynolds, *European Capital, British Iron, and an American Dream* (Akron, OH: University of Akron Press, 2002), 216–217.

31. "The Church of the Pilgrims in Brooklyn," *Evening Post*, June 15, 1870.

32. John H. White, Jr., *The American Railroad Passenger Car* (Baltimore, MD: Johns Hopkins University Press, 1978), 347.

33. For a fuller account of the *Octavia* and its later history, see Daniel E. Russell, "Thomas William Kennard and the Steam Yacht *Octavia* (1865)," accessed April 2021, www.glencoveheritage.com/legacy_site/kennard.pdf.

34. See James Robertson Jr., "English Views of the Civil War: A Unique Excursion to Virginia, April 2–8, 1865," *Virginia Magazine of History and Biography* 77, no. 2 (April 1969): 201–212

35. Smithsonian American Art Museum, *Pre-1877 Art Exhibition Catalogue Index.*

36. "The Offices of the Atlantic and Great Western Railway," *Cleveland Leader*, November 21, 1863.

37. "The Millionaires Gate to Heaven," *New York Herald*, December 3, 1893.

38. "The West Presbyterian Church," *New-York Tribune*, April 29, 1865.

39. "Pulpit Sketches," *New-York Tribune*, December 30, 1883.

40. "Art," *Churchman* 58, no. 12 (July 24, 1886): 94.

41. "Pulpit Sketches."

42. "The West Presbyterian Church."

43. "Amusements," *New York Times*, December 13, 1865.

44. "Art," 94.

45. Kathryn E. Holliday, *Leopold Eidlitz: Architecture and Idealism in the Gilded Age* (New York: W. W. Norton, 2008), 110–111.

46. "Our New York Letter," *Troy Daily Times*, March 4, 1872.

47. "Our New York Letter."

48. "The Church of the Holy Trinity," *New York Times*, May 6, 1865. See also "Church of the Holy Trinity," *New York Herald*, April 30, 1865.

49. "Our New York Letter."

50. "Suburban News," *New York World*, April 12, 1861.

51. "Miscellaneous," *Evangelist*, April 12, 1861.

52. Clarence C. Cook, *A Description of the New York Central Park* (New York: F. J. Huntington and Co., 1869), 95.

53. E. H. Ludlow, *Map of Five Central Park Lots at the Fifth Avenue and 63d Street*, sales prospectus (New York, 1869).

54. Christophe R. Gray, "A Single Brownstone Remains Between 62nd and 63rd," *New York Times*, February 10, 2011.

55. *Map of Five Central Park Lots*, sales brochure (New York: William R. Martin, 1869), 5.

56. Quoted in Nancy K. Anderson and Linda Ferber, *Albert Bierstadt, Art and Enterprise* (New York: Hudson Hills, 1990), 34.

57. Martha Lamb, "The Homes of America, II," *Art Journal* 2 (1876): 45.

58. "Bierstadt's Loss By Fire," *New York Times*, November 11, 1882.

59. J. Wrey Mould to Building Committee of Proposed memorial College Chapel, July 1866. Manuscript and Archives, Yale University Library, New Haven, CT.

60. J. Wrey Mould to Mr. Salisbury [Yale Chapel building committee], August 13, 1866. Manuscript and Archives, Yale University Library.

61. "The Fine Art Museum," *New York Times*, April 30, 1880.

62. Jacob Wrey Mould, "Mr. Mould and the Museum of Art," *New York Times*, May 1, 1880.

63. "The New Presbyterian Church," *Steuben Courier*, August 12 1874.

64. Montgomery Schuyler, "Italian Gothic in New York," *Architectural Record* 26, no. 1 (July 1909): 46.

6. Greater Expectations

1. Mould to Davenport, February 23, 1875, Davenport Family Papers, Olin Library, Cornell University.

2. Watt Stewart, *Henry Meiggs, Yankee Pizarro* (Durham, NC: Duke University Press, 1946), 43.

3. "Personal," *New York Times*, April 9, 1859.

4. James Orton, *The Andes and the Amazon: Or, Across the Continent of South America*, 3rd ed., rev. and enl. (New York: Harper & Brothers, 1875), 396.

5. Orton, 404.

6. Mould to Davenport, April 26, 1876.

7. Henry Meiggs, *Appleton's Cyclopedia of American Biography* (New York: D. Appleton & Co, 1888), 4:287.

8. Mould to Olmsted, April 18, 1876, Frederick Law Olmsted Papers, Manuscript Division, Library of Congress.

9. Quotes from Mould to Davenport, April 26, 1875, and June 19, 1875, and Mould to Olmsted, April 18, 1875.

10. Mould to Olmsted, April 18, 1875.

11. "Peru Seen from the Inside," *Corvallis Gazette*, August 15, 1879.

12. "The Situation in Peru," *New York Times*, July 21, 1879.

13. Mould to Davenport, June 18, 1875.

14. Mould to Olmsted, April 18, 1875.

15. Mould to Davenport, June 19, 1875.

16. Mould to John Davenport, February 18[, 1876].

17. Mould to Olmsted, April 18, 1875.

18. Mould to Olmsted.

19. Mould to Olmsted.

20. Mould to Olmsted.

21. Mould to Olmsted.

22. "El neuvo tempio masonico," A Spanish translation in an unidentified source of an article in English originally published in the *South Pacific Times*. The author's copy is undated, but internal evidence identifies the date as late 1877 or early 1878. Article courtesy of Augusto Tamayo.

23. Untitled article, *Cincinnati Gazette*, February 18, 1876.

24. Mould to Olmsted, April 18, 1875.

25. "A Poughkeepsian Abroad," *Poughkeepsie Daily Eagle*, July 29, 1879.

26. It may have been installed after Mould left Lima by local architect Eduardo de Brugada.

27. Jacob Wrey Mould, "A Well-Known Architect Back in New York," *New-York Tribune*, January 20, 1880.

28. Teofilo Castillo, "Ínteriors Limenos, XIV: Casa de la senora Emilia Gonzalez Orbegoso de du-Bois," *Variedades (1915)*, 2144–2152. Quoted in Juan Jose Pacheco Ibarra, "Una mansi6n en el Centro," *Cosas, una revista internacional* (October 30, 2019). This article also includes detailed information about Edward Dubois's life in Lima.

29. *New York Times*, July 21, 1879.

30. "A Poughkeepsian Abroad."

31. Enrique Bonilla di Tolla, et.al., *Lima Y El Callao: Guia De Arquitectura Y Paisje* (Lima: Universidad Ricardo Palma, 2009), 221.

32. Ulrich Mücke, ed., *The Diary of Heinrich Witt* (Leiden: Brill, 2016).
33. Mould to Davenport, June 19, 1875.
34. Mould to Davenport.
35. Mould to Davenport, October 20, 1875.
36. Mould to Davenport, January 20, 1876.
37. Mould to Davenport, May 19, 1876.
38. Mould to Davenport, July 21, 1876.
39. Quoted in Helen K. Brink, *The First Presbyterian Church of Bath, New York* (Bath, NY: printed by the church, n.d.), 16. Helen Brink, the historian of the church, also furnishes a chronology of the church. In 1897, the sanctuary end of the church was remodeled by Tiffany Glass and Decorating Company. Mould's arcade system was repeated as a flat blind arcade across the south wall. Mould had had the arches face forward from the south wall with a recessed area in the center. Stained glass windows were also replaced, including the rose window in the sanctuary wall. From 1958 to 1959, the church was renovated. At that time, the existing electrical lights were installed. Mould's gas jets across the tops of the side corbels disappeared. Mould's slate roof was replaced in 1956.
40. Mould to Davenport, February 19, 1876.
41. Unfortunately, Mould would never have seen this tower as he had envisioned it for it was completed according to his design only in 1894.
42. Diary of Heinrich Witt, October 2, 1877.
43. "The Situation in Peru."
44. "What he intended to do in Peru—His Death Koncks Everything Endwise," *San Francisco Examiner*, July 22, 1879.
45. "The Situation in Peru."
46. Quoted in B. C. Butler, *Home-Spun and Calico* (Albany, NY: Weed Parsons, 1877), 38.
47. Mould to Olmsted, August 8, 1879.
48. B. C. Butler, *From Home-Spun to Calico* (Albany, NY: Weed, Parsons, 1877), 50.
49. Quoted in Jane Palmatier, *The Story of Saint Mary's Episcopal Church, 1865–1988* (Lake Luzerne, NY: printed by the church, 1988), 51.
50. Except for the tower, St. Mary's calls to mind Mould's design for Holy Trinity Church in New York. Perhaps, the Reverend Tyng, Holy Trinity's rector, had played a role in the general resemblance, for he had conducted services at the Lake Luzerne parish in 1868.
51. Sally E. Svenson, *Adirondack Churches: A History of Design and Building* (Keeseville, NY: Adirondack Architectural Heritage, 2006), 123.
52. Mould to Olmsted, November 28, 1879.
53. Mould to Olmsted, October 29, 1880.
54. Mould to Olmsted, October 4, 1880.
55. "Personal," *Detroit Free Press*, September 26, 1880.
56. Quoted in NYC Landmarks Preservation Commission report on Morningside Park. This excellent history of the park is the source for much of my discussion of Mould's role in the park's design.
57. Andrew S. Dolkart, *Morningside Heights: A History of Its Architecture and Development* (New York: Columbia University Press, 2001), 5.
58. "Morningside Park: The Proposed Plan of Improvement There," *Evening Post*, September 19, 1881.
59. "Mr. Mould's Suit," *Evening Post*, March 12, 1885.
60. Mould to Olmsted, August 3, 1884.

61. Jay Shockley "Morningside Park," Landmarks Preservation Commission, July 15, 2008, Designation List 404 LP-2254, 5.

62. "Concerning Men and Things," *Record and Guide*, July 25, 1885, 834.

63. "Personal Mention," *Steuben Courier*, November 18, 1887. Other notices in the *Steuben Courier* for June 15, 1883, March 27, 1885, and June 25, 1886, provided the information about the other Davenport projects mentioned.

64. "The Funeral Pageant," *New York Herald*, July 31, 1885.

65. "How it Came About," *Salt Lake Herald*, April 23, 1897.

66. *American Architect and Building News* 19 (June 26, 1886): 301.

67. See *The Diary of George Templeton Strong*, ed. Allan Nevins and M. H. Thomas (New York: Macmillan, 1952), 2:381 and 3:490; Russell Sturgis, "Italian Gothic in New York," *Architectural Record and Guide* (1891), 46; and Clarence Cook "Obituary—Jacob Wrey Mould," *The Studio*, n.s. 2 (July 1886): 15.

68. "Jacob Wrey Mould," *Harper's Weekly*, June 26, 1886, 414.

ILLUSTRATION CREDITS

Figures

Frontispiece: *Harper's Weekly* 30 (June 26, 1886): 414. Buffalo & Erie County Public Library.

Figure 1. New York Public Library Digital Collections. https://digitalcollections.nypl.org/items/94b7acd9-dc81-74f7-e040-e00a18063585.

Figure 2. Courtesy of the George Eastman Museum.

Figure 3. Courtesy of William Hudson.

Figure 4. Metropolitan Museum of Art.

Figure 5. Man vyi/Wikimedia. https://www.wikidata.org/wiki/Q4446615.

Figure 6. Photograph by John Salmon. CC BY-SA 2.0, geograph.org.uk/p/3610609.

Figure 7. From the *New-York Tribune*, May 29, 1905. Wikimedia Commons.

Figure 8. Unknown photographer. Public domain. CC-PD-Mark, via Wikimedia Commons.

Figure 9. Metropolitan Museum of Art.

Figure 10. Library of Congress.

Figure 11. Photograph by Victor Prévost. New York Public Library.

Figure 12. New York Public Library.

Figure 13. Photograph by Stephen Cleveland, ca. 1930. Indiana Limestone Company. Courtesy, Indiana Geological and Water Survey, Indiana University, Bloomington, Indiana.

Figure 14. New York Public Library.

Figure 15. Karl Ludwig von Zanth, CC0, via Wikimedia Commons.

Figure 16. Stephen Richards, *Christ Church, Christchurch Road*. CC BY-SA 2.0, via Wikimedia Commons.

Figure 17. Buffalo & Erie County Public Library.

Figure 18. Buffalo & Erie County Public Library.

Figure 19. Photograph by Andrea Bertozzi, CC BY-SA 4.0, via Wikimedia Commons.
Figure 20. YukioSanjo, CC BY-SA 3.0, via Wikimedia Commons.
Figure 21. Steve Farrow, Grimsby's hydraulic dock tower. CC BY-SA 2.0, via Wikimedia Commons.
Figure 22. Buffalo & Erie County Public Library.
Figure 23. Photograph by Robert Linsdell, CC BY 2.0, via Wikimedia Commons.
Figure 24. Courtesy of David Van Zanten.
Figure 25. Indiana Limestone Photograph Collection, Building A Nation: Indiana University. https://purl.dlib.indiana.edu/iudl/media/s45q28ov20.
Figure 26. Photograph by Sara Cedar Miller.
Figure 27. Photograph by Victor Prévost. Courtesy of the George Eastman Museum.
Figure 28. Courtesy of the Municipal Archives, City of New York.
Figure 29. New York Public Library, Robert Dennis Collection.
Figure 30. "The Terrace," lithograph published by Sarony, Major & Knapp (1868).
Figure 31. Photograph by Sara Cedar Miller.
Figure 32. Photograph by Sara Cedar Miller.
Figure 33. From *First Annual Report of the Board of Commissioners of Central Park* (1858).
Figure 34. Photograph by Sara Cedar Miller.
Figure 35. Photograph by Sara Cedar Miller.
Figure 36. Photograph by Sara Cedar Miller.
Figure 37. Photograph by Sara Cedar Miller.
Figure 38. Courtesy of the Municipal Archives, City of New York.
Figure 39. Photograph by Sara Cedar Miller.
Figure 40. Courtesy of the Municipal Archives, City of New York.
Figure 41. Courtesy of the Municipal Archives, City of New York.
Figure 42. Photograph by Victor Prévost, 1862. Courtesy of the George Eastman Museum.
Figure 43. From *First Annual Report of the Department of Public Parks* (1871).
Figure 44. Photograph by Sara Cedar Miller.
Figure 45. Photograph by Sara Cedar Miller.
Figure 46. Photograph by Sara Cedar Miller.
Figure 47. Courtesy of the Municipal Archives, City of New York.
Figure 48. Photograph by Sara Cedar Miller.
Figure 49. From Clarence Cook, *A Description of the Central Park* (1869). Author's collection.
Figure 50. Photograph by Sara Cedar Miller.
Figure 51. From Clarence Cook, *Description of Central Park* (1869).
Figure 52. Courtesy of the Municipal Archives, City of New York.
Figure 53. From *First Annual Report of the Department of Public Parks* (1871).
Figure 54. *First Annual Report of the Department of Public Parks* (1871).
Figure 55. *First Annual Report of the Department of Public Parks* (1871).
Figure 56. Courtesy of the Municipal Archives, City of New York.
Figure 57. Courtesy of the Municipal Archives, City of New York.
Figure 58. Courtesy of the Municipal Archives, City of New York.
Figure 59. Courtesy of David Van Zanten.
Figure 60. Library of Congress.
Figure 61. Photograph by Beyond My Ken. CC BY-SA 4.0, via Wikimedia Commons.

Figure 62. Photograph by Beyond My Ken. CC BY-SA 4.0, via Wikimedia Commons.
Figure 63. Buffalo History Museum.
Figure 64. From *Bicknell's Wooden and Brick Buildings with Details* (1875).
Figure 65. Buffalo & Erie County Public Library.
Figure 66. Reynolds Collection, Allegheny College.
Figure 67. Royal Institute of British Architects.
Figure 68. From Henry Collins Brown, ed., *Valentine's Manual of Old New York* (1920).
Figure 69. New York Historical Society.
Figure 70. Church of the Holy Trinity.
Figure 71. From Charles E. Alison, *The History of Yonkers, Westchester County, New York* (1896).
Figure 72. New York Historical Society.
Figure 73. Brooklyn Museum Libraries. Special Collections.
Figure 74. Brooklyn Museum Libraries. Special Collections.
Figure 75. Yale University Archives.
Figure 76. Courtesy of the Municipal Archives, City of New York.
Figure 77. First Presbyterian Church, Bath, New York.
Figure 78. First Presbyterian Church, Bath, New York.
Figure 79. Photograph by Rosanna Kuon.
Figure 80. Photograph by Juan Jose Pacheco Ibarra.
Figure 81. Courtesy of Juan Jose Pacheco Ibarra.
Figure 82. Photograph by Juan Jose Pacheco Ibarra.
Figure 83. Courtesy of Juan Jose Pacheco Ibarra
Figure 84. From T. Castillo, "Interiors Limenos, XIV: Casa de la senora Emilia Gonzalez Orbegoso de du-Bois," *Variedades* (1915).
Figure 85. Photograph by Dr. Alfonso Castrillón. Director of the Galería de Artes Visuales. Universidad Ricardo Palma.
Figure 86. Courtesy of the Municipal Archives, City of New York.
Figure 87. Photograph by Martin Wachadlo.
Figure 88. Photograph by Martin Wachadlo.
Figure 89. From Silas Farmer, *The History of Detroit, Michigan* (1884).
Figure 90. Courtesy of the United States Department of the Interior, National Park Service, Frederick Law Olmsted National Historic Site.
Figure 91. Museum of the City of New York.
Figure 92. Photograph by Martin Wachadlo.
Figure 93. Courtesy of the Steuben County Historical Society.
Figure 94. New York Public Library. The Miriam and Ira D. Wallach Division of Art, Prints and Photographs: Picture Collection.
Figure 95. Photograph by Danny Callaghan.
End piece: Olin Library, Cornell University.

Plates

Plate 1. Courtesy of the Municipal Archives, City of New York.
Plate 2. Courtesy of the Municipal Archives, City of New York.
Plate 3. Courtesy of the Municipal Archives, City of New York.
Plate 4. Courtesy of the Municipal Archives, City of New York.

Plate 5. Courtesy of the Municipal Archives, City of New York.
Plate 6. Courtesy of the Municipal Archives, City of New York.
Plate 7. Photograph by Sara Cedar Miller.
Plate 8. Photograph by Sara Cedar Miller.
Plate 9. Courtesy of the Municipal Archives, City of New York.
Plate 10. Courtesy of the Municipal Archives, City of New York.
Plate 11. Avery Library Architectural and Fine Arts Library, Columbia University.
Plate 12. First Presbyterian Church, Bath, New York.
Plate 13. Photograph by Rosanna Kuon Arce.
Plate 14. First Presbyterian Church, Bath, New York.
Plate 15. Photograph by Martin Wachadlo.
Plate 16. Photograph by Pat Morin.

INDEX

Note: Illustrations are indicated by page numbers in *italics*.

Francis Kowsky is SUNY Distinguished Professor Emeritus and Fellow of the Society of Architectural Historians. He has written numerous articles on nineteenth-century American architects and is the author of *Country Park and City: The Life and Architecture of Calvert Vaux* and *The Best Planned City in the World: Olmsted, Vaux and the Buffalo Park System*. For many years, he served on the New York State Board for Historic Preservation and took pleasure in teaching the history of art at Buffalo State College.

Lucille Gordon (1929–2021) was a lifelong resident of New York. She founded and ran Gordon Associates, which specialized in marketing books for technical publishers. She volunteered as a docent in Central Park, leading educational tours, and later devoted many years to researching and drafting a biography of Jacob Wrey Mould, the lesser-known third architect of Central Park who created the majority of its decorative elements such as Bethesda Terrace.

SELECT TITLES FROM EMPIRE STATE EDITIONS

Patrick Bunyan, *All Around the Town: Amazing Manhattan Facts and Curiosities, Second Edition*

Salvatore Basile, *Fifth Avenue Famous: The Extraordinary Story of Music at St. Patrick's Cathedral*. Foreword by Most Reverend Timothy M. Dolan, Archbishop of New York

William Seraile, *Angels of Mercy: White Women and the History of New York's Colored Orphan Asylum*

Andrew J. Sparberg, *From a Nickel to a Token: The Journey from Board of Transportation to MTA*

New York's Golden Age of Bridges. Paintings by Antonio Masi, Essays by Joan Marans Dim, Foreword by Harold Holzer

Daniel Campo, *The Accidental Playground: Brooklyn Waterfront Narratives of the Undesigned and Unplanned*

John Waldman, *Heartbeats in the Muck: The History, Sea Life, and Environment of New York Harbor, Revised Edition*

John Waldman (ed.), *Still the Same Hawk: Reflections on Nature and New York*

Gerard R. Wolfe, *The Synagogues of New York's Lower East Side: A Retrospective and Contemporary View, Second Edition*. Photographs by Jo Renée Fine and Norman Borden, Foreword by Joseph Berger

Joseph B. Raskin, *The Routes Not Taken: A Trip Through New York City's Unbuilt Subway System*

North Brother Island: The Last Unknown Place in New York City. Photographs by Christopher Payne, A History by Randall Mason, Essay by Robert Sullivan

Tom Glynn, *Reading Publics: New York City's Public Libraries, 1754–1911*

Mark Naison and Bob Gumbs, *Before the Fires: An Oral History of African American Life in the Bronx from the 1930s to the 1960s*

Robert Weldon Whalen, *Murder, Inc., and the Moral Life: Gangsters and Gangbusters in La Guardia's New York*

Joanne Witty and Henrik Krogius, *Brooklyn Bridge Park: A Dying Waterfront Transformed*

Sharon Egretta Sutton, *When Ivory Towers Were Black: A Story about Race in America's Cities and Universities*

Pamela Hanlon, *A Wordly Affair: New York, the United Nations, and the Story Behind Their Unlikely Bond*

David J. Goodwin, *Left Bank of the Hudson: Jersey City and the Artists of 111 1st Street*. Foreword by DW Gibson

Nandini Bagchee, *Counter Institution: Activist Estates of the Lower East Side*

Susan Celia Greenfield (ed.), *Sacred Shelter: Thirteen Journeys of Homelessness and Healing*

Elizabeth Macaulay-Lewis and Matthew M. McGowan (eds.), *Classical New York: Discovering Greece and Rome in Gotham*

Colin Davey with Thomas A. Lesser, *The American Museum of Natural History and How It Got That Way*. Forewords by Neil deGrasse Tyson and Kermit Roosevelt III

Wendy Jean Katz, *Humbug: The Politics of Art Criticism in New York City's Penny Press*

Lolita Buckner Inniss, *The Princeton Fugitive Slave: The Trials of James Collins Johnson*

Mike Jaccarino, *America's Last Great Newspaper War: The Death of Print in a Two-Tabloid Town*

Angel Garcia, *The Kingdom Began in Puerto Rico: Neil Connolly's Priesthood in the South Bronx*

Jim Mackin, *Notable New Yorkers of Manhattan's Upper West Side: Bloomingdale–Morningside Heights*

Matthew Spady, *The Neighborhood Manhattan Forgot: Audubon Park and the Families Who Shaped It*

Robert O. Binnewies, *Palisades: 100,000 Acres in 100 Years*

Marilyn S. Greenwald and Yun Li, *Eunice Hunton Carter: A Lifelong Fight for Social Justice*

Jeffrey A. Kroessler, *Sunnyside Gardens: Planning and Preservation in a Historic Garden Suburb*

Elizabeth Macaulay-Lewis, *Antiquity in Gotham: The Ancient Architecture of New York City*

Ron Howell, *King Al: How Sharpton Took the Throne*

Jean Arrington with Cynthia S. LaValle, *From Factories to Palaces: Architect Charles B. J. Snyder and the New York City Public Schools*. Foreword by Peg Breen

Boukary Sawadogo, *Africans in Harlem: An Untold New York Story*

Alvin Eng, *Our Laundry, Our Town: My Chinese American Life from Flushing to the Downtown Stage and Beyond*

Stephanie Azzarone, *Heaven on the Hudson: Mansions, Monuments, and Marvels of Riverside Park*

Ron Goldberg, *Boy with the Bullhorn: A Memoir and History of ACT UP New York*. Foreword by Dan Barry

Peter Quinn, *Cross Bronx: A Writing Life*. Foreword by Dan Barry

Jill Jonnes, *South Bronx Rising: The Rise, Fall, and Resurrection of an American City, Third Edition*. Foreword by Nilka Martell

Matt Dallos, *In the Adirondacks: Dispatches from the Largest Park in the Lower 48*

Mark Bulik, *Ambush at Central Park: When the IRA Came to New York*

Brandon Dean Lamson, *Caged: A Teacher's Journey Through Rikers, or How I Beheaded the Minotaur*

For a complete list, visit www.fordhampress.com/empire-state-editions.